DATE DUE

THE SPYGLASS

The book page February 5, 1928, before syndication.

The Spyglass

VIEWS AND REVIEWS, 1924–1930

by DONALD DAVIDSON

Selected and Edited by
John Tyree Fain

Nashville 1963
VANDERBILT UNIVERSITY PRESS

Composed, printed, and bound by the Parthenon Press
Nashville, Tennessee, United States of America
Library of Congress catalogue card number 63-9946

INTRODUCTION

The present volume is a selection of book reviews and comments written by Donald Davidson for the Nashville *Tennessean* from February 4, 1924, to November 30, 1930. Most of the items appeared in the feature column of a book page edited by Davidson for the *Tennessean* during those years. It has often been said to be the best literary page ever published in the South. Probably of greater significance, however, is its close connection with the Southern literary renascence. In speaking of the relationship of the Fugitive and Agrarian movements, recent commentators have noted that this change of interest from poetry to social criticism occurred during the brief period between the last number of *The Fugitive* (December 1925) and the publication of *I'll Take My Stand* (1930). The record of this change can be traced in the *Tennessean's* literary page. Davidson himself puts the matter thus:

The Fugitive magazine had less than a year to run when I started editing the *Tennessean* Book Page. Some "Fugitives" (that is, Ransom, Tate, Warren, and I) were passing into their "Agrarian phase" shortly afterwards . . . The Book Page became more than a book page because of the ideas, hopes, pressures, enterprises, both individual and collective, that engaged us all from about 1925 to 1930 and later.[1]

In January of 1924 John H. Nye, managing editor of the *Tennessean*, approached Davidson on the subject of the book page. The pay, Nye explained, would be ten dollars a week plus the books. Davidson jumped at the chance. He had a wife and daughter to support. It would be ten dollars every week in the year, while his salary of $1800 as instructor of English at Vanderbilt hardly sufficed in predepression Nashville for the nine months of the school year. But aside from the need, he really liked newspaper work—he had

[1] Letter to editor, June 1960.

worked on the *Tennessean* during the summer of 1920—and felt that he had aptitude for it.

The page began the next month. To each Sunday edition of the paper Davidson contributed a column of book news and, during the first year, one or more book reviews of his own. Gradually the news column became much enlarged so that it contained book reviews and comments on literary subjects in general. This was "The Spyglass," so called after the second month of publication and until 1928, when for some unremembered reason the name was changed to "The Critic's Almanac." When "The Spyglass" became longer, the editor cut down on his extra reviews. There were only so many hours in the week, and Davidson was still helping with the publication of *The Fugitive* in 1924 and publishing in it during its last year, publishing two volumes of his own poetry, writing regularly for the periodical *Creative Reading* and occasionally for such magazines as *Forum, Saturday Review of Literature, Sewanee Review* and for several "little" magazines, besides teaching full time. And then there were odd jobs at the *Tennessean* that he simply could not resist, though he told himself only that he needed the money. For instance, during one summer he occasionally ghosted "I Reckon So," a syndicated column written by one of the *Tennessean* editors, T. H. Alexander, who would give him usually, as here, a day's notice and suggest subject matter:

Under separate cover I am sending a bunch of letters—almost all inspired by the columns you wrote which is proof of reader interest. . . . Young feller me lad, I need aid, assistance and moral support pronto. Can you write me a column for Monday. . . . Note what the Montgomery man (see letters) says about the new [Andrew] Johnson biography. Might try that, just remembering that our Knoxville Journal readers think him the cow's tits. . . . Also I have a check for you. Don't you ever want money? Hells bells.[2]

[2] Letter dated "Friday, 1 PM." in file of 1926.

In the beginning of the book page most of the reviewing was done by Davidson and his associates among the Fugitive poets. Of 176 reviews during the first seven months Davidson wrote thirty-five, John Crowe Ransom thirty-one, Allen Tate twenty-four, Stanley Johnson twenty-four, Jesse Wills twenty.[3] This count indicates general proportions only, however, as small reviews were ordinarily unsigned. One of Davidson's 1924 space memoranda to Nye reveals smaller items:

John Crowe Ransom   *Totals*

July 27, The Home Maker	11
August 3, Shadows That Pass	12
August 10, Saint's Theatre	3
August 10, Letters from Senator's Wife	10
August 17, Darkened Windows	3
August 17, The Golden Bed	11
August 17, Places in English Literature	2
August 24, Heliodora	16
August 31, Stiletto	5
September 7, Pipers; After Harvest (2)	9½
	82½

Allen Tate

August 3, Atlas and Beyond	11½
August 3, Negro Poetry	10½
August 10, Nature of Love	7
	29

Jesse Wills

August 3, For Love of a Sinner	7
	7

[3] For a list of contributors see "Appendix," pp. 257–59.

Alec B. Stevenson

August 17, Equipment Obligations	15½
August 24, Handwriting on Wall	3
	18½

William Frierson

July 27, Fata Morgana	10
August 3, Evolution	9½
August 10, City Out of Sea	5
August 17, Advisory Ben	3
August 24, Shantung Garden	9½
August 31, Astronomer at Large	6
September 7, One-Act Plays	5½
	48½

It was necessary to keep this record since in the beginning contributors other than the editor were paid by inches. After the first seventeen months of publication, pay for contributors was eliminated. This space sheet also indicates changes which had already begun to occur among the contributors. By the fall of 1924 Tate was spending most of his time in New York and abroad and through the years contributed only an occasional review. Johnson was no longer on the space sheet at all. He began to work soon after for the Nashville *Banner* and never contributed again.

Partly because of these changes, partly to enlist people of varied interests and talents, Davidson made some effort to enlarge his group of contributors. Actually the list grew almost without encouragement, among members of the *Tennessean* staff, townspeople, Vanderbilt faculty and students, though very few undergraduate students contributed. Since Davidson could get down to the *Tennessean* only two or three times a week, the books were kept in an immense wooden box that sat in the corner of Nye's office on the second floor of the old Southern Turf Building on Fourth Avenue. Nye himself kept the key, and William Kingsbury, one of the news editors at the time, locked up the books when they came from the publishers. With the coming of the literary editor, the newsman's age-old bonus of free books was continued only with the proviso that all free books be reviewed, and some of the *Tennessean* staff members became devoted to the book page, James I. Finney (editor of the morning paper), Barr Moses, Katherine Hall, and Kingsbury being among the most frequent contributors. Robert Rowlett, another staff member, in addition to reviewing, helped with the makeup of the page and saw it through the printing process. He also drew the Spyglass design that headed the feature column. Davidson would distribute review copies to staff members when he came to town. Other reviewers might drop by his office at Vanderbilt or his apartment at Wesley Hall to get theirs, for he had to take great numbers home with him, to scan and decide what to do with them. But in the first years few out-of-town contributors were encouraged, except those who remained permanent members of the intellectual community, like Andrew Lytle, who wrote back from a family farm in Guntersville, Alabama:

I shall want to do about four good books a month, with special emphasis on plays. I shall want to do a few more volumes of poetry than novels, unless there is too great a demand for them. And if you hold the slightest degree of affection for me, don't let another antique book slip away to some clutching hand . . .[4]

In spite of the fact that "The *Tennessean* Book Review and Literary Page" was maintained as a local enterprise as far as possible, it took more and more time, until in the early part of 1928 it had become another fulltime job carried on in the editor's spare moments. And Davidson decided that if they wanted a book page, they should pay for it. To put

[4] Letter of February 18, 1926.

the matter thus is to state it out of context, however. Really
he was wondering if he should not leave Vanderbilt, even
leave the South. The Vanderbilt that now invites some of
the Fugitives back every year for a literary symposium was
not kind to them in the twenties—or in the thirties either,
when Ransom left. The Fugitives themselves have imparted
to recent commentators their own attitude of somewhat
mellowed reminiscence. Thus Randall Stewart has recently
said:

It is interesting, and I think unique at that time, and very much to
the credit of Mims, the Department Head, that he advanced Curry
and Ransom, *pari passu*, through the various grades; that is, he
allowed equal "credit" for a scholarly article in PMLA, and for a
poem . . . This was indeed a remarkable situation at a time when
George Lyman Kittredge dominated practically every English
department in the country.[5]

To those of us who were near at hand and who watched this
literary movement in its development through the twenties
and thirties, Stewart's statement comes as a surprise. Official
Vanderbilt does deserve credit for the qualified toleration
it afforded the Fugitives and Agrarians; it never, to my
knowledge, encouraged them. But this story is a complex
one and would take us too far afield as an interpolation in
the present brief history of the book page.

To Davidson's malaise in the late twenties the reaction of
his newspaper associates was typical, as recorded by Alexander:

I hear vague mutterings that you may leave V.U., because of un-
satisfactory salary, etc. It's none of my damned business, of course,
but before you throw your brass hat away, if you are thinking of
so doing, let me talk to you of a matter I have been discussing with
J. Finney, the editor of the publick print. He and I think you
would adorn the editorial page of The Tennessean each morning.
Keep this under your hat, as an anchor to windward, but there

5 "The Relation Between Fugitives and Agrarians," *Mississippi Quarterly*, XIII (Spring 1960), 55.

may be gold in them thar mountings. In 20 years a bronze tablet will mark your rooms at Wesley Hall. Tourists will gape and spread halitosis from the rubber neck wagons. Even Georgians will know who you are. As Tom Heflin chants: Hold the Line, the Americans are coming! [6]

But regardless of his thoughts about his career in general at this time, Davidson was sure that Colonel Luke Lea, owner and publisher of the *Tennessean*, should put the literary page on a respectable financial footing. It was not so much the pay as the principle of the thing. So after explaining his position—making sure, however, that the page had enough material to continue—he took a brief vacation in Gatlinburg with his family. As he wrote to Tate,

Recently I quit the *Tennessean*, having suffered long enough under the indignity of a pitiful wage. They countered by putting me technically on leave of absence, while they stirred up Colonel Lea. [7]

Two weeks later Nye wrote Davidson that Lea would like to syndicate the book page to two other papers just purchased by him, the *Commercial Appeal* of Memphis and the Knoxville *Journal*, the compensation on this new basis to be two hundred dollars a month, paid jointly by the three newspapers. [8] In accepting, Davidson said,

May I say that I interpret this offer, in its implications, to mean that you have ambitious views as to the possibilities of the book page in relation to the cultural development of this section. . . . I take this offer as, in effect, a challenge and an inspiration. [9]

Excerpts from a sheet of suggestions for reviewers drawn up at about the time syndication began indicate Davidson's high seriousness as he envisaged his expanded task. It is the hope of the editor, he said,

to publish an independent-minded book page of the utmost distinction possible under the circumstances, preserving a generous

[6] Letter of January 1, 1928.
[7] Letter of March 21, 1928.
[8] Letter of March 7, 1928.
[9] Letter to Nye, March 12, 1928.

catholic scope and yet maintaining a characteristic Southern point of view.

Even at best, he said, metropolitan "critical despotism" would be unfortunate, and

when, as is often the case, New York sees the books of the day too near-sightedly or evolves its critical tone from issues and circumstances that will not bear close scrutiny, the condition becomes altogether unhealthy.

With this broader sectional outlook Davidson attempted to get more contributors from the areas reached by the other two newspapers—East and West Tennessee and parts of Mississippi, Arkansas, Louisiana, Georgia, and Kentucky. Most of the nonlocal reviewers began writing at this time. Some of those invited wrote congratulations but did not wish to review. For instance, William Alexander Percy wrote from Greenville, Mississippi,

. . . I was delighted to see your name on The Literary Page of the Commercial Appeal. Judging from the result you have already accomplished, you are going to make this the outstanding page of literary criticism in Southern journalism . . . As for writing occasional reviews, let me confess to you that I have little respect for my own abilities in the role of reviewer.[10]

The book page had now changed its name to "The Weekly Review: A Page about Books," the deadline had to be moved up, mats had to be made and sent to Memphis and Knoxville. Davidson's feature column itself was also appearing in the Miami *News*. Correspondence with out-of-town contributors also increased, and books had to be mailed to them rather than just pulled out of the old wooden box. So Davidson asked Edd Winfield Parks, who was then working on his doctor's degree at Vanderbilt, to do part-time work on the page, paying Parks out of his own salary from the *Tennessean*. On the adjoining page is a letter from one of the later contributors to the page. At the top is a

[10] Letter of May 18, 1928.

25—50M.·826.

Date October 16, 1936

om ....

, ...

bject ....

Dear Donald,

I enclose a review of a book which I enjoyed very much, for which many thanks. I found the Mary Gladstone journal uncompromisingly dull — ugh! review it if you wish, but Dutton won't like it! I am O'Flaherty's "Two Years" is most interesting but strikes me as not valid — another "Call of the Deep"; however, I have not finished it yet. I am so very pleased with the books you've been sending me, and hope I can continue to note the same sort. Regards & best wishes — Bill S.C.

Signed

typical note to Parks. The independence expressed in this note had been recognized as one of the chief merits of Davidson's page from the beginning. Davidson had always practiced it and had always urged it on his reviewers. And the chips that fell were just as likely to bark a friend's shins as anybody else's.

But it was really the sincere desire to give justice that attracted more and more readers. Files for the book page years contain numbers of letters like the following one from Addison Hibbard:

> I've been waiting for the blast on "The Lyric South" from your book page . . . most of the reviews have been idle chatter. . . . I know you'll write what you think and I honestly want to benefit by what you say.[11]

And there are just as many like this one from Louis Bromfield:

> This is just a line to thank you for the profound and intelligent article about "Miss Annie Spragg." As you may have guessed in the case of such a book—complicated as it is and with the idea behind it left for the reader to discover—the suffering from the hands of crude and hasty reviewers is intense and the blunders extremely annoying. Therefore I appreciate more than I can say the way you have treated "Annie." [12]

The book page continued two years and seven months after syndication. It was a common activity that made for continuity and integrity among its contributors. As Davidson says, it had become

> a part of our general group concern about the arts, and the position of the South . . . and there was a general understanding among us that the Page was open to the group and their supporters as a "medium" of publication.[13]

The book page, then, was functioning as a testing ground for Davidson, John Crowe Ransom, Allen Tate, Robert

[11] Letter of August 3, 1928.
[12] Letter of April 2, 1929.
[13] Letter to editor, March 14, 1960.

Penn Warren, Andrew Lytle, Frank Owsley, Lyle Lanier, H. C. Nixon, and Henry B. Kline—nine of the twelve Southerners who issued *I'll Take My Stand*.[14] And Davidson, as editor, continued to exert his customary influence.

The truth is that Davidson, because his intensely emotional nature interpenetrates a mind of great critical flexibility, has always inspired his associates. For instance, in the following typical letter he comments on Tate's "Ode to the Confederate Dead" as he read it in manuscript:

> The poem is beautifully executed. I do not quibble with a single word. Its economy is striking: its tone is sustained: it has very fine individual passages . . . it is coherent, structurally unimpugnable. But its beauty is a cold beauty. And where, O Allen Tate, are the dead? You have buried them completely out of sight—with them yourself and me. God help us, I must say.[15]

The justice of the first part of this statement, then the unshaken conviction that Tate is wrong, then the complete giving of himself at the end—these are the qualities that were so highly prized by Tate and others in Davidson's criticism. Louise Cowan rightly recognizes in Davidson the strongest cohesive force in the Fugitive movement.[16]

The end of the book page was sudden. Though Davidson was not surprised—it was the beginning of the Great Depression and everybody expected the worst—some of his deep feeling for the page shows through his circular letter of November 26, 1930, to publishers and reviewers:

> I regret to inform you that the book page which has been published under my editorship . . . has been discontinued . . . What the *Tennessean* itself intends to do in the future I am unable to say. My own connection with the *Tennessean* ceases completely on November 30. . . . entirely aside from my personal part in the

---

[14] John Donald Wade, another one of the twelve, contributed very little to the book page, though he was closely associated with the group in other ways.

[15] Letter of February 15, 1927.

[16] *The Fugitive Group: A Literary History*, Louisiana State University Press, 1959.

matter, I feel very sorrowful that the book page, as a medium of contact between the readers of this section and the world of current books, is apparently about to be entirely lost. . . . To all, my best, my sincerest good wishes, with the deepest regret that our acquaintance in the world of book reviewing—in some cases of several years standing—must be thus broken.

Many of the replies were written on the assumption that the book page would resume publication later, as was that of Mary Rose Himler from Bobbs-Merrill:

And before I get madder and begin to bite keys off the typewriter, let me say that we do certainly appreciate your fine cooperation and the high grade of your reviews and we regret very much indeed that our five years of association must cease—even if only for a short time.[17]

Luke Lea, Jr., encouraged the assumption in answering protests: "We have decided to discontinue the page and intend to put it back later on." [18] This evidently was the intention, but the *Tennessean* went into receivership some time later, and when it became solvent again, Davidson was not reinstated. Other recipients of Davidson's letter assumed suppression and wrote deploring the fact. But the book page was not suppressed. It just ceased publication, and at the very time when Davidson believed it was ready to exert the kind of influence of which he had dreamed.

Mention has been made now and again, in this narrative, of the place of the book page in the Fugitive tradition. It should be made clear in closing, however, that the book page was not a joint enterprise which the group had commissioned Davidson to carry out. Commentators have often made too much of the communal aspect of Fugitive affairs, too little of the fact that they were individuals following their own paths, stimulating one another more often by opposition than otherwise. As Theodore Hoepfner correctly puts it, "The Fugitives were not a football team, com-

[17] Letter of December 1, 1930.
[18] Letter to Henry Hart of Scribner's, December 1, 1930.

plete with coach and captain." [19] The book page was Davidson's own independent undertaking, in which he was trying,
as he says,

within the narrow limits available to me in a newspaper book page,
to make up to some degree for the lack of a good literary magazine
in the South.[20]

A word might be said here also of the climate of literary
opinion prevailing in the nineteen-twenties. For many readers of this volume will not remember a time when Glenway
Wescott was well known and William Faulkner was not,
when James Branch Cabell was seriously spoken of as one
of the great satirists of all time, when H. L. Mencken was
the most powerful American critic, when Sinclair Lewis
was and T. S. Eliot was not an object of reverence, when
Hardy and Bridges and Masefield were the leading British
poets, when the *Saturday Review* was really a review of
literature, and Robert Frost was not the patriarch of American poetry. For those who do remember such a time much
of the interest in Davidson's reviews (judging from my own
experience) will come from thinking back on their own
reactions when first reading books now acknowledged
masterpieces, or those which have been forgotten. Such
readers will realize too some of Davidson's difficulties as an
independent critic, as a Southerner who demurred at the
exorbitant praise of Ellen Glasgow in the New York *Times*
and the *Herald Tribune*. And if he attacked Mencken, did
he not place himself on the side of Bruce Barton or Senator
Heflin?

The selections begin with a column written for the first
issue of the literary page that appeared after it was syndicated. Here Davidson discusses his own concept of provincialism, revealing incidentally the chief sources of his

[19] "Economics of Agrarianism," *Mississippi Quarterly*, XIII (Spring
1960), p. 62, note 2.
[20] Letter to editor, March 12, 1961.

motivation for editing the page and writing the feature column. This explanation to his new readers in 1928 may therefore serve a similar purpose for readers of the present volume. The rest of the selections are divided roughly according to subject matter and arranged chronologically within each group. The first group is composed of reviews and comments on Southern fiction. The book page itself gave a more or less complete coverage of the best current books regardless of origin. One of the main purposes of the feature column, however, was to encourage whenever possible what Davidson considered the right kind of Southern fiction, to discourage the wrong kind. So the number of Southern selections reflects Davidson's predominant interest in the nineteen-twenties, as well as afterwards. As Theodore Hornberger says, "Davidson has been the leading proponent of literary regionalism in our time." [21] Among Southern authors, he seems to have preferred Elizabeth Madox Roberts. She shows, he says, "the excellences and advantages of provincial art at its best." [22] In this acclaim, however, there may be a reservation, perhaps an implication that the best art transcends provincialism, even as Davidson interprets the term. If so, then I believe that, during the book page years, he would have chosen Stark Young as representative of Southern fiction at its best.

The Southern regional note is never far from the surface in the succeeding groups of selections on other American fiction, on poetry, on critics and commentators, and in a general group including Davidson's comments on folk art, the book business, music, war books, and other topics. In the last group, on the backgrounds of Agrarianism, the South again occupies the central position. Here are grouped the reviews of such books as Bowers's *The Tragic Era,* Phillips's *Life and Labor in the Old South,* Borsodi's *This*

[21] *Journal of Southern History,* XXVI (May 1960), p. 268.
[22] *Infra,* p. 47.

Ugly Civilization—books of the sort that the Fugitives were handing around to each other in the days when they were passing into their truly Southern phase. It is possible to follow in Davidson's reviews of these books the incremental growth of convictions that appear in *I'll Take My Stand* (1930) and in his own *Attack on Leviathan* (1938).

The last entry in these selections did not appear in the book page at all but in *Bookman* for May 1931, six months after the page was suspended. It is Davidson's evaluation of his seven years of experience as editor. And here again, as in the first entry in the selections, he emphasizes provincialism, a concept which—though often used with half-humorous contrariness—held within itself, for a time, the literary and social idealism of a whole school of writers.

J.T.F.

CONTENTS

ILLUSTRATIONS

ABOUT DONALD DAVIDSON

Donald Davidson was born in 1893 at Campbellsville, Tennessee, of the old pioneer stock whose history he has celebrated both in poetry and in prose, without ever neglecting the no less absorbing modern scene. His gaze, Allen Tate recently said, "is into the past but the glance is at the present, and this glance is sharp and exact." Both his parents were teachers, and Davidson himself has been teaching and writing since he was seventeen years old, the only major interruption being during World War I when as a lieutenant of infantry he saw action with the 81st ("Wildcat") Division in France. A graduate of Vanderbilt, he returned to his *alma mater* in 1920 to teach and to study for his M.A., and eventually he mounted the professional ladder, without benefit of the usual Ph.D., to the Vanderbilt professorship in English that he has held since 1937. Summers, however, have generally found him in Vermont as a faculty member of Middlebury's famous Bread Loaf School of English. Davidson's mature acomplishments as a writer date from the nineteen-twenties when, with Ransom, Tate, and others, he became one of the founders and editors of *The Fugitive*. His earlier publications are largely related to the Fugitive movement, but much of his work after 1927 reflects his own characteristic interests in affairs, ideas, and the arts. A large part of his vigorous periodical writing of both earlier and later years remains uncollected. In 1952 he collaborated, as librettist, with Charles F. Bryan in the opera *Singin' Billy*. The most recent of his four volumes of poetry are *Lee in the Mountains* (1938) and *The Long Street* (1961). Among his published books are three volumes of literary and social criticism, *The Attack on Leviathan* (1938), *Still Rebels, Still Yankees* (1957), and *Southern Writers in the Modern World* (1958); a two-volume history in the Rivers of America series, *The Tennessee* (1946-1948); and several textbooks.

ACKNOWLEDGMENTS

To the publishers of the *Nashville Tennessean* and to Vanderbilt University I wish to express thanks for making possible the reprinting of these selections, and to those who have aided me in their preparation my grateful obligation: Donald Davidson, William W. Davidson, Andrew Lytle, Edd Winfield Parks, Gertrude Morton Parsley, John Seigenthaler, Allen Tate, and Lucile Welch Fain.

JOHN TYREE FAIN

University of Florida
Gainesville, January 1963

THE SPYGLASS

Provincialism

In many of its forms, the provincial habit of mind is dangerous enough. Whether you discover it on Main street or in Greenwich village, it can be dull or smart with equal deadliness, and it is always a question which is deadlier—the sophisticated provincialism found even in metropolitan areas, or the narrow rural type which is awkwardly intolerant without being picturesque. Between these, we should dread to choose. The deadly sort, at any rate, may be known by its closed mind or its limited experience or both; it has generally too much self-sufficiency and swagger; it is noisy and egotistical. We are naturally fearful of this repulsive thing, and we do not need to choose it or to submit to it; but we ought not to let our dislike for its manifestations blind us to another sort of provincialism that is not to be despised.

Provincialism may be a bad name for what I am talking about, but I defend the term on certain grounds which will appear. Furthermore it is always a pleasure to explore words that are used as epithets, for sometimes we tend to condemn people for having qualities we have not and make it seem that a virtue is a defect. Those who toss the term "provincial" loosely about as, say, it has been tossed at the South, might well remember that there is a kind of provincialism that is allied to the self-reliance of Emerson's teaching and to the "know thyself" of the ancient sages.

Critic's Almanac, April 22, 1928. In this essay, Davidson sets forth his theory of the purpose and function of a "provincial" book reviewer. The following six sections demonstrate how he put his theory into practice. The final essay in the volume is an evaluation of the theory and practice.

It is important in modern times because the currents of
the age are continually tempting people to merge their individual characters into the nervous, fleeting patterns of
thought that rise and shift and change in response to every
stimulus from without, which our means of communication,
so apt and quick, bring to us instantly. In subtle, imperious
ways we are constantly being urged to conform, to forget
our old centers and origins—in short, to be in fashion.
Cosmopolitanism is the virtue of an industrial age, but it is
also a defect, so far as it destroys diversity. It is fitting to
remember the difference between the civilization of Athens
and that of Rome. Athens was, in a sense, provincial; for
while it did not refuse wisdom that came from without, its
main strength was in its own Greek character. But Rome,
which began and for long years maintained a genius for
government, rapidly became cosmopolitan, and almost as
rapidly lost its sturdiness, falling a fairly easy prey to
decadence, partly because it was too comfortably tolerant.
It consolidated and selected, but it did not originate.

The analogy of Athens and Rome may perhaps be
attacked. But a student of provincialism does not need to
insist on such examples. He can see that a city civilization,
such as ours is becoming, will gain all the more color and
interest if it can maintain a certain diversity in its parts, and
it will profit by resisting forces within it which may serve
to bring out both its weaknesses and virtues. A modest
amount of provincialism, in fact, becomes almost a necessity,
if we are to have any peace of mind and fruitful repose.
Provincialism, in the favorable sense I am thinking about, is
a philosophy of life that begins with one's own rooftree.
It is rebellious against the modern principle of standardization, as it is carried over from science and machinery into
habits of thought.

It believes in unity as a principle of convenience and
beauty, but not in uniformity. It knows that harmony

comes not from exact correspondence but from a certain amount of diversity. It begins its reasoning, not with the new, but with the old and established things, wherever they are the marks of a native character and tradition that seem to have contributed something valuable and interesting to life; but it does not reject the new when the new seems valuable and interesting. Only, in the midst of a hue-and-cry after the modish and startling, it makes certain reservations and waits to see developments. In the time of mass-thinking, it keeps an independent mind, storing this, like a quiet citadel, with resources selected widely but discriminatingly. Above all, it does not put on airs. It does not pretend to be something other than what it is. It believes in integrity of soul and self-possession, but it hopes also to be kindly and it allows to others their own rights of differentiation.

The relation of such a philosophy to books may not be at first clear. But it has two or three important bearings on the subject of current literature, especially in the South. It means, first, that the growing tendency of the remarkable new school of Southern writers to fit themselves into modern literary patterns, although it is proper and advantageous in many respects, may become dangerous when it causes them to dilute and subvert and forget their own native inheritance; they cannot help being contemporary, but they need not be any the less Southern. This is not the most fundamental of all literary questions, but it is an important one at the moment.

The second bearing of a possible philosophy of provincialism would be on the general Southern audience. It may be true, as some of our critics have said, that the Southern audience has long been provincial in a bad sense, and needs to be scolded and admonished out of its obstinate wicked habits. But I cannot altogether agree, for the greater need seems to be that the South should explore its own mind and rediscover itself. For the time being it has had a sufficiently hearty dose of scolding. Let it now determine its own qualities, while not being hostile to foreign ones. And in the field of literature or the discussion of literature, that self-discovery which is what I mean by provincialism, is just as important as any modernizing process. It is, in fact, one true way of progress.

A warm but generous independence of mind may be all that we seek, in literature as in any other department of life. And here I may seem to be forgetting—what a recent correspondent pointedly admonished me about—the function of the critic as entertainer. But in this, no doubt, tedious preface I have aimed mostly at laying down a platform, and I could not forget the saying of the eminent English critic, Middleton Murry, that criticism "should openly accept the fact that its deepest judgments are moral." I am writing thus because I believe, as I trust those who read this page believe, that the South, in the new day of its prosperity and progress, is not ready to forswear its own character. While we take all good things to ourselves—and even a page so small as this may bear some relation to those good things— we are but reawakening certain interests that always were ours and we are confirming them as a part of what we are now becoming. The world of books, as well as the world of finance, religion, or politics is a route to self-discovery as well as to the discovery of new regions.

Under its new title,* this column does not necessarily lay claim to the function of long-distance forecasting to which the old-fashioned almanacs pretended, although a certain amount of forecasting may naturally, though riskily, occur. But almanacs are miscellaneous; they discuss other things besides the weather. They are domestic. They are homely things that used—in the old days—to hang by the

---

* This was the first column after "The Spyglass" changed its name to "The Critic's Almanac."

mantelpiece, and got into their pages some of the smoke and flavor of a log fire. They belong, maybe, among the Lares and Penates of a Southern hearth. This particular almanac, composed from week to week, does not claim to reflect the oracles of the gods. It may be as untrustworthy as most almanacs. But it will serve as a catch-all for memoranda, critical accounts, pictures of contemporaries. Literary philters and curiosities may be slipped in here, to be read or passed by, but at least printed with some regularity.

This has been no attempt to state a critical credo—only to discover some foundation or vantage point from which to observe the panorama of current literature—so to speak the procession of the literary zodiac. And the best vantage point, it seems, is close at hand, and it takes only a little trouble to reach it. Dr. Johnson said (I cull the quotation from the essay by Middleton Murry):

> The irregular combinations of fanciful invention may delight a while, by that novelty of which the common satiety sends us all in quest; but the pleasure of sudden wonder is soon exhausted, and the mind can repose only on the stability of truth.

And such a stability of truth we are all looking for, in one way or another. On this occasion I find it in a certain kind of provincialism; but, such is the vexatious nature of truth, in another week I may find it in cosmopolitanism.

Southern Fiction

T. S. Stribling

Critic's Almanac
April 18, 1926

"Has T. S. Stribling really written the Great American Novel?" ask the publishers of *Teeftallow* in a recent advertisement. The question, except as an example of unscrupulous publicity, is pointless. One might with equal justice ask if Mr. Stribling has written the Great American Magazine Article or the Great American Feature Story, for Mr. Stribling's book is as topical and temporary as either of those types. Considered as an unfavorable commentary on the customs and beliefs of the hill people of Mr. Stribling's native state, the book is, to say the least, an effective piece of writing, strong, nasty-tasting medicine for Tennesseans, of course, but probably useful in the long run. But judged, as a novel should be, by the canons of the best art, it will not meet the test. It is not only not a great novel; it is, in some ways, a poor novel, touching only the surface phenomena of Southern life.

Mr. Stribling, however, as a writer with four substantial novels to his credit, cannot be dismissed with a hasty indictment. His first book, *Birthright*, portrayed a Harvard-educated Negro returning to a Southern town, with results tragic for the Negro and uncomplimentary to the Southerners (Tennesseans, they were). *Red Sand,* his third book, is the story of a Venezuelan bullfighter, done with beautiful objectivity, a clear-cut, powerful novel. *Fombombo,* his second book, presents a rather grotesque combination of the exotic theme, so well managed in *Red Sand,* with a sort of Sinclair Lewis touch appearing chiefly in the main character, an American drummer selling firearms and hardware in an opera-bouffe South American republic. And now comes *Teeftallow,* which exhibits the most impolite cruelty to Tennesseans.

11

Only one of these books, *Red Sand*, possesses the clear detachment and inner stability which are the marks of good art. It is a tragedy of naive gallantry that is its own excuse for being. But let us observe that Mr. Stribling had to go to a foreign country to get such a theme. Toward his own land his gesture is one of rejection. In his own state of Tennessee people appear to Mr. Stribling in nonhuman disguises. His disgust with the wrongness of life in Tennessee transfigures it into a world of monstrosities, hollow puppets animated only by the most gross and vulgar ideas. So if he deals with Tennessee (or at least that section of it which is white and lives in the hill country), his indignation drives him into a specious sort of satire. In Venezuela, he can be artistically cool; in Tennessee his rage destroys all judgment. He can round out a Negro character (such as Peter and Caroline Siner in *Birthright*) with perfect sympathy; but white Tennesseans take on, in his books, the distortions of caricature and become the empty symbols of a social problem.

This is what we find in *Teeftallow*. The book gets its name from Abner Teeftallow, a mountain youth who is first exhibited to us on his journey from the poorhouse to the county court, where his guardian has been summoned to answer a charge for violation of the compulsory school law. Abner is saved from the law by the wire-pulling of Railroad Jones, the illiterate village Croesus, whose ideas of education may be summed up in his epigram that "Readin' and writin' 'll ruin anybody's ricollection." The amiable creature appears henceforth in the role of Abner's protector and benefactor, gives him a job with Railroad Jones's own construction gang, and uses him as a pawn when it is convenient to exploit the estate which Abner unexpectedly inherits. Railroad Jones is Mr. Stribling's best creation in *Teeftallow*. His sharp tricks, his feats of memory, his triumphs over smart city lawyers and wandering Yankees give him a slightly heroic quality which none of the other characters possesses. But Abner's personality is flat as a punctured balloon. He is a colorless rustic, distinguishable from other rustics only by the fact that the events of the book center around him. Even so, he has no motives, only automatic reflexes like a dung beetle or a gas engine. He is the familiar Uncle Josh, in a youthful edition, with none of Uncle Josh's "rube" quaintness and shrewdness. Nothing comes to him by his own action; things just happen to him. He falls in love when some friends playfully bump him into the arms of a yellow-haired country girl. Later he seduces her, apparently because he wakes up too late to attend a lynching-bee which the rest of the villagers are attending, and has nothing else to occupy his time. He carries a pistol and shoots craps because other people do. He is whipped by "whitecaps" and "run out of town," only to fall into the clutches of Adelaide, Railroad Jones's sophisticated daughter, who makes a monkey of him to pull her father's chestnuts out of the fire. When Railroad Jones is dead and Abner's prospects for a noble alliance are gone, Abner returns to his first love as casually as a fox to his vixen. He has neither thoughts nor emotions, only reactions, chiefly biological, slightly modified by a rudimentary herd-instinct such as sheep possess. He has not even the dignity of ambition and consuming passion that somewhat dignify that other worm of modern American fiction, Dreiser's Clyde Griffiths. He is a pinheaded hero.

As for the book in general, it might be described as pseudo satire, or synthetic satire, done with devastating cleverness and flashes of real wit, and based on remorseless observation. But it is not true satire, for true satire deals in frank mockery, and *Teeftallow* purports to give a serious picture. It has been called "realism," but it is only the sort of realism that turns up stones in Tennessee pastures in order to display the slime and the crawling, hideous creatures underneath. Indeed, Mr. Stribling might have made a check list of all the matters on which Tennesseans need to be admonished, for the book clicks these off neatly as an adding machine, with a very unpleasant sum-total. What about education in Tennessee? Well, here is Abner for an answer, with a "brain unspoiled by book learnin'," and Railroad Jones, who cannot read the contracts with which he is cunningly able to win lawsuits. What about religion in Tennessee? According to *Teeftallow*, there is only sanctimonious hypocrisy. The pious bank president in one moment engineers a crooked deal, and in the next moment stops his ears against profanity, with the exclamation, "God hears every word!" The equally pious and self-righteous Mrs. Biggers is a purveyor of scandal and an instigator of lynching; and, like the smirking villagers in Griffith's "Way Down East," heartlessly turns the poor wronged girl (a sinful scarlet woman) from her door. (I must not neglect to add that *Teeftallow* has a good deal of the smeary exaggeration of a typical Griffith movie.) The county court obediently sign a petition for the passage of an anti-evolution law, when an itinerant preacher shouts: "Air ye goin' to let the deceivin', agnostic, hell-bound college professors send our children to hell?" Tennesseans go to church; yes, but they also get drunk, shoot craps, tote pistols, practice seduction, bully Negroes, commit murder and arson, and meet in the village garage to tell dirty jokes, saving all their religion for the strenuous emotional outburst of a protracted meeting. They have government of a sort, but much prefer lynch law. The only decent people in *Teeftallow*, in fact, are the village atheist and a visiting Northerner who informs us that Northern people, in their daily conversation, "are occupied with sports, fiction, drama, pictures, dancing, science, philosophy, and such things."

To be sure we do not miss the point, Mr. Stribling

solemnly adds: "It was noteworthy that every single item in Mr. Ditmas's list was reckoned sinful by the hill folk."

Oh, the refined, heavenly Northerners! Oh, the smutty, boorish, ugly Tennesseans! Oh, the divine sarcasm of Mr. Stribling, who is also a Tennessean!

But let exclamations pass. Mr. Stribling presents, to my mind, the spectacle of an author who has perverted his great skill to cheap and obvious ends. He has seized the opportunity to administer a swift kick to Tennessee at the strategical moment when Northern ears were favorably attuned to entertain enthusiastically the sonorous thud of such a kick. The applause (in New York, for instance) is naturally almost deafening. At the same time I have not the slightest wish to imply that a kick of some sort is undeserved. I have not one atom of comfort to offer to patriotic Tennesseans who may wish me to rush to the rescue with the Southerner's conventional protest when he is under criticism. The most worthy result that could come from the publication of *Teeftallow* would be that it might shock Tennesseans into realization of their follies and shortcomings; they have, by certain actions, let themselves in for just the sort of thing that Mr. Stribling has done. From this point of view I accept *Teeftallow*, even with all its obvious injustices, as a valuable and perhaps timely book.

But as a specimen of the novel, I cannot accept it, in spite of the author's undoubted ability. Mr. Stribling has evaded, not solved or even tried to meet, his artistic problem. It is an easy trick to make an arbitrary arrangement of sensational features and call the result fiction. The writers of syndicated "sob-stuff" and high-life scandals understand that trick perfectly. It is another and a more difficult thing to plumb a people to the depth in the search for the essentials by which they live, and then to give these the clear, fully-rounded representation of art, with complete respect to every individual, whether noble or ignominious. In *Red Sand* Mr. Stribling did this, or came very near it. In *Teeftallow* he has not even attempted to do it and by that act he has neglected an opportunity rich as a Thomas Hardy or a Knut Hamsun ever had.

Elizabeth Madox Roberts
Spyglass
September 5, 1926

It is an extreme statement, no doubt, to say that up to the present time there have been very few really adequate novels dealing with rural life in America. Yet such a statement might be defended. Lay patriotism aside for the moment and try to make a list of novels of the American countryside comparable to any of Thomas Hardy's best. You will find plenty of books with "local color," all the way from Bret Harte to Emerson Hough and T. S. Stribling. But how few of abiding merit! How few that are free from sentimentality or from its opposite, caricature! How few that have the inner dignity and self-sufficiency of great art! To find the reasons for this condition would involve long investigation and debate. But one reason may be suggested here. It is a foolishly obvious one. Seldom in American literary history have we had the necessary combination of an artist who was an artist by nature and training and who at the same time lived so intimately with the people of hill or plain that he knew them as well as he knew his own soul. Seldom have we had a real artist who was able to approach people with the perfect sympathy and yet the detachment demanded in the highest art.

Of late there has been a tendency which the blurb-writers are fond of calling a "return to the soil." It has had some very healthy manifestations. I do not refer to the dull chronicles of Ruth Suckow—drab tales of drab Iowa farmers; or to the peevish compositions of T. S. Stribling; or to the popeyed investigations of Percy MacKaye. I mean rather a book like Glenway Wescott's *The Apple of the Eye*, which by the way is now being republished, and a few other books that have headed in the same direction. And at this particular moment I mean a book by a Kentucky woman—*The Time of Man*, by Elizabeth Madox Roberts, who has previously published only a book of poems, *Under the Tree*.

And now I am prepared to place Elizabeth Madox Roberts in the department of my mind which I had hitherto reserved mainly for Glenway Wescott. I am ready to say that she and Glenway Wescott are the two Americans of the twentieth century who have written most beautifully and intelligently of country people. She and Glenway Wescott approach, if they do not fully attain, the ideal which I indicated in the first paragraph. And in coupling Miss Roberts with Glenway Wescott I want it understood that I am paying one of the highest compliments I can command. Miss Roberts has what so few others have, at once the power of fine expression and a perfect command of the materials which are to be expressed. I am almost ready to say, though I do hesitate to say it on the evidence of one book alone, that she has by one stroke placed herself among the best novelists of contemporary America.

The Time of Man is a novel of the country people of Kentucky, especially those "poor whites" about whom you hear so much. It follows the life of a girl, Ellen Chesser, through the stages of adolescence, womanhood, courtship, marriage. She is a daughter of "travelers"—families who rove gypsylike through the country, now working, now

begging, always rather shiftless. Her people settle down as
tenants on a tobacco farm. After a while they grow dis-
contented and move on. Gradually they better themselves
a little, but not much. Always there is toil and some misfortune. And little of great importance ever happens to
Ellen. Although she is depicted as beautiful, kindly, unusually sensitive and ambitious for a country girl, the
round of her life is the same as that of other lives. She takes
the world as it comes, with some questioning and pain, but
little protest. Her wish is always going out to another
world, but her wish is never realized. Life is quiet for her,
even in the midst of violence and disappointment. But it is
deep. It is full of loyalties and loves. The tobacco plants
must be set. The turkeys must be fed. Men must be com-
forted. Children must be born. It must rain, it must snow,
and people must die. Ellen is a part of all this and accepts it.
She is different from other people of her world only in the
keenness of her realization of all that goes on about her and
beyond her, all she wants to have and can never hope to
have. Perhaps this is a defect of the book, that Miss Roberts
has made Ellen more self-conscious than she might naturally
be. Even so, I doubt whether the book could have been
written in any other way.

It might be thought that a book of this sort would be
dull. It would be dull in the hands of the plodding Middle-
Westerners, for example, Ruth Suckow again. But Elizabeth
Madox Roberts is not like that. She has the power of in-
forming all she writes with great beauty. She is a stylist
who knows what the art of language is capable of, and the
simplest incidents, the most familiar actions of country life,
the most usual features of landscape receive in her prose
treatment the vitality of poetry. Nor is this a mere business
of decoration. Miss Roberts does not overlay her writing
with strained literary effects. The beauty of the style is
native to the content and to the slow tranquil mood of the

book. There is a lyrical softness which is no affectation.

There are many people in the book, and they are all just right. But I am not going to speak of them. What most amazes me in this book is the dignity and naturalness with which Miss Roberts uses the old colloquialisms of the countryside, the brogue which has defeated so many in-expert writers. Miss Roberts gets it down just as it ought to be. The dialect of her characters is a triumphant example of just what Southern country dialect really is, and seldom is represented as being. But beyond that, dialect becomes in her hands a real literary instrument. It is not a trick, a superadded flavor of realism. You feel that it belongs in the narrative. It is a kind of poetry in itself. And as a final point, I must add that Miss Roberts has humor, too, for which let us be thankful. So few of the novels of the "poor whites" have shown any evidences of humor.

For example, here are some young people at a party, sitting by a fire. Somebody sees a spider, and the joshing begins, in the rough country way:

> "Durned if here ain't a louse," one said.
> "Oh, shut up!"
> "Keep it to yourself, hit's your'n."
> "Well, it is one now."
> "Well, kill hit then."
> "Hit's a tater bug."
> "Hit's a gnat or a flea, maybe."
> "Flea your hind leg! Hit's a body louse."
> "Step on it with your feet."
> "What was it, Dorine?"
> "Hit was a spider, Mammy."
> "Call hit a spider for manners!"

But it isn't quite fair to give such a boisterous passage as typical of *The Time of Man*, I suppose, though there is plenty of country crudeness in the talk of its characters. I close with some contrasting bits that indicate the quality of Miss Roberts's prose:

She heard the cattle come down to the creek to drink; heard them slopping in the water and pulling at the locust sprouts beyond the fence. The warmth of the bed shut around her and after a while the sounds of night became remote in their setting of stillness. The well-being of sleep stole over her limbs and she could see white clovers in a pattern, designed against dark threads of cloth. "I'm lovely now," this well-being said. "It's unknowen how lovely I am. It runs up through my sides and into my shoulders, warm, and ne'er thing else is any matter. I saw some mountains standen up in a dream, a dream that went down Tennessee. I will tell somebody what I saw, everything I saw. It's unknowen how lovely I am, unknowen."

*   *   *

They heard the voice of the preacher as it broke and parted among the corners of the room and flattened against the ceiling— Rehoboam and Jeroboam, kings, and the kingdom divided, never again to unite. Rehoboam and Jeroboam, great words striking the wall, great words with jagged fringes of echoes hanging from each syllable, and the lonely kingdoms, divided and apart forever, the great sadness of the lonely kingdoms settling upon them as they sat.

Julia Peterkin

Spyglass
April 3, 1927

Interest in Negro literature continues apace, and some of the manifestations of that literature have been duly noted in this column. None, however, seem at this moment so striking to me as the novel *Black April*, by Julia Peterkin, a white woman who for many years has lived on Lang Syne Plantation, in the low country of South Carolina. And here it is necessary to distinguish between three kinds of Negro literature—I use the term in a very broad sense. There is the folk literature of the Negroes, which is not in a sense literature at all, because it is unwritten; it is the most genuine and pleasing of the three kinds in many ways, as all know who have studied Negro songs and stories in their naive and unperverted state. Next is the literature written by educated Negroes themselves who strive to interpret their race and in so doing use the forms and fashions of the white man; and interesting as have been the attempts of Walter White, Countee Cullen and others in this field, the sophisticated Negro writers have not so far produced much that is finally convincing. The third type is the literature of the Negro which is written by the white man; one thinks of Joel Chandler Harris, Thomas Nelson Page and others, and is forced to believe, for the present, that the white man has rendered the Negro into artistic terms better than he has rendered himself, except in the folk literature. And this seems true despite the obvious fact that the white interpreter of the Negro cannot go beyond a certain point. Ultimately his knowledge, and therefore his art, is imperfect because his understanding must needs be imperfect.

Among writers of this third class I believe that Julia Peterkin will have to be assigned a very high rank. She, more than any other writer I know, seems to come close to transcending the limits I have indicated. She writes without either condescension or idolatry. She has no other object, I think, but to let the Negro speak in full character through her pages. She is a wonderfully sympathetic and faithful reporter, and I hazard the guess that she has forgotten more about Negroes than Joel Chandler Harris (for all his greatness), Thomas Nelson Page, and that prurient modern, Carl Van Vechten, ever knew. Her knowledge is so intimate, so detailed, so exact that one is overwhelmed and asks how a white person could ever know so much (if what she knows is true) about Negro life. And at the same time Mrs. Peterkin has, in a quiet way, great literary power; we knew this from her first book, *Green Thursday*, but it had

hardly led us to expect such an effective piece of work as
Black April.

The novel has no particular plot. It is a chronicle, rather,
of the slow, even stream of life among the Gullah Negroes,
who are considerably different from the types encountered
heretofore in literature. Their language at least is different,
so different as not to be understandable to one who is not
trained in it. And therefore Mrs. Peterkin's first problem
was to adapt this dialect to literary purposes, and her
rendering, whether or not it is actually near to the Gullah
talk itself, is unobstrusive and effective.

Most of the events of the book are reported as seen
through the eyes of a Negro boy named Breeze, who was
one of the putative children of April, the hard-ruling, tall,
imperious foreman of the Blue Brook plantation. Nobody
knew how many children April had, outside of his lawful
or "Yard-children"; he did not know himself. His reckless
yet shrewd and very human ways are the chief motive of
the book. He is a fine savage in trousers, ruling body and
soul the life of the Blue Brook plantation—judge, jury,
executioner, advocate, lover, human being. He catches a
rattlesnake and chokes it to death for the purpose of making
"rattlesnake tea." He quarrels with the preacher and dis-
misses him by the barbaric process of biting a piece out of
his cheek. When his best workman becomes impudent, he
strikes the rash man down with his overseer's stick and
"runs him off the plantation." The quarrel between Big Sue,
who is Breeze's foster-mother, and Leah, who is April's
wife, results in a killing. Then Zeda conjures April by
putting Leah's death-sheet over his feet while he is asleep.
April's feet deaden. Even the white man's medicine, dropped
into "hottened" water, fails to cure, and at some far off
hospital, April's legs are amputated at the hips. But when
he comes to die, he gasps with his last breath: "Bury me in

a man-size box—you un'erstan'?—A man-size box—I been—six—feet—fo'—Uncle—six feet fo'!"

Yes, April is "man-size," and so is the book. It is powerful, serene, good-humored, tempestuous by turns, with all the varying primitive passions kept for so many years in their undisturbed original state. The folklorist may read this book, if he wishes, for its infinite store of superstitions and sayings; the sociologist may read it for its account of a definite social group which has maintained itself practically untouched by civilization; everybody else may read the book for what it is, perhaps the first genuine novel in English of the Negro as a human being.

Conrad Aiken

Spyglass
August 14, 1927

> For he saw everything, and, in the centre
> Of corrupt change, one guileless rose; and laughed
> For puzzlement and sorrow.

These lines from a poem of Conrad Aiken's will pass as the insufficient yet significant epitome of a good deal of his writing. Aside from some exceptionally beautiful earlier lyrics, he has seldom spoken with an affirmative voice. Disaster and a sort of sweet despair are his fundamental tone—the disaster and despair of the modern who has looked, Actaeon-like, upon a knowledge forbidden, perhaps because it is too terrible to endure. But at all times his complete mastery of the art of language, his power of evoking a sensuous beauty from the images of decay, his lyrical faculty which disillusionment has not been able to kill, his absolute intellectual integrity—these qualities have attracted us to his work, though we may have come to it often with a half-grudging morbid fascination and considerable bewilderment. But now he has written a novel, *Blue Voyage*, and what do we find?

By and large, the same thing, only on a grander scale, with more fierceness, and with more direct relation to reality. *Blue Voyage* falls loosely into the category of novels which follow the lead of James Joyce in exploiting the "stream of consciousness" technique. In that great sprawling book *Ulysses*, what the characters actually do is of minor importance and indeed is not always clearly discoverable; but what they think—even to half-thoughts, inconsequentialities, and perceptions only vaguely realized —is all-important, and that is what is put down, so mixed with the chatter and movement of the superficial world of action as to compose an incoherent picture of life, which one gradually realizes is nevertheless a jagged but unified pattern of a personality. That is Joyce's method, and it is also Aiken's; but where most of the imitators of Joyce have been mere pettifogging apes, Aiken is a sound artist. His novel (and it is his first one) is a success; at the same time it makes somewhat the same impression on you as a suicide, well-planned, that comes off perfectly.

The central plan of *Blue Voyage* is simple. Demarest, a young writer, takes a second-class passage for England to see a girl he is in love with in a dazed, half-spiritual way. His shipboard friends are Silberstein, a gross but intelligent Jewish businessman; Smith, an honest and wistful Babbitt; Hay-Lawrence, an Englishman and philanderer; Mrs. Faubion, a clever and attractive divorcee; sundry other men and women, ordinary or vulgar. Strolling surreptitiously on the first-class deck where he has no business, he runs into the very girl he is going to England to meet, is told that she is going home to marry another man, and at a later encounter gets a polite snub. There is much chess-playing, small talk in the smoking room, sly love-making, all the usual actions of a voyage, but not much drama. The voyage has indeed become purposeless for Demarest, tragically purposeless, but purposefulness is supplied (if you will pardon a confused repetition of words) by working on the very theme of purposelessness, and the mind of Demarest is the channel through which this is accomplished.

The mind of Demarest, we may well guess, is also the mind of Conrad Aiken, and whether or not we like this sort of book depends on whether we like Conrad Aiken's (alias Demarest's) mind, as fully revealed by the Joycean method, or the particular view of the universe which is here presented with one person as the focal point, the center of circumscription. I am inclined to think that Aiken has himself described the book in a passage of a letter which he had Demarest write to his lady (and never sent).

It is my weakness as an author (so the critics have always said) that I appear incapable of presenting a theme energetically and simply. I must always wrap it up in tissue upon tissue of proviso and aspect; see it from a hundred angles; turn laboriously each side to the light; producing in the end not so much a unitary work of art as a melancholy "cauchemar" of ghosts and voices, a phantasmagoric world of disordered colors and sounds; a world without design or purpose; and perceptible only in terms of the prolix and fragmentary. But I have often wished that the critics would do me the justice to perceive that I have deliberately aimed at this effect, in the belief that the old unities and simplicities will no longer serve—if one is trying to translate, in any form of literary art, the consciousness of modern man.

A modest enough statement! And indeed what attracts us most in the book is its modesty, for in spite of the "immodest" revelations which naturally come to light when a modern mind is opened for inspection, there is no revolting presumption of cleverness such as afflicts many of Aiken's contemporaries. His presentation of the modern conscious- ness varies from the vulgar to the rhapsodical; but instead of the precocious bitterness of, say, John Dos Passos, Aiken has a poet's own tenderness. His people are all fully alive. His Mr. Smith, for example, is a truer Babbitt than Sinclair Lewis's own creation. And Aiken's use of language is nothing short of astonishing. On the one hand he can write small talk with stunning variety; on the other, he can write Demarest's subjective soliloquy, covering nearly eighty pages of rumination as Demarest lies on his bunk trying to go to sleep, with a fecundity, color, richness of invention and pursuit of associations and images that overwhelms you and leaves you breathless. Readers of *Marching On*, *A Good Woman*, and similar straightaway novels will not comprehend Conrad Aiken's devious ways, for Aiken is not so plausible a writer as Boyd and Bromfield; Aiken's book is indeed a sort of sweet poison, dangerous to the system; but I prefer his poison to many modern kinds I can think of.

Frances Newman

Critic's Almanac
May 13, 1928

After reading all of the 295 pages in Frances Newman's book *Dead Lovers Are Faithful Lovers*, I turned over and read what was on the back cover. The publishers had thoughtfully recorded the opinion of James Branch Cabell, H. L. Mencken and other important people that the mind of Frances Newman of Atlanta is profound, interesting, witty. It was encouraging to come upon these plain-spoken words, because they restored my faith in the English language. I may not believe H. L. Mencken, but at least I know what he is after when he says: "You have done an original and first-rate job." Who can tell what Frances Newman is after when she writes the following:

And since she did not think he could feel what she had felt if she was only able to whisper with her lips against his ear, and if she was only able to remember the moments when she had been thinking about him, she laid her lips against his smooth warm ear and murmured her wondering about what he had been thinking at fifteen minutes after three, when she had been listening to Mrs. Perryman's conversation and thinking, and what he had been thinking and doing at half past three, when she had been listening to Mrs. Abbott's conversation and thinking of what he could be thinking.

To quote the specimen sentence is a sufficient criticism of Miss Newman's book. That she is a "stylist," that she has a fine mind, that she has much learning, may all be true. But her "style" is a wilful forcing of the good English tongue into stiff monotonous patterns that are generally dull rather than quaint. With its eternal "which's" and "when's," its studious antitheses and parallelism, its leaden repetitions, it simply leaves me in the same disgusted condition I experience when I read a batch of very poor freshman themes. In fact, I am not sure but that Frances Newman, possibly from her long association with libraries, exploits all the worst faults of freshman themes.

Her mind is clearly a superior one, and it is original, else she would never have been able to write *The Short Story's Mutations*. It is also vulgar and uncreative in its direction. Both of her so-called novels, *The Hard-Boiled Virgin* and now *Dead Lovers Are Faithful Lovers*, strike the suspicious reader as mere autobiographical documents, slightly disguised but barely concealing the vitriolic social criticism which animates them. *The Hard-Boiled Virgin*, it is true, had a slight smear of tragedy in it, but there was hardly a

page without its malignant intent at puncturing some convention, especially the conventions of the Old South as
represented in the St. Cecilia Society of Charleston and the
aristocracy of Peachtree Street, Atlanta. The second
"novel" changes the theme a little to display to us the
entirely boresome mind of a Virginia daughter of the
Pages (not the North Carolina Pages) who marries an
Atlanta corporation lawyer. So far as the events of the
story can be deciphered, it seems to deal with the decline
and defeat of this dull, aristocratic lady at the hands of
another more intelligent but possibly unaristocratic lady
who works at a library. Yet whatever the difficulty in
digging out the story, there is never the smallest doubt that
Miss Newman is attacking the marriage convention and
again prying into silly Southern ways and exhibiting a
thorough knowledge of the physical mysteries of life.

Miss Newman's "novels," if such they be, resemble the
ugly whisperings of a repressed and naughty child more
than they do works of art; there is no use in our being impressed with them because they are advertised, because
they are recommended by Mr. Cabell, Mr. Mencken, and
their host of assembled worshippers, or because they have a
correct modern acidity. I hate to be so unpatriotic—indeed
so un-Southern—as to make disparaging comments on the
work of so distinguished a feminine writer as Frances
Newman. But I am compelled to believe her method is
perverse and sterile. It seems to be affected. It links up
with the writing of defeated Europeans like Joyce and
jabbering expatriates like Gertrude Stein, thus expressing
complete artistic weariness rather than the vitality of
thought and feeling that a Southern writer at this time
might well experience. It parades its intellectuality; but
a book like this latest one, when you grind it down to its
elements, tells no story and establishes no characters, except

so far as it gives cross-sections of their remarkably unin-
teresting and commonplace minds.

Nor does it seem to have any ideas that a reader can
grasp with satisfaction. Frances Newman apparently thinks
she is going to make us think she is thinking (if I may
borrow her style for a moment) by simply making all her
sentences walk on stilts. It is a pretentious way of being
dull. And if there is a sort of social criticism in her books,
I am unable to see that it is effective. We Southerners may
deserve Frances Newman, as the United States deserves
Sinclair Lewis. If she can shake us out of mental sloth and
too-easy conformity by her peculiar methods, I am all for
her. But I greatly fear that these books are not written in
terms that will penetrate far or shock very much, since
they are admittedly prepared (Mr. Cabell says) for the
very sophisticated few.

An Author Divided against Himself

Critic's Almanac
February 3, 1929

DuBose Heyward has enjoyed a considerable popularity
in the last few years, and has been looked on as a leader
among the new writers who have brought the South forward in literary matters. That the popularity is well deserved, I think no one can deny. But Mr. Heyward's third
novel, *Mamba's Daughters,* shows him to be wavering
between the demands of his own artistic integrity and the
demands made by outside influences, including no doubt the

public, the metropolitan critics, and the publishers—all three
as likely to operate for ill as for good.

The memorable *Porgy* was first of all a good story.
Perhaps it did not rise to great heights, but in an even,
mellow tone it unfolded the drama of an obscure and
pathetic life, strong in the primitive values for which our
jaded civilization is now greedy. It was faithful to the
Negro character it depicted, as Thomas Nelson Page and
others were faithful in the old days. Yet it has a novelty
of attitude. The Negro was allowed to stand forth as a
human being in his own right, with the white world not
merely put in the background but shoved completely out
of view. The slight tone of indulgence that Southern
writers have used toward the Negro was almost entirely
absent, though it was replaced by a somewhat elusive tone
partaking of the peculiar modern sentimentalism affected
nowadays. Furthermore, *Porgy* dealt with the Gullah
Negro, a regional type belonging to the Carolina coast and
not widely known. It was published at a time when it got
the full advantage of New York's sudden fancy for Negro
art of all sorts, and indeed for everything pertaining to
Negro life.

The second novel, *Angel*, toyed with Fundamentalist
themes against the social background of the North Carolina
mountains. It did not go well, for it was somehow artificial.
It had little conviction of purpose. It was not a very good
story. But public interest in Mr. Heyward's work continued, for the play, *Porgy*, made from the novel by Mr.
Heyward and his wife Dorothy, entered on a very successful run in New York and proved in many ways to be
even more interesting and satisfactory, from the artistic
standpoint, than the novel. There is also Mr. Heyward's
poetry to be considered. His *Skylines and Horizons* and
Carolina Chansons stand at the beginning of the poetry
revival in the South. His work as leader and organizer of

the Poetry Society of South Carolina was notable in many ways. Since he has now apparently gone over entirely from poetry to fiction, I do not need to prolong critical comment, except to observe that his poetry, like his fiction, is regional. It exploits the Negro, the mountaineer, the picturesque ways of Charleston. It reflects fine feelings and good taste and has a gentle lyrical charm. But it never shows great strength or originality.

Considering Mr. Heyward, then, as a regionalist, we are obliged to ask some primary questions. If we observe the works of Hardy or of the European novelists of the soil, or, in this country, of Elizabeth Madox Roberts and Julia Peterkin—all, in my opinion, true regionalists—we see at once that they write of their chosen section as if no other region existed. They bring to their interpretation of a locale no extraneous attitudes, being quite unconcerned about special "problems" and contemporary manias. They have no particular philosophy devised for an occasion merely and applicable only to mountaineers, cowboys or English milkmaids. But these special types are accepted as human beings, costume and place being pervasive but incidental; and whatever philosophy is applied is a philosophy of humanity in the large. Singularly enough, these writers get their universality by narrowing their gaze to the extremely particular.

Without wishing to put myself in too authoritative an attitude, I am nevertheless forced to believe that Mr. Heyward does not resemble the writers I have mentioned. As a regionalist, he does not possess their traits. And *Mamba's Daughters* is example enough.

If I did not know Mr. Heyward is the author, I could easily have imagined the book to have been written by some fly-by-night millionaire novelist from the Riviera or Gopher Prairie, who put his yacht into Charleston harbor for the winter season and picked up enough local color to

fill out his contract for a fifteenth best-selling novel. Not
that DuBose Heyward does not know his Charleston! Not
that he does not depict it accurately and with enough
humor to make us like him and it, even in spite of his
faults! But the voice and tone are not the voice and tone
of DuBose Heyward. They are of New York. They echo
its fashionable platitudes about the Negro and to some
extent play up to its curiosity about Charleston. The book,
in brief, though seeming to be an "inside" interpretation, is
without the passionate absorption in the subject that we
must demand of a regional novelist. It is written as if to
order.

As such, it is a rather astonishing mixture of things. First
of all, there is the story of Mamba, the old crone from the
vulgar Negro set who attaches herself to the patrician
Wentworths and makes herself an indispensable retainer
by shrewd ways that Negroes have. She is a real creation,
as well conceived as Porgy, or better. What Mamba does
is by way of sacrificial labor for her daughter, Hagar, a
giant incoherent child of earth, and more especially for her
granddaughter, Lissa. The story of Hagar and Mamba
alone would have been enough to make a fine book, and
I feel that Mr. Heyward has erred greatly in not sticking to
their simple tale.

But there is also the mixture. We are shown the pathetic
secrets of the proud-but-poor Wentworths, and in much
too obvious contrast to them the tawdrier secrets of a
family of wealthy social climbers from the North. The
mother of this latter family attempts in vain to break into
the exclusive St. Cecilia circle. Victory is attained only
when the father, a coolly efficient businessman, maneuvers
a business deal to the advantage of the Charleston men,
and through them wins the coveted entry. The son of
the Wentworths succumbs to the charm of a Northern
girl, whose love brings him to his real self—and he vanishes

weakly, rather vaguely, into the mists of New York. The unholy system by which workers in the phosphate mines are kept under the company's thumb is revealed; in this there is a little more than a hint of doctrinaire attitudes, and though the whole episode involving Hagar, young Wentworth, and others, has its dramatic and lively parts, it is rather detached from the main story. Then there is the story of Lissa, Mamba's talented granddaughter. She works her way into Negro aristocracy in Charleston and finally flees to New York after Hagar's sacrificial death and there her golden soprano charms exclusive circles and plays a distinguished part in making a new art. This last strand of narrative, especially inorganic, is an unexplainably pat echo of the Harlem school of rhapsody and propaganda, very surprising in Mr. Heyward.

The general treatment, too, smacks of conceptions extra-Charlestonian rather than indigenous. On one side is white Charleston, consciously patrician, idealized against the background of its romantic past, but a little infertile and chilly, yielding gradually before the onset of a commercial, hustling world. On the other side are the Negroes—full of primitive strength and zest, superstitious but humorous and wise, somewhat abused yet on the whole pampered and indulged by the white folks, curiously faithful to the "quality" white folks and to Negro codes at the same time. In this contrast, as in occasional touches on social conditions, Mr. Heyward ceases to be a local colorist and leans in the direction of sociology.

Reluctantly, one comes to the conclusion that in *Mamba's Daughters*, despite many excellent strokes of character and incident, Mr. Heyward has faltered uncertainly. He is divided against himself, and it is still impossible to say what he is going to make of himself. But in justice to him—and he is a writer for whom one would cheerfully make every possible excuse—it is well to remember that *Mamba's*

Daughters was first published serially. In the serialization, a stretching and filling out process may have occurred to the great disadvantage of the book and the disappointment of those who wish Mr. Heyward well.

Stark Young and Others
Critic's Almanac
October 6, 1929

Of the many people writing novels about the South, Stark Young is, so far as I know, the only one who sees the Southern way of life as a whole and communicates it with the grace and conviction that it deserves. Others, no matter what their distinction, too often seem special pleaders; bright or gloomy features distract them. They are not able to get beyond the case of the Negro, the poor white, the mountaineer. Like Ellen Glasgow, they are stricken with a contrary itching to deride; or, like Cabell, they achieve a bitter escape into romance, or like William Faulkner, they become terribly conscious of pain and decay. Let us value their special gifts as much as we please and admire them for their various excellences. Yet why should we forget that their views are partial? They plow narrow fields and plow too often, but Mr. Young strikes deep into a richer, wider ground. He explores the quiet provincial life that is most characteristic of the South. He works from the central body of society, which is sensible to change, but still abides; he does not skip around the circumference.

Consider the characters, the theme, the manner of Mr. Young's new novel, *River House*. We can easily imagine what the special pleaders would do with any one of the

characters in *River House* or with any particular angle of
its theme. His Major Dandridge would be served up by
Ellen Glasgow as a nice, silly old gentleman, wagging his
beard over modern follies quite uncomprehendingly while
witticisms (at the expense of Southern chivalry) crackle
around his futile head. Yes, Miss Glasgow would make a
whole book of the Major and have some witticisms left
over for the next book or two.

Mr. Cabell would begin with the extra-marital affair
of young John Dandridge, and Evelyn would pluck John
dreamily out of the office of the St. Louis bank where he
smoothes troubled brows of angry clients, would find him
a disguised reincarnation of Don Manuel, and then would
proceed to illustrate his sexual prowess in a series of adventures with reincarnated princesses, who would all turn
out to be Evelyn in disguise.

Elizabeth Madox Roberts and Maristan Chapman would
never get beyond the borders of the Dandridge plantation.
They would enter some remote and ramshackle cabin and
sob in picturesque accents over the "inner life" of its un-
washed tenants.

William Faulkner, whose eye sees further than most,
could use any or all of the *River House* people, but he
would probably prefer to concentrate on young John, who
would be all broken up by the wars and would wander
about doing violent and unaccountable things, hearing
bronze bells of twilight ring in his brain while all around
him his uncles and his cousins and his aunts would mutter
a chorus of Joycean-Aeschylean complaint.

DuBose Heyward would see nothing but the Negro
servants, Awce and old Uncle Amos. With joyous primitive
hearts, they would chant melodious spirituals in their delightful shacks on the Mississippi, and, turning away con-
temptuously from the wretched paleface, would stab one
another to death for the love of a buxom black wench,

while Ol' Man River still kept rollin' along. And so would Julia Peterkin, with more style and more scruple for reality.

And T. S. Stribling? What ornery two-faced cusses the Dandridge household would turn out to be under his morosely sarcastic eye! They would be nigger-beaters, grafting politicians, and adulterers, all loudly protesting virtue and gentility while they went about their incredibly low and vulgar ways.

And as all these dealt with the characters, so likewise would they deal with Mr. Young's theme, which concerns a point of family honor viewed differently under the codes of two Southern generations. Imagine their possible remarks. "How amusing," says Miss Glasgow. "What fools," says Mr. Cabell. "Nasty old hypocrites," says Mr. Stribling.

Of course, one might find ways to caricature Mr. Young's methods as I have caricatured these others—with, I hope, not too much injustice. Perhaps Mr. Young conceives his novel too much as a play, with repeated exits and entrances, stage "business" of picking up guitars and fumbling with books, and almost constant dialogue to carry the thread of the story. Perhaps, too, he is in a limited sense a special pleader. Obviously he dislikes the "New South" and progress and hates to see good old Southern ways submerged under cheap and easy gospels of prosperity. Good-humoredly, but a little too obviously, he lets us see his dislike; his doctrine would carry further if it were altogether implicit.

Yet he can be defended on all these counts. His novel is like a play, but its structure is taut and secure, and it is not "stagey." *River House* is not, like so many modern novels, an impressionistic hash; it has form as well as feeling. As for dialogue, are not Southern people the last remaining animals in America who can talk in anything but monosyllables—yes, who like to talk, even to converse, despite the invasions of bridge? If there is any American or European novelist who can make people talk more delight-fully than Stark Young, let him be dragged from his hiding place at once and advertised, for he is not yet known. And as for doctrine, his antiprogressivism (which is after all a subordinate feature) has the modern virtue of being quite heretical. It is fashionable either to damn the South or to gush over it; Mr. Young's heresy is that he does neither. His asides are aimed at worse monsters than any Southern contributor to the *Mercury* has yet discovered.

Mr. Young's *River House*, like his *Heaven Trees* and *The Torches Flare*, is essentially a novel of family rather than of one or two people. This time there is no observant Henry Boardman on hand to act as chorus and narrator, and Greenwich Village characters are absent. The scene is a little Mississippi town, Le Flore, or rather it is River House, the home of the Dandridges, who are "land people" and have been all their days. But as in *The Torches Flare*, Mr. Young gets the best part of his effect by putting old folks and young folks in contrast.

The main difference between the two generations is that one has a code and the other hasn't. Young John Dandridge, who comes home with his new wife, casually acquired, to lead the life of a country gentleman, which he thinks he would like, runs tragically headfirst into his father's code when he has barely settled down. It is a matter of a land dispute and an old estrangement between John's father and his dead mother—an affair which he has never known much about until now, when he somewhat too insistently worms the whole secret out of his reluctant father. Despite mutual love between father and son, despite John's affection for the old place and his home folks, he is gradually driven to realize that his father's ways and his own ways do not harmonize. So he abruptly walks out of the house one night and takes the train for St. Louis, where his banking job is presumably still waiting for him. There is no great dramatic crash, no heated struggle. The story works slowly and delicately to the impasse between the two parties, and John walks out. That is all there is to the story.

But there is much more to the book. It is exceedingly rich in its rendering of personalities. John and his somewhat flighty young wife Evelyn have all the mixture of sensitivity and insensitivity of moderns. They go by their feelings altogether, and are thus excessively generous and excessively untactful by turns, and in the wrong places. John can sympathize with the woes of his absent Cousin Ned, who, he thinks, has been mistreated, but since he has no sense of the past, he can't get the point of view of his father, who will not forget an old woe. Evelyn tosses off fine old wine as if it were cocktails, smokes cigarettes and appears "pour le sport" in a dress of the Major's dead and exiled wife, quite unconscious of being rude. John is a little better. He can see what he is missing, though he can't clutch it. Rather wistfully he says:

> How much stronger their generation is than mine, than ours. We just get slap-dashes of ideas and of what we want to do; they have a point-of-view. They know what they think about everything, right where they stand. And we think something different every time we turn round.

And these contrasts between young and old generations are the more evident because Mr. Young crowds his book full of delightful characters of the older generations, up and down the scale, all in their proper places. Major Dandridge is a little stiff, perhaps, but he is real. Slight as the ground of the dispute between father and son may seem, it is just like a Southern family to have such a skeleton in the closet and to be sensitive about it for half a century. John's aunts, Ellen and Rose, are done to perfection. They are the familiar, devoted maiden aunts who know all the family legends and cover up all the little rough places of life with a flow of pleasant talk, and they know, too, the things that must never be mentioned, the time when it is better to play the guitar or gather flowers than to talk. And Cousin Tom, with his hatred of crickets and his infatuation for correspondence between the Book of Revelations and Confederate history, and Mr. Bobo, perpetual guest and feudal hanger-on—how curious and how true they are. Five old folks and two young ones, thrown together in the "last old house" in a too-rapidly modernized country town—what opportunities they afford for the long, pleasant chatter and anecdotal allusion in which Mr. Young excels. He knows, too, the thousand miscellaneous things that give Southern life its flavor—how people pronounce words; the "wise quietness" with which they (at least the older generation) take life, when they have suffered much; and why Negroes don't commit suicide. (Awce says: "I reckon hit's because evy time I sets down and gits to thinkin' about my troubles, I goes to sleep.")

No great thunder of tragedy rolls from Mr. Young's book. No remorseless plumbing of "life forces," no psychological analysis, no "social problem" engages his pen. But he has written in this novel, as in his former ones, something altogether his own, something that moves in a direction nobody else has taken, something that seizes you irresistibly but quietly and goodhumoredly and puts you in the living presence of a reality so warm and true that it does not fade. All Southern or non-Southern aspects aside, that is achievement enough for any novelist in America or wherever you please.

Farewell—and Hail!

Critic's Almanac
February 16, 1930

Odious and unjust as comparisons may be, one must perforce reflect now and then on the singular conjunction of events. It so happens that James Branch Cabell says farewell to the novel at the time when Thomas Wolfe makes his first appearance as a novelist. And although *The Way of Ecben* and *Look Homeward, Angel* are not of a like order, it is not stretching the truth to say that they come from the same condition of mind. It is not exactly a lamentable condition, for the by-products and incidental features are such as give delight to many persons; but it gives no firm assurance to those who may look for the shadow of a great rock in a weary land.

Mr. Cabell, already a veteran of a distinction that we must all respect, tells one of his old stories over again, or a variation of his perpetual theme that "the dream is better," that beauty is elusive and not to be held for more than a moment, and that nevertheless, men do well to prefer to spend their lives seeking it rashly, in spite of the certainty of defeat. What happens to Alfgar, in this brief tale, is hardly more than a rewriting of what has happened to all Mr. Cabell's heroes; and Ettarre and Horvendile and other shadowy creatures of the Cabellian mythology make their ironic appearance as before, with cues, entrances and exits intoned in Mr. Cabell's beautiful and deprecatory prose manner.

When this is done, there is still about a fourth of the book to read, which is called the "Colophon." Here Mr. Cabell delivers his personal confidence about his generation, his own writing, and his firm determination to bring the biography of Manuel and associated projects to an end with this book. Some of his statements have already had great publicity—notably his opinion that novelists ought to cease writing at the age of fifty. But not so much has been said of this comment on his own generation.

"It was," he says, "the first generation which said flatly: 'All is not well with this civilization.'" But it also is "a generation of which the present-day survivors appear a bit ludicrously to go on fighting battles that were won long ago." And it "is destined to be huddled away, by man's commonsense, into oblivion." For it has not only said, "All is not well." It has offered no panacea to correct the ills it denounced. And though possibly, in Mr. Cabell's opinion, no panacea may exist, it maybe seems a little unfortunate for the perpetuity of his generation that it had nothing in particular to suggest.

As to the perpetuity of Mr. Cabell's generation and of certain of his own works, I think we can easily give solid reassurances. But in acknowledging the refusal of himself and others to "offer a panacea," he has come very near the truth. Yet "panacea," which is spoken, I fear, out of secret and mistaken pride, is the wrong term. Mr. Cabell's generation, after subjecting us to a series of drastic purgatives, now can neither heal us nor feed us; in fact, it has rendered us practically incapable of taking nourishment at all. What Mr. Cabell should have said is that his generation has offered no convictions alive enough to straighten the disordered pattern of our lives, no sure direction that we can take with comfort, no centrality and no doctrine. For literature, this is a barren legacy, equivalent almost to a curse. To the generation of rising younger novelists, Mr. Cabell and his fellows bequeath fine words and a bucket of ashes.

In Mr. Wolfe's fine novel, I believe, one may discover more than a trace of this inheritance. One gives *Look Homeward, Angel* much the same sort of disturbed admiration as to Ernest Hemingway's works. The performance is superb; it is already enough to captivate an entire chorus of New York reviewers into warm twitterings of praise and prophecy. Yet surely virtuosity of performance is not enough. I feel the lack in Mr. Wolfe's novel of what must be called, for want of a better term, "point of view," or conviction, or purposiveness. Or to put it differently, there is evidently no real harmony between this artist and the materials he deals with; and the result is inevitably a kind of inner confusion, which, though it does not destroy the incidental merits of the book, does hurt its total effect.

The materials here are the materials of Southern life. Specifically, the story is of a large Southern family, begotten and reared in some mountain town (let us say Asheville, North Carolina). The progenitor is a stonecutter named Gant, of English-American extraction, who strays into the country, carpetbagger-wise, in the wake of the Civil War, marries Eliza Pentland, one of an old and numerous clan, and settles down. The incurable romanticism of Gant, which vents itself all through his long life in rhetorical maundering and wild bursts of energy, is thus wedded to the stable, property-loving nature of Eliza. And this dual nature, a combination of the vulgar and the sensitive, is exhibited in their various progeny, whose history the novelist chronicles in detail. Incidentally, the chronicle of the Gant family is also the chronicle of the mountain town as "progress" and a modicum of wealth, acquired by hotelkeeping and investments, impose a veneer of change.

So far, so good. The reader is prepared to consider this to be something like an American Forsyte Saga; but it has, with all its detail and involved stratification, none of the solidity of Galsworthy. As it gradually develops the book is about Eugene Gant, the youngest son, and the most sensitive and poetic creature of the lot. It is almost sufficient to say of Eugene that he is both tortured by his environment and drawn to it. In the end, after a long riot of sensitivity and seeking, which often expresses itself in impulsive outbursts, much like those of the elder Gant, he simply runs away to Yankeedom forever.

This account seems to give the book more coherence than it actually has. Eugene goes through the years of his life in alternate puzzlement and disgust, with only occasional spasms of delight. His confusion and hurt are, I am convinced, identical with the confusion and hurt of the author. The book must be considered, in a very real spiritual sense, autobiographical. Indeed, the author practically tells us in so many words that Eugene (who is evidently himself) entertains a certain hatred and loathing for the South, perhaps all the more because he recognizes it as a part of himself, which he has now honestly put on record. Therefore we must deduce that the real subject of the novel, so far as it has a single subject, is some mixed and not very clear thesis, which might be stated thus: "Why Young Men Leave the South."

Is this not a tragic condition of mind for an ambitious and able novelist, at the very outset of his career? With all the equipment for his craft that could be wished—power of observation, insight into character, robustness and largeness of manner, an extensive vocabulary, and a supple style whose range includes the armchair coziness of a good Victorian method as readily as the wilder methods of Joyce and Proust (perhaps too readily)—with all this, the novelist must yet assume a negative attitude and must betray the disorder of his mind in a general desultoriness. The detail of the book is everywhere good. Take it piecemeal, and you have remarkable pictures and incidents of family and individual life, of newspaper offices in drear mornings, of the slinky, blowzy atmosphere of resort hotels, of the furtive harlotries of small towns, of youth in a Southern university (the University of North Carolina, perhaps?), of the tumult and fever of love. And perhaps few novelists of our time have created, at a single stroke, such an interesting gallery of individuals—for they are individuals, rather than types.

But brilliant and powerful as it is—even magnificent, at times—*Look Homeward, Angel* has a sickness in its marrow, a sickness of divided aims and of dislikes that are everywhere stronger than likes. "Eugene," says the author, "was quite content with any system which would give him comfort, security, enough money to do as he liked, and freedom to think, eat, drink, love, read and write what he chose. And he did not care under what form of government he lived—Republican, Democrat, Tory, Socialist or Bolshevist —if it could assure him those things." Maybe Eugene could be indifferent to "systems" without harm, but I do not think that Mr. Wolfe can be. The separation of art from life can only be injurious and confusing. Let us hope it will not be a permanent separation, for Thomas Wolfe is too fine a writer to succumb to the defeatism which might be called Cabellian.

Elizabeth Madox Roberts
Critic's Almanac
March 16, 1930

Elizabeth Madox Roberts's fourth novel, *The Great Meadow*, shows all her fine qualities at their best. . . . What is the subject matter? In general, this time it is the westward push of the pioneers from Virginia across the mountains that brought the Watauga and Cumberland settlements into Tennessee, and Boone's Fort and Harrod's Fort into Kentucky. Of course Miss Roberts is writing specifically about Kentucky, which is her own state, and about people that are her own people in a real ancestral sense. *The Great Meadow* is thus as historical a novel as I ever read before. What made the Albemarle people want to go into Kentucky; how did they feel about going; what did they think and feel about their journeying and arriving and settling down; how did they behave in all the dangerous shifts of wilderness life?—these, I take it, constitute the matter that Miss Roberts is interested in giving. All the time, it is evident, she wants to be inside the minds of the Kentucky pioneers, and is not much concerned about telling a brisk story, with the wilderness a stage—which is what James Fenimore Cooper or Winston Churchill would have done.

What happens, then, in the novel, for something must happen in any novel? A great deal, when one comes to think about it. Diony Hall, a girl of an Albemarle family who has "the marryen mouth," marries bold Berk Jarvis and sets forth with him on the very day of her wedding, to follow Dan'l Boone's Trace into the Promised Land of Kentucky. When the long journey is over, they settle at Harrod's Fort, and experience all the hardships of pioneer life. Diony is saved from prowling Indians by the sacrificial devotion of Elvira Jarvis, Berk's mother, who is slain and scalped. Berk goes against the Indians to avenge his mother's death and does not return for a long period. And in the meanwhile Diony, thinking him dead, marries Evan Muir, who is devoted to her in her loneliness. But finally Berk does return, worn and spent with captivity among Ojibways, and the rough pioneer code decrees that Diony must choose between her two husbands. It is a wilderness version of the old Enoch Arden story, boldly and beautifully handled, with the American Revolution but a rumor of wars in the far-off background and the privations of Indian warfare and settlement building furnishing the main episodes.

Yet there are really no episodes. *The Great Meadow* is no tale of action. All this passes as in a glamorous dream where all things pass with the slow, equal intensity of thought. The narrative is like the bright steady flow of a river which does not change even while it changes. All is in the mind of Diony. And this leads to the next question:

What is the manner of the telling? It is the same as in *The Time of Man,* but more carefully shaped and confined to a unity, less straggling, and therefore less tedious. Seek for words to describe the effect, and you will have to say somewhat about reveries, or trance, or even hypnosis. Perhaps the second word is best. In this style, people, things, events are fixed as in the soft glow of a trance. It is as if these figures of wilderness people struggling and loving in the magic land of "Kaintuck" never had more than the muted reality of a dream spun in the thought of Diony Hall, like bright or dark threads on a smoothly humming wheel whose sound is a simple melody yet is rich with overtones.

The overtones, which are not to be separated from the melody, are to be found in the language and in the sharpness and particularity of the physical detail. What Elizabeth Roberts does is to make archaisms of speech, which appear quite forthrightly in the dialogue, the basis of an entire prose style which is not in itself archaic. The archaisms somehow strike a pitch for the sweet monotone of the prose; lying beneath it, they still invade and color it. And into this monotone are worked the thousands of little ways of life, as a painter would work in bits of color to make a harmonious composition—the manner of dress, the talk of distant happenings, the look of forests, the sounds of human and animal life, the strands of social behavior. It is all so skillfully done that I am quite at a loss how to describe it.

Then how does one estimate the performance in general? Certainly it is far above even the average good performance in contemporary English and American fiction of today. Miss Roberts's writing has an excellence all its own. There is nobody to compare her with, unless it would be Virginia Woolf, with whom, in method at least, she has some slight kinship. Whether or not she is founding a literary tradition that may be used by others is another question.

How she differs from her contemporaries is an easier question to answer. First of all, she has no special prejudice, so far as we can tell, for which she is making her novel a vehicle, and she is not writing about country people or pioneer people because it happens to be the fashion to write about them. Somehow one feels that in writing as she does she is doing the perfectly natural and inevitable thing, which has come spontaneously out of herself as a natural-born Kentucky person.

This, I suppose, is what one calls literary sincerity. No doubt it is what Glenway Wescott is driving at when he writes of Elizabeth Madox Roberts at the University of Chicago:

> There was the young Southern woman, alone, absolutely original, unimpressed by the setting of evils and plagiaries, meek and insinuatingly affirmative, untouched by but kindly toward all our half-grown basenesses. [Or again] Wherever she was, it (Kentucky) evidently underlay the outbranching experience, folded shadowily into the typical scenes of an author's life—an immense territorial ghost.

(One must somewhat cruelly observe that Mr. Wescott, the author of *Goodbye, Wisconsin*, does not have a similar feeling for his own state, which, instead, he patronizes.)

And being, so far as we can tell, without social programs and preconceptions, Elizabeth Madox Roberts does show the excellences and advantages of provincial art at its best. Happily, she has never learned to abhor nature and simple things; they are not for her something to reform or to condescend to, nor have they for her the false romantic attraction of offering a convenient literary attitude. What they are, she is. Her subjects, her vocabulary, her style, her thought, and herself must surely be all in harmony. Out of this harmony come her scrupulous and beautiful books and her sureness of purpose, which contrast so remarkably with the works of our numerous muscle-bound and be-fuddled literary athletes.

Is the critique all praise, then? This question might be side-stepped by saying that her work has definite limits. Certain things it does well; it cannot do everything. Per-haps at times it is dangerously near to fastidiousness and affectation. It is of course absurd that a young pioneer woman could be metaphysical, as Diony seems to be. Hardly does it seem possible that the pioneers thought so intensely, and Bishop Berkeley's theories of mind and matter, which provide one of the minor motifs of this curious novel, could hardly have been in the conscious purpose of the Long Knives who won Kaintuck. There is a mystical strain in Miss Roberts that is a little confusing and strange. One fears that the poetic richness it provides carries with it a risk of downright queerness. But Miss Roberts will probably slide safely between Scylla and Charybdis by virtue of a quiet sense of humor.

Ellen Glasgow—Social Historian

Critic's Almanac
April 13, 1930

More than four years ago, the late Stuart P. Sherman discovered in Ellen Glasgow a novelist who treated "provincial life from a national point of view." Sherman was not the first to "discover" Ellen Glasgow; in fact, he was a little late in improving his mind to that extent. But one wish of his, expressed at the time, has come to pass: he hoped for a collected edition of Miss Glasgow's works, since he had been put to much trouble in rummaging through bookshops to find them. The *Old Dominion* edition of Ellen Glasgow's novels is now a reality in which we may all rejoice. To have it in hand confirms not only Stuart Sherman's good opinion of her, but the general one as well. . . .

The first issue of the *Old Dominion* edition includes four volumes: *The Battleground*, originally published in 1902 (when Miss Glasgow was 28); *The Deliverance*, 1904; *Virginia*, 1913 and *They Stooped to Folly*, 1929. Each volume has a short preface in which Miss Glasgow sets forth her intention as to the particular novel. Whether she has revised the text itself, I do not know; but I imagine she has not heeded Sherman's humble petition to reduce her novels twenty per cent in bulk "out of tender regard for the brevity of man's life." For they are spacious novels—especially the early ones—that take their own time about getting under way and finishing up. Often they are laborious. Nearly always they are more loquacious than they need be—even in the entirely modern *They Stooped to Folly*. For a mind alternately goaded and enervated by the galvanic excitement of modern literature, they make slow reading; but what a pleasure to read something that stays a while!

In the earliest of the group of four novels, *The Battleground*, Miss Glasgow began the program which, in 1902, only a rather strong-minded writer could have undertaken. She wanted to write, she explains in her preface, "a complete social history of Virginia since the Civil War" and "to look beneath the costume into the character of civilization."

Her first claim to distinction among American novelists today is that she has carried out her plan consistently and seriously. While novelists in general have been a wavering, unsteady tribe, her novels can honestly be described in her own terms as "a continued comedy of manners which would embrace the whole varied structure of Virginian society." Her resolution to hew to one mark is all the more striking when one considers that it was taken during the giddy days of the Graustark romance, while the Mauve Decade was still casting a faint, dying glow. Critical intelligence, strong-mindedness, independent feminism have put her on one path and kept her there. And so, strangely enough, Ellen Glasgow, a Southern writer, anticipated by some fifteen years the realistic trend that has lately become a pronounced feature of American fiction.

However, a writer of such pretensions must suffer a very close examination. And when that writer proposes to interpret a society of which she is an intimate part, her point of view needs to be studied. Intelligence, with which Miss Glasgow is unusually gifted, is not enough by itself. After all, a writer is expected to feel as well as to observe and analyze. There must be a real communion between the interpreter of the society and the society, for a novelist can hardly hope to attain, or want to attain, the strict and critical detachment of the academic historian. The historian's task is scientific in a sense; the novelist's is artistic.

Too much aloofness in the novelist is deadly. It results not so much in "artistic detachment" (a quality that I defy anybody to explain) as, more dangerously, in coldness and condescension.

I feel sure that Miss Glasgow has always had intelligence, and with it, in large measure, the general technical equipment of a first-class novelist. But I am doubtful whether her feeling has been in the right place. She has not always been at one with her own people. She has looked at them from the outside as often as from the inside.

We may leave *The Battleground* aside as a fairly minor book. It is not much of a novel, although it gives a pretty systematic picture of what Miss Glasgow thinks of Virginia society. All the types are in it, from glorious gentlemen and fine ladies to obstreperous sons and humorous mountaineers; but tragic-romantic themes simply don't fit Ellen Glasgow's spirit. Her works really do "drop groundward." *The Battleground* has only a historic interest.

The Deliverance, however, really comes alive. It is a fine novel of Reconstruction times, showing very sympathetically the social disorder of the period and the struggle of codes that inevitably took place when landowners lost their patrimonies and the daughters of overseers were sent off to finishing school. The well-conceived plot of *The Deliverance* somewhat exaggerates the jostling of classes. The Christopher Blake of this book drudges too obstinately in the shadow of the family mansion which his father's overseer (he thinks) has filched from him. Too grimly he swears eternal revenge on the vulgar thief; so neatly does he slide into a love match with the overseer's educated daughter. But the characters and the scenes are, with one exception, splendid.

That one exception, I fear, betrays the worm in the bud of Miss Glasgow's ambitious intentions as social historian.

It shows that she sees Virginia people perfectly on the surface; but one doubts whether she intimately understands them.

One of the memorable characters in *The Deliverance* is the blind old lady, Mrs. Blake, who has been kept in ignorance of the South's defeat and of the loss of her family home. For her, the Confederacy still exists; she lives on illusion, and loses her mind forever when the illusion is broken roughly. Of her Miss Glasgow says, with unhappy explicitness: "I saw in her not one old woman alone groping blind and nourished by illusion . . . but Virginia and the entire South, unaware of changes about them, clinging with passionate fidelity to the empty ceremonial forms of tradition."

The task of the sympathetic novelist, one would think, would be to show the "passionate fidelity"; but not necessarily to disapprove it or patronize it. Miss Glasgow not only gets up theses and writes novels to fit, not only makes human beings into symbols—she passes *ex cathedra* judgments on the people and the civilization she is writing about. She is thus more the social critic (not always a good one) than social historian.

So in *Virginia*, another very fine novel, Miss Glasgow apparently seeks to demonstrate the inadequacy of Southern female education in fitting young women for motherhood and wifehood. It is a study in maladjustment. But quite unwittingly, Miss Glasgow does what Tolstoi said Tchekov did in his story, "The Darling"; he intended to show how silly the "Darling" was; he ended by making her a very fine character. About the same thing happens to the heroine in *Virginia*.

Miss Glasgow's system of ideas that furnishes her with theses and attitudes toward Southern society would be, I suppose, difficult to trace. Perhaps it has a good deal of Walter Hines Page's liberalism, in the earlier novels; and in the later ones, such as *The Romantic Comedians* and *They Stooped to Folly*, it derives a good deal from the "modern temper." One suspects that there is a flavor of Frances Newman in these two novels. Whatever it is it subtracts more than it adds. One feels like discounting her attitudes and reading her books, distinguished though they are, for incidental rather than major rewards. No doubt Ellen Glasgow is, as the critics have frequently said, the wittiest novelist in America; but witticisms hardly do the social historian any good, except in dealing with drawing-room varieties of civilization. Yet I make the complaint with hesitation, being well aware that there is much more to say for Ellen Glasgow than I have been able to say in making this one small point.

Roark Bradford

Critic's Almanac
April 20, 1930

There have been so many unpleasant books. We have read them dutifully as a concession to "culture." And having improved our minds by the usual process of psychological torture, we ask for some pleasant books, just for a change. To begin with there is Roark Bradford, who has arrived in our midst without producing a single reform from his vest pocket. Mr. Bradford's latest collection of Negro stories, *Ol' King David an' the Philistine Boys*, follows the line of his first success—the well-remembered *Ol' Man Adam an' His Chillun*. Furthermore it comes at the moment when the play *Green Pastures*, which Marc Connelly based on *Ol' Man Adam*, is greatly exciting the theatrical world of New York. The old-time religion, Negro-style, with God appearing as a "natcheral man" and Gabriel ready to blow his horn, has just about completely captured the most un-Christian and totally irreligious audience in America. A curious sidelight on the situation is the controversy that has grown up, as to whether Marc Connelly or Roark Bradford deserves the credit for the play; and Hasty Heywood Broun has stopped talking about Communists long enough to testify in the matter.

About the play, I can't speak, not having seen it or read it. But I should like to make a rash guess as to what Mr. Bradford's secret of success may be. It is not merely in his faithful rendition of Negro character, which follows the Joel Chandler Harris rather than the Heyward-Peterkin mode, and, I think, rightly so. It is not in his humor, which, like all humor deriving from Negro subjects, is countrified —and therefore shrewd and wholesome.

It must surely be in his rendering of religion itself—a rendering which I am inclined to believe is serious rather than comic in its final effect. Mr. Bradford, in his quiet and unpresuming way, has slipped up on the American public and taken a left-handed advantage that no minister of the Gospel could assume. Without seeming to intend it, he has got a hardheaded people interested in religion. And this is the way I should elucidate the matter.

For divers complicated reasons, it has become "bad form" to be religious in any thoroughgoing way. You may liberalize, and sociologize, and do welfare work, but you mustn't *be* religious—unless you are a Fundamentalist. However, the religious instinct does not surrender quite so easily. It revives immediately when it can be enjoyed vicariously, as we may enjoy it in the Bible stories of Mr. Bradford. It is not "bad form" to take delight in spirituals or to read stories and see plays that present Old Testament characters, even God himself, in Negro guise. We applaud and approve; we may even confess an unashamed rapture when we are permitted to walk with God without violating the social proprieties of the modern age. Nobody is going to condemn a Negro for picturing God as a benevolent but rather subtle old gentleman with the white beard. We hide from the world our secret affection for the same image of God, and use the Negro as our proxy. It is much like the privilege of the mask for gala occasions or of children's games played by adults.

In the end, it shows the power of the myth, which science has tried so hard to destroy or to displace with shoddier myths. The most powerful appeal is never through logic and reason; but when ideas attach themselves to a certain manner of speaking which by common consent is privileged against hard and fast criticism, and which has rules of its own that suit our inmost sense of rightness—then a myth is created to which we ally ourselves only too gladly. Roark Bradford is, in a moderate but nonetheless certain way, a mythmaker. Far from cheapening sacred lore, he strengthens it, or makes it strengthen ours. Of course I don't mean to claim that this particular point is an original and unique idea of mine. Others have said, quite properly, that neither Mr. Bradford, nor Mr. Connelly, nor Negro ways of talk deserve as much credit as the Good Book itself, from which grand source they all derive.

The delightfulness of the stories in their telling needs no particular comment. They win their way without special advertisement. Some are a little strained, perhaps; some are just ordinary; but many are very good, indeed—among the most notable, to my notion, being "Elijah and the Meal Barrel," with its moral beginning: "About the time you git to whar you figgers you don't need de Lawd to he'p you out, dat's about de time you needs Him mostest."

Other American Fiction

Glenway Wescott, *The Apple of the Eye*

Extra Review
December 21, 1924

Some American novelists can write well, but have nothing to write about; such is Carl Van Vechten, for instance. Others, like Dreiser, have much to say, but cannot say it with any distinction. The combination of fine style and great thoughts is so rare that the field of American fiction looks to be an assemblage of illiterate giants on the one hand and featherheaded dilettantes of literature on the other. But here comes Glenway Wescott with a first novel that proves the combination can be made.

Here is a writer who at his first effort (so far as we know) turns off a book that is very nearly a perfect piece of prose. Words glow like jewels under his hands. His effects are studied, yet there is no specious glitter about them. You see his striving, you feel that it comes from a deep sincerity that wants to express itself harmoniously in absolute consonance with its subject.

More than this, Glenway Wescott has had the courage to treat a difficult and serious subject without making the slightest compromise with popular taste. His novel—which is really more a series of episodes than a novel proper— deals with the course and the consequences of repressed, struggling passion in the lives of country folks in southern Wisconsin. In places it is an ugly, terrible tale, so far as the facts go. At others it has the clear, warm beauty of a Grecian idyl. But at all times the author's sympathetic restraint and his beautiful prose temper sordidness into serenity and terror into pity.

One gropes for words to describe the story, and finds none that will do. Baldly, it is the story of Bad Han and Rosalia and Jules Bier and Mike, all of whom in their own days and times struggled with a love either unrequited or forbidden and who had to endure in bitterness the cold and inflexible way of the world. They are caught by blind forces they do not comprehend. They perish in sorrow, or flee in dismay, or bitterly hold their tongues. It is all the same; tragedy is the end. But not a tragedy bleak and complete. Life somehow lies fair enough beneath it all.

The tale is of southern Wisconsin, but though Wescott describes an American landscape and American persons, both his scene and his people seem remote. About his book there is an air of brooding and contemplation; we seem to be in a far land, only half-familiar. It is more like a European than an American novel.

The episodic structure has been unfavorably criticized in some instances. It does perhaps give resemblance of fragmentation; the unity of structure is not perfect. There is no plot in the usual sense. But no longer in this time can restrictions be put on the structure of the novel. Novelists do what they please, and we have only to ask whether the result pleases us. In Glenway Wescott's case it does, for he has a unity of mood.

The book comes dangerously near morbidity, and Mr. Wescott, like most of the younger writers of the day, has read his Freud and his D. H. Lawrence. To a certain extent he does what Sherwood Anderson does in interpreting obscure lives and obscurer sentiments. He objectifies his materials, sometimes almost too severely, but he never grows maudlin.

Sherwood Anderson's *A Story Teller's Story*
Extra Review
January 18, 1925

The easy thing to say about Sherwood Anderson's autobiography is that it is Sherwood Anderson's best novel. And it is true in a large sense. Sherwood Anderson, as protagonist, reconstructs a drama of self-realization in the midst of the antagonistic forces of American life. Since "the true history of life is but a history of moments, the record of significances rather than mere facts," it is his aim "to be true to the essence of things." Therefore, while his book has "form," in the most modern sense of the word, it is, compared with the usual autobiography, apparently straggling and disorganized. With only the loosest regard for time-relations, he works backward and forward as he pleases, with always a leaning toward parentheses. For he is seeking to bring out the history of his inner consciousness, to characterize the forces that made him a "word-fellow," rather than to depict mere physical events in chronological order.

One may say in the first place that this method, which may prove a little distracting to some readers, operates to give us some of the best writing that Sherwood Anderson has done. The pictures of his boyhood days are clear and serene, never blurred; the portraits of his father and mother and other characters are singularly attractive; and certain dramatic episodes stand out as stories within themselves, as pointed and as moving as any of the stories in *Winesburg, Ohio*.

Beyond this we necessarily seek to find the composition of the man, and we find it, without any question. The book indicates the part heredity played in the making of this artist: for there was his father, a broken-down signpainter who could more easily tell tales than support a family, a natural artist who was suppressed by an environment hostile to art—"Dreams were then to be expressed in building railroads and factories, in boring gaswells, stringing telegraph poles, and since father could not do any of these things he was an outlaw in his community." The dreamy-minded boy, born of a dreamy-minded father and a mother of foreign strain, likewise finds himself ill at ease in this environment. Always accompanied by his dreams (which are his real, hidden life) he works in factories, rolls kegs of nails, drinks terrific quantities of beer, enlists in the army, tries to be a manufacturer. None of these pursuits satisfies. And at last, Sherwood Anderson, manufacturer, breaks off in the middle of a sentence which he is dictating to a stenographer, and walks out of the room forever, to become Sherwood Anderson the artist—the "word-fellow." And from this purpose the smart-alecks of New York whom he afterwards meets cannot divert him, either by praise or by scorn.

An artist, then, what is he trying to do? The book reveals him as a rather wistful figure, somewhat inchoate, struggling toward a creative ideal. He feels himself to be the advocate and interpreter of humble lives, bringing to light the hidden and unsuspected currents that make up the "undistinguished mixture of life," as Stuart P. Sherman has called it. And in the world of fancy where he, as artist, lives, "no man is ugly—even the most base of man's actions sometimes take on the form of beauty." This portion of the book (in which he gives his aesthetic creed) may be read with benefit by those who think Anderson is preoccupied with sex themes out of sheer morbid perversity. He may make mistakes and he has made them—notably in *Many Marriages*—but his purpose is a poet's purpose, and his inadequacies come probably from an insufficient literary background and possibly an atrophied sense of humor, rather than from deliberate sensationalism.

Like most of the "Younger Generation," he feels out of tune with the Industrial Age, or at least does not like what it does to people. But his philosophy, as given in this book, is positive, not destructive, and his love of things American is as great as his distaste for certain particular things American.

Henry Adams, in *The Education of Henry Adams*, examined the Industrial Age and turned pessimist thereby; that was your scholarly, effete New Englander! Sherwood Anderson, a man more rudely formed, who sees what Henry Adams saw, retains a sense of the integrity and value of humanity which is his salvation. "A man and a woman in a garden," he writes, "had become the center of a universe about which it seemed to me I might think and feel in joy and wonder forever."

Sherwood Anderson has his crudities, which strike you sometimes as a kind of illiteracy deliberately exploited and exhibited. But on the whole he seems gentle and sincere, a man with his own way of speaking. And *A Story Teller's Story* is the best possible route to an appreciation of his work. As a personal "apologia," it is a most convincing and impressive document.

Sinclair Lewis

Spyglass
March 15, 1925

Two and a half years ago Sinclair Lewis astounded all of us, and maybe piqued not a few of us, with his portrait of the sonorous and wistful Mr. Babbitt, whose name speedily became a byword. "What next?" we curiously queried, implying in the question a certain amount of doubt. Could Sinclair Lewis rise any further than this easy level of caricature: Could he give his pictures of American life depth as well as surface? Was he capable of drawing more than synthetic heroes with traits plucked shrewdly from the temporary melee of American mannerisms? Could he go beyond cheap and spectacular effects? Could he, in short, exercise the complete function of the novelist, which is to record, in artistic form, a full section of life with all its lights and shadows, with all its complex interplay of forces, with all its hopes, defeats and ardors, presenting Man, that incalculable being, with imagination and sympathy?

Now comes a work which permits the reader to answer those important questions, and to answer them, for the most part, in the affirmative. Sinclair Lewis's new novel *Arrowsmith* is surely his best novel so far. It is a moving story, honestly and completely told. It abounds in satire, yet the satire is tempered often with gentleness, and fully balanced with elements of genuine humanity. It presents a hero who is not a half-ludicrous, half-pitiful joke, as Babbitt was, nor a tedious doll, as Carol Kennicott was, but an aspiring, peculiar, very human person. It presents a very admirable philosophy of endeavor and devotion to a cause. It does not grow tedious in the reading, as *Main Street* did, though it covers nearly 450 closely printed pages. It is, in short, a very fine achievement, and a book that everybody ought to read, though perhaps it may not, because of its fundamental seriousness, have the wide popular appeal that *Babbitt* enjoyed.

The hero of Mr. Lewis's book is Martin Arrowsmith, whose fortunes and misfortunes are followed through from the time of his eager days as medical student in the University of Winnemac to the height of a triumphant career, when, as the eminent bacteriologist of McGurk Institute, he dramatically conquers the bubonic plague in an island of the West Indies. Arrowsmith's unflagging devotion to medical science, particularly in the field of research and preventive medicine, furnishes the theme. And a very happy choice of a theme it is, in this age when science plays so important a part in American life. Naturally, such a subject gives the novelist an opportunity (which we should hardly expect Sinclair Lewis to forego) of executing a number of satirical pokes at the medical profession. But doctors and medicine afford the incidental machinery of his story, which is not primarily satire. It is Arrowsmith's struggle to realize himself that attracts our main attention. He wins his fight, but at severe cost, and in the end we are liable to wonder whether he is, after all, so victorious as he would outwardly seem.

The book is loaded brimful of characters and scenes that stick in the mind and refuse to be forgotten. There is Leora, quiet, indispensable, warmhearted Leora, whom Arrowsmith met when she was playing at being a hospital nurse. She could never remember to sew on buttons; she could be savagely tart when Arrowsmith needed to be answered back; but she could also wait patiently at home, without demurring, when Arrowsmith missed his meals and engaged in frantic all-night sessions at the laboratory. Surely she is one of Sinclair Lewis's best creations, and we cannot help feeling that Mr. Lewis was shamefully cruel to have her die of the plague at the very moment when Arrowsmith was philandering with the aristocratic Joyce. There is Max Gottlieb, the devoted, sardonic German bacteriologist, whom Arrowsmith worshipped; who always asked embarrassing questions just when Arrowsmith thought he had solved an experiment, who was victimized and mistreated by physicians of cheaper ideals, but who nevertheless finally became director of the great McGurk Institute. There are the friends of Arrowsmith's student days, particularly Cliff Clawson, later automobile salesman, a Babbitt on a small scale. There is the invincible Bert Tozer, Arrowsmith's loquacious brother-in-law, who thinks that it is a "blame sight more dignified to be seen shoving a wheelbarrow than smoking the dirty cigarettes all the time." There is Dean Silva of the medical school, type of the general practitioner; the redoubtable Doctor Pickerbaugh of Nautilus, "the two-fisted fighting poet-doc" and health-officer, who overwhelms the citizens with his Better Babies Week, Banish the Booze, Clean-up Week, Tougher Teeth Week, and Stop the Spitter Week, not to speak of his atrocious "health poems"; the "divine Tubbs," director of McGurk Institute, "a glory of whiskers, ready to blast any of the little men who stopped being earnest and wasted time on speculation about anything which he had not as-signed to them; the oily Holabird called "the Holy Wren," who succeeded the divine Tubbs; and so on through a host of characters over which you may alternately chuckle and weep.

It is this wealth of characterization and variety of scene which gives richness to the book. By the same sign it also gives perspective, for in this procession of types which verge on caricature are blended normal persons, real individuals whose qualities you may admire without re-serve. At the same time, it must be noted that Sinclair Lewis is not a man for fine distinctions. Subtle shades of variation are not for him. I find it objectionable that so many of his characters should talk like Babbitts, and that he should transfer to the medical profession all the jargon of *Main Street*. All his noble characters are inevitably made of rough stuff, as Arrowsmith himself is, with a vocabulary of "damns" and uncouth tendencies toward gray flannel shirts and bootleg whisky. On the other hand, all the most despic-able characters are either aristocratic persons who insist on immaculate linen or else cheap-Jacks of the blatant Pickerbaugh variety. Undoubtedly also, though one may take a great deal of delight in the resounding thwacks which Sinclair Lewis administers to the doctors, I am inclined to wonder whether that excellent profession quite deserves all the knocks this novelist gives it. Surely all clinics, for instance, do not resemble the suave Rouncefield clinic, where the debonair Angus Duer, to Arrowsmith's disgust, cultivated wealthy clients.

But Sinclair Lewis is what he is. He is not, for instance, a Henry James. He is all for broad effects. He capitalizes vulgarity and makes of it his chief strength. *Arrowsmith* is racy with the speech of everyday America. And if you object to the crassness and cheapness of the vocabulary used by Pickerbaugh and Bert Tozer, the only remedy, no doubt, is to imitate the methods of Pickerbaugh and engineer some sort of "Better Adjectives Week." And after all, there is something delightful in the manner with which Mr. Lewis catches and faithfully renders the flavor of American life today.

Theodore Dreiser

Spyglass
January 31, 1926

Theodore Dreiser's new novel is in two volumes, with fine print, some eight hundred pages in all. But to those who have the wisdom and the courage to undertake it, the reading will bring an unforgettable experience. It is a complete presentation, methodical, unsparing, and yet somehow tender and pitying, of a being who could perhaps exist at this time in no land but America, yet who is so

fully and poignantly imagined that he partakes of universality. Clyde Griffiths, Mr. Dreiser's hero, is a weakling, a
trivial worm crawling vainly through a complex morass of
social and moral forces that he cannot understand, forces
which rule and blind and bewilder and finally kill him. But
he aspires, this poor worm, in his fumbling and uncertain
way. He dreams eagerly of some state better than his
trodden wormhood, and would rise, treading down other
worms in his turn. The dream brings disaster, and at last
death to which he goes with dignity yet with wonder that
the immutable laws of the universe can inflict such extinction on a being so conscious of life's warmth, its brightness,
its beauty.

Therefore *An American Tragedy* is, in a sense, a moral
and spiritual allegory depicting man as the victim of the
complicated civilization he himself has made. But of course
it is not actually an allegory. It will generally be put in the
class of "realistic" novels. Such in truth it is, and as such it
has in it material enough for a dozen or so sociological
treatises. It has all the defects of Dreiser's work—uncouth,
rambling sentences; prosiness, lumbering, dry, matter-of-
factness; enormous masses of details apparently trivial. Yet
really nothing is trivial in this book. Nobody but Theodore
Dreiser would have had the courage and patience to write
it. The very multiplicity of detail arises from an honest and
sympathetic desire to allow nothing pertinent in this man's
life to remain undiscovered. Nothing, absolutely nothing,
must be shirked which will disclose him and the society in
which he moves. And even the gawky, sprawling sentences
may be the product of the same unflinching honesty.
Artistic effects? Artistic selection? Let all be abandoned for
the sake of the truth. And Dreiser, so far as he is concerned,
is right. The result is an overwhelming book; a book convincing, terrible, and true; a book that tears you away from
whatever you are doing and incorporates you into itself;

a massive and pitiful document of human verity; a book from which may be gained, as from George Eliot's *Romola*, an overpowering sense of the reality of evil.

["The Spyglass" continues after summary of plot]

To summarize the story in such terms is really to give no idea at all of the book—its masses of psychological detail and inquisition; its host of minor characters; its revelation of the inner workings of American social life from higher to lower strata; its tremendous dramatic moments such as the scene on the lake when Clyde takes the innocent Roberta to her doom, and his last hours when he is facing, in the death house, the remorseless fact of the waiting electric chair. In his study of motives, especially, Dreiser is amazing. What is there, I ask myself, that this man Dreiser does not know about human beings? Clyde turns and twists from subterfuge to subterfuge, always justifying himself while he is acting, yet always repentant for his errors when they are at last evident. Even in the death house, when tragedy has finally achieved its purgation, his mind still puzzles over the question of his guilt. To save his soul (literally, for he faces the problem of religious salvation) he cannot decide whether he really was guilty or not, in the ultimate sense. He has a feeling that he has somehow been wronged, though he has undoubtedly done terrible things. He thinks of all the people who condemned him as a monster.

He had a feeling in his heart that he was not as guilty as they all seemed to think. After all, they had not been tortured, as he had, by Roberta with her determination that he marry her and thus ruin his whole life. They had not burned with that unquenchable passion for the Sondra of his beautiful dream as he had. They had not been harassed, tortured, mocked by the ill-fate of his early life and training, forced to sing and pray on the streets in such a degrading way, when his whole heart and soul cried out for better things. How could they judge him, these people, all or any one of them, even his own mother, when they did not know what his own mental, physical and spiritual suffering had been?

At the last he has his moment of dignity, when word comes that the Governor has refused to pardon him—

So they've decided against me. Now I will have to go through that door after all—like all those others. They'll draw the curtains for me, too. Into that other room—then back along the passage—saying good-bye as I go, like those others. I will not be here any more.

It is, after all, the universal human exit. Those words are fraught with a symbolism; we are all pressed toward that Door—all of us poor puzzled creatures, born willy-nilly into a world we do not understand and forced to leave it before we have really had a chance to understand it, not always perhaps like Clyde Griffiths, with innocent blood on our hand, but certainly, like him, finding it terrifyingly difficult to adjust ourselves and our fine dreams to all its complex forces. That is the tale told by Dreiser in this great and powerful book—a sombre tale of an ignoble and curious creature, that paragon of animals, that quintessence of dust, Clyde Griffiths, or in other words, "Homo sapiens."

Edna Ferber

Spyglass
August 22, 1926

Erna Ferber explained in *So Big* that cabbages are beautiful, and a multitude of readers, including the Pulitzer Prize committee, agreed with considerable exhibitions of pleasure. In *Showboat*, her new book, she tells us that the Mississippi and Ohio rivers are beautiful, or were beautiful in the days of the 1870's when floating theaters went leisurely up and down Southern rivers; that the life of people moving on or around these rivers was beautiful; that Chicago was at least partly beautiful in the bad, mad days of Gambler's Alley, and that modern theatrical New York with its cut-and-dried sophistication is rather feverishly unbeautiful.

That is to say, both *So Big* and *Showboat* are differently pointed adventures in Miss Ferber's determined search for the romantic element in American life. Selina Peake, the heroine of *So Big*, was placed by unfortunate circumstances in a dull world of cabbages and stolid Dutch farmers; she refused to be defeated, and bravely made the commonplace romantic. *Showboat* presents the obverse of the same theme. Here again Miss Ferber's people (and shall we say Miss Ferber herself) flee from dullness. They escape to the Cotton Blossom Floating Palace Theater and are removed from the boredom of a stationary existence. They enjoy the changing pageantry of river banks and river towns; they have a colorful world of their own. And Magnolia Ravenal, the heroine of *Showboat*, is the creature of this world, a flesh-and-blood symbol of the universal human yearning after the exotic, a wistful gypsy pertinaciously clinging to her own dreams. Thus while Sinclair Lewis and the Main Street school condemn American life, Miss Ferber follows the lead of those who extol it, at least in the manifestations of its immediate past. It is interesting to observe that she, like Sherwood Anderson recently, has been drawn in her new novel to the "magnet-South" significantly described by Whitman. And here again Southerners have left their own rightful and native themes to be exploited by alien hands. Decidedly, the "newness" of the novel *Showboat* is that it depicts the river life which nobody has touched since Mark Twain, and at that a phase which Mark Twain, so far as I remember, did not explore.

To describe the book more definitely I find it very handy to quote from the title page of the beautifully bound and excellently printed copy furnished me. This says:

The Time—from the gilded age of the 1870's, through the 90's up to the present time. The Scene: The earlier parts of the story take place on the Cotton Blossom Floating Palace Theater, a showboat on the Mississippi. The background—is panoramic. Twice a year the unwieldy boat was towed up and down the mighty river and its tributaries; it was a familiar sight from New Orleans to the cities of the North, from the coal fields of Pennsylvania to St. Louis, and stirring presentations of *East Lynne*, *Tempest and Sunshine*, and other old dramatic favorites, by the actors and painted ladies of the Cotton Blossom troupe, are still remembered in Paducah, Evansville, Cairo, Cape Girardeau, Natchez, Vicksburg, Baton Rouge and in many other river towns and cities.

This panoramic feature gives the author a grand opportunity for descriptive work, and she makes the most of it. The novel is as much pictorial as dramatic. It evokes a mood of lazy contemplation through which scenes and people move gracefully transfigured into romantic shapes. Edna Ferber writes vividly and deftly, never too much, always just a right amount, perhaps too tastefully so. And her style has a richness and flexibility I do not remember to have observed in her work before. Episodes merge gently into each other. There is no frenzy or dash, no splashing of emotion. All is subdued, restrained, measured, carefully turned, almost retrospective. The book has structural peculiarities which may bother a few impatient readers. Miss Ferber uses very deftly the back-and-forth type of narrative which Joseph Conrad liked so much. But in her hands this device does not serve for quite as powerful ends as in Conrad's novels. And here and there one sees marks of the "serialized" novel!

Magnolia Ravenal, Miss Ferber's heroine, grows up on the showboat, a yearning, inquisitive child, and such she remains all her days. She is romantic and rather selfish, but doesn't achieve any great dignity. Even when she makes a reckless marriage with the gentlemanly gambler, runs away to lead a rocky up-and-down existence in Chicago, and narrowly escapes being sucked into the "underworld" of those days, she is still just childish, wistful, innocent. She is surpassed by her parents, two creations vastly more interesting. Captain Andy Hawks, the playboy owner of the floating theater, and that indomitable Puritan house-keeper, Parthenia Hawks, the solidest person in the book. The various minor characters, including the urbane gambler-actor, are well done, but Captain Andy and Partheny have the real stuff of life in them. Their queer mating, their odd administration of the floating theater, their opposite philosophies of life are treated in a somewhat Dickensian, almost slapstick manner. But there is an ex-uberance about them that Miss Ferber does not allow her other characters. They are fun.

Some major criticisms might be made. The ending of the book is quite incongruous. Miss Ferber becomes ironic and satirical in treating theatrical life in New York, with Magnolia's daughter, Kim, depicted as a successful ready-made actress. Miss Ferber does not play fair, either, in introducing at various points in the narrative certain prescient references to the Negro spirituals so popular nowadays.

It seems an illegitimate foresight, even a truckling to the mood of the moment, to equip her heroine with a perhaps unnatural admiration for "I Got Shoes," "Go Down, Moses," and "Deep River." It is a cheap trick. And Miss Ferber's pictures of Southern people, though always in-teresting, are generally in the conventional, sentimental vein. A more general fault is that the book seems always on the point of becoming very serious, without ever really becoming so. Miss Ferber delicately skirts the edge of tragedy, never plunging in. Just so much tears, so much pathos, so much wickedness, so much ugliness—just enough to make us faintly aware that all might not be quite as beautiful as it seems, and then, plenty of movie sunshine to dash away the clouds. It looks as if Miss Ferber had carefully mixed her ingredients for a large popular audience. And I will not question her right to that audience, and it would not make any difference if I did. *Showboat* will please lots of people, and why shouldn't it? Doubtless it will be a best seller, and who cares if it is? I'll prophesy right now that it will be chosen by the Book-of-the-Month Club.

At this point one remembers what some notable critics have said about the superiority of women novelists over men novelists in America. Didn't somebody say once that Dorothy Canfield, Willa Cather, Elinor Wylie, Edna Ferber, Ellen Glasgow, et al., had made a much better showing than any similar number of men novelists in this country? Maybe it is only the masculine ego which makes me unwilling to concede this superiority. At any rate, I for one do not see it. I certainly see the defects in the work of Theodore Dreiser, James Branch Cabell, Sinclair Lewis, John Dos Passos and others. But their writing has a substance which I do not find in the novels by women. Dreiser, for example, is as crude as an old fence post; neither he, nor any of the men except Cabell and Thomas Beer, have anything like the finesse and clear serenity of Willa Cather or Elinor Wylie. But they somehow go deep. They get down to strata that the women seldom reach. Perhaps it is too obvious a comment to say that the men have "virility," and too foolish a derogation to claim that the ladies are . . . well . . . ladies! Still I can't help wondering whether any of the women have written a novel as solid, as strong, as portentous, as Dreiser's *An American Tragedy*. I don't believe so. Shall I say, then, that the men have (convention prohibits me to use an Elizabethan term, so I choose a rural word) . . . "innards"? Maybe so, maybe not. At any rate, Edna Ferber's books, charming as they may be, have no . . . "innards."

Tragedy of Limitation:
Tarkington and Hemingway

Spyglass
January 22, 1928

Booth Tarkington's remarkable gift for making common-place people interesting was never more evident than in this new novel, *Claire Ambler*, which has just been issued as the first publication of the Doubleday-Doran merger. As in *The Plutocrat*, the theme is (at least in large part) the performance of an American type in contact with European civilization. But the protagonist of *Claire Ambler* is an American girl, beautiful and wealthy, as confident of the power of her beauty as the Plutocrat was of the all-sufficiency of his riches and vulgar directness. And the book, though it plays lightly back and forth between satire and pure comedy, also leans towards tragedy. It might be called a tragicomedy, and it would be a tragicomedy of limitations, or rather of not knowing limitations, for the winsome Claire Ambler, with typical American blindness, never for a moment dreams that European males have a psychology in any respect different from the psychology of the youngsters back in the old home town in the States. Her straightforward coquetry, operating in a Mediterranean summer resort, therefore produces the most surprising results, and she has to learn a difficult lesson.

Observe the beauty and simplicity of Mr. Tarkington's methods. His novel is in effect a shrewd criticism of the typical American girl—not the vulgar title-hunter, but the typical fair daughter of any wealthy dad who is bullied into paying for a European jaunt. But most readers, I dare say, will be taken up with the story and the delightful chatter (quite empty, most of it) in which all the American characters indulge, without ever perceiving the true inwardness

75

of Mr. Tarkington's design. He portrays Claire Ambler as having all the outward evidences of the sophistication for which the younger generation is noted. She has, indeed, a little more, for she is conscious of her dual nature; she never is quite sure whether that winsome self of hers, which goes through all the maneuvers of the old drama of life, is in earnest or merely play-acting. But her poor little mode of sophistication, which is based on sheer frankness and not much else, is revealed as completely inadequate when it is measured against the sophistication of Europe. She is charming, she sweeps all before her, but she is unable to conceive of other persons as real until her play-acting reaches a serious pass, and other persons take on an almost too poignant reality.

She thinks she can play with the fates of the crippled English war hero who has but a few months to live, of the handsome Italian prince, and the two monocled confidence men, with as great disregard of consequences as when she played with youthful suitors in America. But Europe is old, subtle and complicated. Before she knows it, she has played into a first-class tragedy. Worse than that, she has fallen seriously in love with the English invalid. Mama steers her safely home, but wounds have been made. She arrives at the dangerous age of twenty-five without ever having found a suitor to her taste, and finally snatches a man almost in desperation. But she knows somehow that she has missed a certain real savor of life, and missed it because of the silly little egotism which Americans think is self-sufficiency, but which really is very like the self-sufficiency of cats and dogs, for it recognizes only the Me and has no imagination for dealing with the Not-Me.

It is entirely possible that I am mistaken in my interpretation of *Claire Ambler*. At any rate, I have described what I get out of the book, and I furthermore would put it very high among Mr. Tarkington's writings. It seems to be more

subtle than most of his writings, but of course Mr. Tarkington is too much interested in merely ordinary folks, particularly ordinary Americans, to attempt either the sublime
or the difficult. Among contemporary American novelists,
he alone has the saving grace of humor; he alone is not defeated by the oppressive apparatus of modern civilization.
He takes his people wherever he finds them, lets them be
themselves, lets them talk and play and show themselves
off—and the whole proceeding he finds to be not merely
amusing but delightful and human. He is the Dick Steele
and the Oliver Goldsmith of our day. He has their gift
of simplicity and tenderness, with the addition of a definite
amount of Yankee shrewdness. And when you have read
Claire Ambler, you will consider yourself to have been
entertained in a way which you experience so seldom in
these days as to consider the experience rather remarkable
and worth repeating.

The oddest person to compare Mr. Tarkington with
would be Ernest Hemingway, whose *Men Without Women*
has by this time gone the round of all the reviewers and
been praised, and of all the readers of book-of-the-minute
and been duly admired. Mr. Hemingway also writes about
commonplace people: bull fighters, gunmen, prize fighters,
peasants, travelers. His purpose, however, is not in any
respect to elevate them, but to make them seem in fiction
exactly as dull, foolish, banal, and ugly as they are in real
life. There is this one addition to be made; he also makes
them just as tragic, and that quality is what makes his
stories important, I suppose.

How has he gained his vogue? That is a question to
puzzle over. There is his prose, for example, which has
been greeted with the most extravagant critical superlatives.
And he writes wonderful dialogue, they say. Well, his
prose seems to be like this. He puts down only the words
that will convey his idea with the utmost economy and

precision. There must be no ornamentation, no grace, no heightening of color.

The sentences must be as flat and brief as possible. He never attempts a complicated sentence, except when at intervals he gives a long succession of clauses tied together with "and," like a child's story of an adventure. And as his people are like people in ordinary life, his sentences are like the sentences we speak every day—simple, severe, casual. The result is that he has developed a style of his own, which I am obliged to respect because it is so perfectly done after its design; but I cannot read it with any great pleasure, unless you would say it is a pleasure to see a butcher carving a hind quarter or slicing lamb chops. There is exactly the same sort of execution—cut, slice, whack. And that's the way Mr. Hemingway writes.

Nevertheless, the method has its virtues. You can't get away from it. It won't let you go. I think it is at its best in the story of the bullfighter called "The Undefeated," for which, if for nothing else, Mr. Hemingway would deserve the crown of the American Academy if there were an American Academy. And this story, too, indicates Mr. Hemingway's general field. Visceral sensation, it seems, is what he is after. Be rough, be hard-boiled, put all daintiness and elegance aside. A pox on the people who say that literature is intellectual, that it has subtle ties, indirections, philosophies. Have done with prettiness and the virtues of the drawing room. Show that life has no meaning except the desperate and perhaps foolish striving after something to eat, after sex satisfaction, after the approval of one's fellows. Show that folks are a dirty set of animals whose virtues are muscular. Feel sorry for them, if you want to, but be careful not to show your sorrow openly. That sort of thing seems to me, in general, the program of Mr. Hemingway, and his program is no particularly new thing in literature. It looks a good deal like Naturalism, and may always be one of the accepted literary methods, bobbing up in every generation. But whatever it is, you cannot ignore Mr. Hemingway, even if you dislike him.

Mr. Nicholson's Jackson
Critic's Almanac
July 22, 1928

A man who had come from the far North of the United States to live in the South was talking about Andrew Jackson. Until he came here, he said, he had thought the old story about country districts still voting for Andrew Jackson was just an empty joke. But he found the legend had, if not a certain reality, at least an emphatic symbolism. Andrew Jackson, he discovered, was a name still on the lips of the people, spoken almost as familiarly as if the Old Hero was yet alive. It was astonishing that the spiritual presence of a historical character should be felt nearly a hundred years after his death. This surprised observer might have added, as some of our critics have been only too eager to say, that our affection for Andrew Jackson is but another instance of our backwardness. But he did not, and I suppose he took the other view that, after all, it may be something of an advantage for us to have a feeling of continuity with our own romantic past.

At any rate, it is this feeling that makes us look closely at all attempts to put our past into literature, and we look with particular solicitude at all portraits of Andrew Jackson, because he represents that part of our past which gives this section its individual character in the general Southern tradition, or, more broadly, in the American tradition. So no matter what the absolute merit or demerits of Meredith Nicholson's historical novel, *The Cavalier of Tennessee*, we will feel obliged to give it our consideration, and we will be asking ourselves whether the image of Jackson which Mr. Nicholson conjures up compares favorably with the grand image of Jackson that dwells intimately in our bosoms.

There is first of all the matter of facts. Has Mr. Nicholson handled them with proper respect? I am no Jackson scholar and am quite without minute documentary knowledge, but it seems to me that Mr. Nicholson has exercised considerable care in essential historical matters. I am doubtful, to be sure, whether the frontiersmen of Jackson's day actually disliked the Spaniards as much as Mr. Nicholson represents; Mr. Arthur P. Whitaker's recent book, *The Spanish-American Frontier*, seems to show the contrary. Some people, too, may object that Mr. Nicholson makes Jackson drink too much hard liquor and break too often into vituperative flights, hinted rather than recorded. And there is the usual coloring we expect in historical fiction, in the way of hypothetical conversation and fictitious characters. But on the major points the gentleman from Indiana seems to be all right. His book covers the early half of Jackson's career, beginning with his appearance as public prosecutor and closing with the death of Rachel Jackson. It is, indeed, the romance of Rachel and Andrew Jackson that is Mr. Nicholson's main story. His principal theme, as indicated in the title, is the struggle between the tender and chivalric side of Jackson's nature and his strong impulse toward action and combativeness. And thus he is the first writer of historical fiction, so far as I know, who deliberately emphasizes the private rather than the public life of Jackson, bringing into a strong and favorable light the love story that deserves all the immortality possible in art. I think the admirers of Jackson and his wife will find little or nothing to cavil at here, and everything to applaud.

But mere fidelity to fact is not the only thing that counts in the historical novel. We still have to ask whether Mr. Nicholson has written a genuine historical romance or disguised history. We must remember the two main schools of historical fiction. One—the school of Walter Scott, of Bulwer-Lytton, of Hugo—tells the story from the outside, depending upon a vast amount of pageantry and scenes reconstructed in detail to give verisimilitude. A few major historical characters are prominently mingled with a host of lesser imaginary ones. But it is the omniscient point of view of the author, looking backward on history, that prevails, and that gives the tone. The other school—represented, let us say, by so recent a comer as James Boyd—attempts to psychologize the past; it tries to get inside and adopt a point of view contemporary with the times depicted. It dwells also on sensations and moods rather than on events pure and simple. Mr. Nicholson, generally speaking, belongs to the older rather than the newer school. He does not revitalize as much as reconstruct. He shows us the people of an elder time, makes them walk, talk, fight, love, and die; and he tries to show them in characteristic thought and actions convincingly.

For example, here is a passage:

"Not if you behave yourself," Overton replied amiably, tossing his three-cornered hat on to the bed in the corner.

The three-cornered quality of the hat is not implicit in the action; it is put in as a detail of information, to remind us that men in that time wore three-cornered hats. A more modern technique would have handled the detail less obtrusively and more indirectly. Compare the way James Boyd handles a detail of apparel:

Dismounting on the farther side, he washed his face, put on his tie and coat and tried to smooth the wrinkles out of his tight mustard-colored trousers.

(It is James Fraser trying to primp before a call.)

It is not necessarily true that one school is better than the other. But it is true that the public has been trained to the modern school of historical fiction and its representatives—Thomas Beer, Naomi Mitcheson, James Boyd, even Edith Wharton, and all the people who do "period" novels —have the call over the old-fashioned writers, who seem naive by comparison, a bit stiff, lacking in overtones. You may deny—as one of my acquaintances who has studied historical novels denies—that it is possible to "psychologize" the past as moderns try to do. But modern readers have grown accustomed to subtle effects. The straightforward expository character of Mr. Nicholson's novel makes it tame in comparison with historical novels of this day that employ all the tricks of concreteness and sensation learned by modern writers and that above all adopt and preserve an inner rather than an outer point of view. The device at least gives a color and tone that Mr. Nicholson's rendering of Andrew Jackson does not have.

The Cavalier of Tennessee is an honest and commendable work, nevertheless, because Mr. Nicholson, whatever his failings of technique from the modern standpoint, has had the genius to perceive that there was in the story of Rachel and Andrew Jackson a story worth telling and needing an affirmative, romantic treatment. The book is wholesome and worthy and painstaking. It will reach many readers who might be repelled or confused by a more subtle method. It is worth while because of its subject and because of Mr. Nicholson's care and integrity. But we should not allow either Andrew Jackson's or Meredith Nicholson's reputation to delude us into thinking that the story has been told as well as it could and ought to be told.

Irony: Edith Wharton, Louis Bromfield

Critic's Almanac
September 23, 1928

There are various ways of distinguishing superficial from profound art. Beauty, sincerity, reality are the usual catchwords of differentiation, the only trouble with them being that, while apparently everybody knows vaguely what they mean, nobody ever has exactly and completely defined them. Another test, not quite so general, is to ask whether the artist has irony. If he has genuine irony, he must be approached with utmost respect; if he does not have it, or has only the seeming of it, he may be interesting in a dozen different ways, but he cannot be a really serious interpreter of human life. If other qualities were equal, Shakespeare would still be superior to Jonson by the test of irony. In a similar way, irony alone would differentiate the sonnets of Shakespeare from the sonnets of a hundred technically capable but unironical contemporaries. In modern times, it might be a mark to separate a play by Eugene O'Neill from any typical Broadway success; or Thomas Hardy from Harold Bell Wright; or Edith Wharton and Louis Bromfield from the glib and plausible Edna Ferber.

Is irony easier to define than the other qualities mentioned? Yes, because it is an attitude determining the artist's approach to his material. On the negative side, it means a refusal to simplify too readily; it declines the narcotic lull of easy philosophies; it will not put on ready-made garments of meaning. On the positive side, it is a conviction that the apparent unity of life is based on diversity and that life is essentially dualistic, with evil and good continually merging, changing places, as well as standing opposed. Irony sees contradictions; the animal as well as the god in man; confusion as well as a moral order; discords as well as harmonies. Irony is a part of wisdom, which sees a complex structure where the simple-minded behold but a simple line, yet it does not ignore the simple line. Irony aspires and mourns; laughs, and is distraught. It is the white light in which all colors are blended. It is the sympathy that makes a poet know how each man kills the thing he loves. It is the detachment of love that says, "Forgive them, for they know not what they do."

Among American novelists, irony is rare. The popular mind which wants to be charmed and not puzzled (Socrates was executed for puzzling people) is always at first glance drawn to the unironical; I named Edna Ferber. But, since it does not want always to be merely amused, instinctively it finds out at last the serious artist, as for example, Willa Cather, long neglected, now worshipped. Miss Cather has irony of a warm and lingering sort. Dreiser has the dry, mechanical irony of a dull but earnest reporter. Cabell has an irony which is both malicious and melancholy, and therefore of an inferior sort. Van Vechten's irony is only a superficial kind; it is essentially wit, not irony, and the same is true in large part of Cabell. But Edith Wharton, through a long career, has fully developed the quality of irony; and Louis Bromfield, though as yet more brilliant than mature, has irony in most of his writing, and it is this and not his enormous facility and keenness as a reporter that makes his novels distinguished. Both of these last-named writers have just published new books, which I shall consider briefly. Both are worth any reader's while.

In *The Children* Edith Wharton seems to have written a "topical" or "problem" novel dealing with one of the familiar effects of divorce. "If children don't look after each other, who's going to do it for them?" says one of the characters. "You can't expect parents to, when they don't know how to look after themselves." Superficially, the theme is the hard lot of children of modern parents who are divorced and remarried repeatedly. A bluff American millionaire and a fashion-mad wife rush from one fast European resort to another, while seven children, a mixed but charming group, are left to shift for themselves in Palace Hotels with only governesses, nurses, and a bewitching elder sister to manage their rearing. Subjected too early to a false world of glitter and unmorality, the children maintain among themselves a kind of modern innocence and a remarkable family spirit. But their fortune is nearly all misfortune. They are not only left to grow like weeds; they are blown about by the winds of domestic fury and whim, until in desperation, led by the elder sister, they run away to the mountains together, declaring their firm desire never to be separated again.

If this were all, the book would be only one of those "devastating rebukes" of society that critics are always fondly discovering. But the novel, for all the gay prattle of the youngsters (a company reminding us slightly of the *Constant Nymph* household) is less about the children than about one Boyne, a middle-aged engineer, who gets involved in their affairs. He is on his way to a rendezvous with the sweetheart of his youth, whom the convenient death of an inconvenient husband has now made romantically attainable, when he is veritably annexed by the seven little Wheaters. And now comes the irony that distinguishes Miss Wharton's novel from those popular "studies of life" that are always so plausible and specious. Boyne's good-natured interest in the children draws him further and further until he becomes practically their guardian and protector. And this at first purely benevolent human interest cuts squarely across the track of his own love affair, so that finally he has to make the hard choice between his fiancée, a lovely but too logical woman, and the children from whom he can have no reward but gratitude, and at last not even the consolation of knowing that he has saved

them. Thus do good deeds bring a good man to disaster.
And thus we have, not a problem story, but a human drama,
based on an irony proceeding from a conflict, not between
evil and good, but two different kinds of good.

Mr. Bromfield's novel, *The Strange Case of Annie Spragg*,
has a less subtle irony, more easily detectable, rougher and
more primly humorous (if also pathetic) in its action. The
intent of the book is apparently to show how widely separated series of events in lives far aloof from each other,
both in geography and in social strata, may, by the peculiar
operation of the cosmos, at last all draw together to an
intense focal point, and how those lives and events combine to show that the spiritual and the sensual are closer
than we think, or that paganism and Christianity or the
primitive and the cultured, still exist side by side in modern
civilization. Maybe this is not wholly a serious intent; Mr.
Bromfield's cool amusement with his own characters leads
me to think he may be half joking.

And the book is in fact the more curious mixture, almost
a hocus-pocus, a regular prestidigitation of people and
events. A statue of Priapus, unearthed in an Italian garden
owned by a desiccated "new thought" devotee, has a most
happily disturbing effect on her companion, the suppressed
Miss Fosdick, and on an English bachelor, the well-behaved
Mr. Weatherby, who wrote poems for the *Yellow Book*
and has spent his life on a magnum opus about miracles.
Miss Annie Spragg, of American origin, a primitive Meth-
odist, daughter of Cyrus Spragg (whose practices quaintly
resemble the alleged ways of the "House of David"), dies
in an Italian city with the marks of the stigmata of St.
Francis on her body; and the Catholic Church debates
whether she is a saint or not and buries her in consecrated
ground. Like St. Francis, Miss Annie Spragg had an unaccountable way with birds and animals; but in her "strange
case," too, there are hints both of diabolism and of the old

primitive earth-magic associated with the rites of Priapus. There are other diverse lives, too, that her death affects: the priest, Father D'Astier, and his simple-minded son who is killed by the Fascisti; Anna D'Orobelli, wistful and suffering princess of not too good a fame; Sister Annunziata, the ugly but devoted nun who believed that St. Francis had personally spoken to her through Miss Spragg.

I cannot detail these complicated strands. Mr. Bromfield weaves back and forth from Europe to America, with side excursions to British "pubs" and Victorian pursuits; folklore and religion, Greece and Italy, religious fanaticism and religious disillusionment are strangely mixed. You hardly know whether to accept the book as serious. It looks almost like a parody, with its study of separate lives that come together in one critical event.

But it has irony—an irony which tends to show that neither simplicity nor guile, love nor madness, religion nor mysticism, are quite what they seem on the surface. As it depends on mechanical means for its composition—that is, the more or less arbitrary relation of various series of events and characters to one another—it is naturally more artificial than Mrs. Wharton's irony, which depends solely on the elements of character and on acts proceeding from character. The irony of *The Strange Case of Annie Spragg* makes it a provoking rather than a satisfying book; but it also gives a robustness and strength, which lifts Mr. Bromfield's work, even in a book which may be considered somewhat inferior to his series of "panel" novels, above most contemporary performances.

Perfect Behavior*

Critic's Almanac
November 3, 1929

Ernest Hemingway's novel *A Farewell to Arms* is like a direct and most remarkable answer to the recent wish of Dr. Watson, prophet of behaviorism, that somebody would write a novel containing people who act in a lifelike and scientific manner. That is exactly what Mr. Hemingway does, with such astounding verity as to overwhelm, befuddle and profoundly impress all readers. Mr. Hemingway here is playing scientist, and he is watching people behave. It is a mistake to suppose that people behave morally or immorally, becomingly or unbecomingly. That is not the point at all: they merely behave. There is no good, no ill, no pretty, no ugly—only behavior. Behaviorism argues that there is stimulus and response, nothing else, and Mr. Hemingway's books contain (ostensibly, but not quite) nothing else. The novel is a bold and exceptionally brilliant attempt to apply scientific method to art, and I devoutly hope that all the scientists will read it and admire it immensely.

This comment on a book that is apparently taking the public by storm requires further demonstration, which I shall attempt to give.

Look first at the people of the book, who happen to be people, not cockroaches or mice, acting and reacting in

---

* Davidson's letter to Tate of December 29, 1929, comments as follows on this selection: "I am afraid I sacrificed Hemingway (to some extent) in order to make a point against science. But I should add that I did this the more readily because I felt that he was exposed to criticism, at least to debate, on this particular point. I certainly respect him and I'm glad to have your opinion of him to take to heart. And what you say about literary judgments in general, as not to be made from a sectional basis, but on a higher level, I'm in perfect agreement. I've felt for quite a while that I was in danger of losing balance and becoming merely a cantankerous localist, and your admonishment warms my conscience to its task."

wartime Italy rather than in a laboratory. But they are only people, not highly differentiated individuals. That is to say they are, in a manner of speaking, laboratory specimens. In the interest of the scientific "experiment" or observation, they must be as normal and average as possible, and so they are. It is regrettable, perhaps, that they are nice healthy creatures, not without animal charm (even if without souls), but we must presume that their occasional sufferings are in the interest of some scientific investigation which will eventually declare the "whole truth" about something, possibly war and love.

Thus we have first a Male with no characteristics other than might be noted in a description like this: Henry, Frederick; American; commissioned in Italian ambulance corps; speaks Italian (with accent); reactions, normally human. And then of course a Female: Barclay, Katherine; nurse; English; normally attractive and equipped with normal feminine reactions. The subordinate characters, too, are just as colorless: Rinaldi, Italian officer, inclined to be amorous; a priest, unnamed; other officers, soldiers, police, nurses, surgeons, bawdyhouse keepers and inmates, restaurant keepers, Swiss officials, family folk. All of these, notice, talk alike and all do nothing but behave, offering given responses to given stimuli.

Then we must have a situation. It is simply this. Put the Male and Female under the disorderly and rather uninviting conditions of war, including battle, wounds, hospitalization, return to the front, retreat and bring the Male and Female into propinquity now and then. What will happen?

I am tempted to describe what does happen—it is all, of course, "natural"—in such a catechism as James Joyce uses in one part of *Ulysses*. It would run something like this:

Question: What do soldiers do in war?

Answer: They fight, drink, eat, sleep, talk, obey commands, march, go on leave, visit brothels, are tired or sick or dead or alive, wonder when the next battle will be, sometimes meet respectable women, sometimes fall in love hastily.

Question: Was the same true in the case of Henry, Frederick?

Answer: It was invariably true.

Question: What do nurses do in a war?

Answer: They eat, sleep, drink, talk, obey commands, tend the wounded, are tired or sick or dead or alive, wonder when the next battle will be, sometimes meet attractive officers, sometimes fall in love hastily.

Question: Was the same true in the case of Barclay, Katherine?

Answer: It was invariably true.

Question: What not very special circumstances modified the case of Henry, Frederick?

Answer: He was wounded in the leg, and was thus entitled to prosecute a love affair with Barclay, Katherine.

Question: What wholly natural thing did Henry, Frederick do during the Caporetto retreat?

Answer: He retreated, was arrested, saw police shooting fugitives, jumped in the river, escaped, joined Katherine, quit the war, went to Switzerland.

Question: What not unnatural consequences to Barclay, Katherine, attended her love affair with Henry, Frederick?

Answer: Ineffective labor in childbirth, Caesarean operation, death.

Question: And what were the results for Henry, Frederick?

Answer: Results unknown. He merely walked back in the rain.

The application of the scientific method may be further demonstrated by a scrutiny of other features of the novel. A scientific report of events requires that there be no comment, no intrusion of private sentiments, no depreciation or apology. The "bare facts" must be given—or tabulated.

Therefore style (as style is generally known) is wiped out, or is reduced to its lowest, most natural, terms. It will take the form of simple, unelaborated predications, not unlike the sentences in a First Reader. For instance: The dog is black. The sky is blue. Katherine is pretty. I did not love Katherine at first but now I love Katherine. I drank the wine and it did not make me feel good. She was unconscious all the time and it did not take her very long to die.

And that, as I see it, is the gist of Mr. Hemingway's hypothetical case, which by the unthinking may be called an indictment of war or of civilization or an apology for free love or what you will. But its method does not justify any of these interpretations, however latently they may exist.

What of it, then? On the surface it is assuredly a most remarkable performance. To those who take pleasure in contemplating a world of mechanisms doing nothing but acting and reacting, it must be a nearly perfect book. Let us leave them with their admirations, which are no doubt justifiable under the circumstances.

But what of those who, without knowing exactly why, have an uneasy sense of dissatisfaction with Mr. Hemingway's book and ask for something more than a remarkably natural series of conversations, daydreams, and incidents? Mr. Hemingway's book will have plenty of defenders to fly up and condemn those who are dissatisfied. I want to supply a little ammunition to the dissatisfied, out of pure sympathy for the underdog if for no other reason.

First of all, don't complain about vulgarity or obscenity. There you lose the battle. For to a scientist, nothing is vulgar or obscene any more than it is genteel or pretty. And Mr. Hemingway apparently is trying to be a scientist. Attack him instead at the point where a fundamental contradiction exists. Can there be such a thing as a scientific work of art? The nature of the contradiction can be immediately seen. Mr. Hemingway could treat human affairs scientifically only in a scientific medium. That is, he would have to invent equations, symbols, vocabularies, hypotheses, laws, as scientists are in the habit of doing. By so doing he would achieve all the "reality" that science is capable of achieving —which might perhaps be of practical use, but could not be vended as a novel, even by so respectable a house as Charles Scribner's Sons.

Obviously Mr. Hemingway did not, could not, go to such a logical limit. He was forced to compromise by using the vocabulary and the forms of art. The minute he made the compromise, he failed fundamentally and outrageously. His novel is a splendid imitation, but only an imitation, of science. It is a hybrid beast, ill-begotten and sterile. It is a stunt, a tour de force, and no matter how blindingly brilliant, no matter how subtle in artifice, it is in effect a complete deception (possibly a self-deception) and can exist only as a kind of marvelous monstrosity.

Note that he falls short even of science. Committed to the form of the novel, he must be selective where science is inclusive. He cannot destroy his own personality and bias, for from his book we get the distinct impression that he wishes us to believe war is unheroic, life is all too frequently a dirty trick, and love may be a very deadly joke on the woman. Even in his effort to get away from style he creates a new style that is in effect a reaction against all decorative imagistic prose.

A Farewell to Arms, which is apparently intended to give us a perfect example of pure behavior, turns out after all to be only the behavior of Mr. Hemingway, stupendously overreaching himself in the effort to combine the role of artist and scientist and producing something exactly as marvelous and as convincing as a tragic sculpture done in butter.

Painful Literature

Critic's Almanac
December 8, 1929

While I was reading *The Dark Journey*, by Julian Green, I kept wondering, "What on earth? What makes him do it? Why does the man write about such things, anyway?" Possibly no decent critic ought to ask such questions; it is not critical politeness to be curious about an author's reasons. One is supposed to take the finished product for whatever it is worth, and it is the general opinion of various notables that Mr. Green's product is worth a great deal. Indeed, I think that nobody can cavil about the procedure of Julian Green's art in *The Dark Journey;* it is perfection itself, unquestionably inclining the reader to put it alongside the art of certain great performers.

Still I am curious. It is the objects upon which that perfect artistic procedure is exercised that bother me. What a hideous lot these people of *The Dark Journey* are: a writhing, miserable group of worms, blindly feeling their way through the petty sub-bourgeois life, and now and then striking out venomously at each other. Mme Londe, a grotesque hag (depicted, it is true, with a faint touch of humor) pathetically bullies her boarders, a weak and nasty set, all of them. And Mme Londe regards complacently the furtive activities of her good-looking niece Angele—in effect a prostitute who goes out with the boarders, each in turn. For of course Angele is a help to the establishment.

Enter this scene of distrust and malevolence a veritable Tertium Quid, the incoherent guinea-pig M. Gueret, unhappily married and tormented by evil desires. Guinea-pig Gueret is mad for love of Angele. He patters around dark corners, makes assignations at which nothing is accomplished, timidly squeaks his desire and is brusquely put aside.

93

But observe the passion of a guinea-pig. Foiled in love, he becomes a gorilla. Denied once too often, he tears a limb from a tree and beats Angele nearly to death. In the madness of flight he becomes still braver; he actually kills an old man. Then he runs around in circles, hides in a coal pile, is finally, after some months of village sensation, beguiled and trapped by Mme Grosgeorge, a cruel, pathetic wretch who is secretly in love with him and jealous of Angele. Angele, with her fair face scarred for life by Gueret's blows, dies in wretchedness when Mme Londe makes her the instrument of Gueret's betrayal; Mme Grosgeorge, with feelings badly mixed, shoots herself just as the police arrive; Gueret, one supposes, is nabbed; Mme Londe's establishment is ruined. Everything goes to the bad entirely, and in the gloomiest possible manner. All of the feelings exhibited are perverse and terrible; it is agonizing lust that drives Gueret into stupid violence. All of the people are malign, crooked, or petty—except possibly the prostitute Angele, who is an honest but misguided girl.

And here is your Harper Prize Novel, written by an excellent young American-Frenchman, who lives in Paris, and is translated for American consumption. At the age of twenty-nine he is being crowned with a master's laurels.

Maybe, as William Bennet Munroe says, we have simply progressed from the Eocene and the Pliocene to the Obscene Era. But I had rather take refuge in a phrase of Gorham B. Munson's. He dropped the remark, with reference to a certain woman novelist, that she was extremely "conscious of pain." The phrase certainly applies to a great many moderns, and to Mr. Green among them. Just as for the dying Angele, all that remains of life for them is pain.

They do not, we must imagine, go out of their way to choose examples of ignoble and wretched lives, but in contemplating the spectacle of humanity and in trying to record their impression of it, they are conscious above all of pain. This is true, I am convinced, of Ernest Hemingway; it is true of Zona Gale's *Borgia*, another mad novel of dully suffering people; it is true of William Faulkner, whose work has close kinship with that of Green; it is true of a fine new novel by Thomas Wolfe, *Look Homeward, Angel*. Pain is in the foreground of their books all the time, and it is not at all concealed by the cool objectivity which this age practices apparently to perfection.

Do they, then, have weak stomachs? Are they thin-skinned creatures, inordinately sensitive? Surely there have been plenty of writers in the past who were "conscious of pain" and who, out of sorrow and suffering, composed great tragic works.

Yes, but the great writers of the past never felt the full impact of scientific teaching as we have felt it. They always had something to fall back on: Fate, the Gods, Divine Providence, a Moral Order, or at least some belief in the divinity or nobility of Man. They had some sort of ethics behind or underlying their tragedies. They were more conscious, perhaps, of Evil, as a reality, than of Pain.

But our writers have passed beyond good and evil, beyond the moral order, beyond even a sense of the dignity of man. They have no religion other than a very vague religion of Well-being, and so their Satan, their Evil Principle, their Hell is Pain. It becomes quite doubtful whether, in any old and well-understood sense of the word, they can write tragedy at all; but they can and do produce painful literature.

Poetry

Poetry

John Masefield

Spyglass
January 24, 1926

In the minds of far too many people, the term "modern" when applied to literature suggests something dubious at least, and possibly dangerous, or even obscene. This is an unfortunate and mistaken conception which I will not now undertake to discuss. When we come to modern poetry, the term, alas, also suggests the bizarre, the peculiar, the incomprehensible, along with those other things. Again I say that this is too bad. People who labor under this misapprehension really don't know what they are missing. And as an instance in point, I want to refer rather extensively to the newly published *Collected Works of John Masefield*, which include two volumes of plays, both verse and prose, besides the two volumes of poems representing all his work in this field. And I want to dwell on his poetry rather than his plays because the former, without being bizarre or incomprehensible or obscene nevertheless is distinctly "modern" in tone and execution, and being so, is a bulky refutation (some seven hundred pages in all) to the charges made by those who dismiss all modern poetry with a wry mouth and a lifted nose.

To begin, Masefield is well within the English tradition as it is generally conceived. Chaucer was his first master— indeed, we have his own word for it that he did not desire to become a poet until . . . he ran across an old copy of Chaucer's poems and felt that a new world had been unclosed to him. What he learned from Chaucer, perhaps, was mainly the art of storytelling, for he has little of Chaucer's gift for psychologizing or his humor or his satire. But with storytelling we can afford to be content. Masefield restored the verse-narrative to a place it had lost

in English literature, and there is no modern poet writing
in English who can equal him in the art of telling a tale.

His first volume, *Saltwater Ballads*, was not, however,
in this field. It was a collection of lyrics in the manner of
Kipling, representing on the whole a rather harsh and dis-
illusioned view of sailor life with partial romantic features.
He kept to the purpose expressed in his "A Consecration,"
to write,

Not of the princes and prelates and periwigged charioteers
Riding triumphantly laurelled to lap the fat of the years—
Rather the scorned—the rejected—the men hemmed in with the
spears.

Thus he marked out the "school of life" rather than the
"school of artifice," to use his own words, that he has
fairly well followed ever since.

Nevertheless, fine lyrics though they were in the first
volume (for instance, "The West Wind"), his first real
triumph came later when he published "The Everlasting
Mercy," the first, and I believe the finest, of his verse-
narratives. In its striking subject and its swift, even fierce
rush of language, it remains unequalled in modern poetry,
and I believe we should have to go far back in English
poetry to find anything to compare with it. The picture of
Saul Kane, the violent wastrel and poacher, turned from
reckless contempt of God and man to gentleness by the
power of sudden revelation, is done unforgettably, done
once and for all. It mingles the uncouth and terrible with
the warm serenity of a sudden spiritual exaltation, and the
tale is told with a series of rapid descriptive strokes that
are remarkable. For example, among many passages, I remember this particularly, where Saul leans out of the window of the "pub" into the cool night air—

I opened window wide and leaned
Out of that pigsty of the fiend
And felt a cool wind go like grace

> About the sleeping market-place.
> The clock struck three, and sweetly, slowly,
> The bells chimed Holy, Holy, Holy;
> And in a second's pause there fell
> The cold note of the chapel bell,
> And then a cock crew, flapping wings,
> And summat made me think of things.

It is this mingling of the rough with the gentle, this urge to examine life's realities, this desire to exalt the lives of obscure and homely persons that help to make Masefield's poetry "modern," for in it appears the tendency to cast off romantic illusions which has been characteristic of modern poetry and modern writers generally. In most people's opinions, it will be in Masefield's favor that he does it without ever offending our ear or our moral sense, and he does it simply, without torturing the language, even at the risk of letting his poetry run thin in places. His other narrative verse tends to be of the same character; "The Widow in the Bye Street," "Dauber," "The Daffodil Fields," "Reynard the Fox," all celebrate, in greater or less degree, the story of the underdog. "Dauber," next to "The Everlasting Mercy," I should put as his greatest success, but even as early as this there appears a quality which has somewhat overmastered Masefield's later work. He cultivates a vague yearning after something which he generally puts under the head of Beauty, but which cannot perhaps be so readily defined. Romance gets the better of him, so far as narrative is concerned, and in "Enslaved," beautiful as it is, we have simply a romantic story of the escape of two lovers, with a setting remote from the England which Masefield knows how to depict. "Roses" is another almost-failure, and we are led to the suspicion that Masefield is not at his best in historical pieces.

But we haven't said (somebody may remark) that he is a great writer of the sea. Well, so he is—but everybody else has said that, just as everybody else has said it of Joseph

Conrad, and in both cases it is only a very small and incidental part of the truth.

"Sea Fever," "Roadways," "Biography," "Ships," and
"Dauber" carry out the tradition of the sea that has come
down from the Anglo-Saxon "Seafarer" through all of
English poetry. But, much as I like and admire those poems
(and I do), I find in them the lesser Masefield, the yearning, slightly tearful, much too romantic Masefield, who is
a weaker person than the hot-blooded half-daredevil Masefield of "The Everlasting Mercy." Nor could I rank as his
best work the sort of strain that begins "Beauty, be with
me for the fire is dying." For I prefer to take my beauty
straight; I don't like to hear a poet mouthing over beauty
and mooning over his devotion to it; let him go ahead and
put beauty in his poetry and the rest will follow. I would
even prefer an honest ugliness to a sentimental apostrophe
to beauty.

I like stronger meat—the great sonnet series, for instance,
where at last Masefield becomes philosophic to some degree
and faces without flinching the problems of life in the
rough, although even here he keeps invoking beauty in a
too-insistent fashion

Thomas Hardy

Spyglass
March 7, 1926

The publishers were too quick about issuing a volume of
Collected Poems, as they did for Thomas Hardy a few
years ago. The old master isn't ready to stop yet, not until
they put him in those "six boards" that he discusses with

funereal humor. Thomas Hardy is eighty-five or over; he has already written so many great novels that the trouble of writing any more seemed long since useless; he has written at least one great play, *The Dynasts;* and in his old age he has undergone a rebirth and come forth as a poet who is, many think, the greatest English poet living today. His newest volume, characteristically named *Human Shows, Far Phantasies, Songs and Trifles,* contains some poems that date far back to the days of his youth; but without the dates it would be impossible to distinguish them from the numerous others, written in later years, for Thomas Hardy is always Thomas Hardy, the same yesterday, today, and forever. And I can think of no more striking comparison between the old and the new generation than is indicated in the publication of this new volume of Hardy's, with its 152 poems as an addition to an old man's exuberant store, and the publication recently of T. S. Eliot's "collected" poems, in which the young expatriate American puts together all of his work that "he cares to preserve" (a slim volume indeed!) and thus signifies the drying-up of the springs of poetry in his soul. It would be indeed remarkable if Eliot could write anything important after the triumph of defeatism and fastidiousness, "The Waste Land."

Thomas Hardy is not defeated and is not fastidious, although he feels, as much as Eliot or any of the younger pessimists, the irritating pressure of an incomprehensible universe that never seems to go quite right. But Thomas Hardy makes disillusionment into a virtue, because he has, back of all his despair, a sturdy kind of Anglo-Saxon fatalism that at least leaves him a joy in this unequal battle. Man and other forms of life are exciting objects, no matter how misdirected; and life in general is exciting no matter how old one gets. Therefore Hardy keeps on making his shrewd observations and putting them down as they occur to him, pouring out from the richness of his own soul, taking freely

from the richness all around him. His way of writing, while
it is modern in its tone and often in execution, is casual,
free, and positive, differing in this respect from much that
is called "modern." Hardy expresses this very well when
he writes—

> Any little old song
>   Will do for me,
> Tell it of joys long gone,
>   Or joys to be,
> Or friendly faces best
>   Loved to see.
>
> Newest themes I want not
>   On subtle strings,
> And for thrillings pant not
>   That new song brings:
> I only need the homeliest
>   Of heart-stirrings.

To read a book of Hardy's poems such as this is, to
quote one of his own descriptions, like passing through "a
gallery portrait-lined and scored with necrologic scrawls."
But it is a depressing experience only as a tragedy of Shakespeare or Sophocles is depressing, because Hardy's array
of "human shows" comes out of a mind profoundly philosophical and warmly aware of life's mixture of elements, a
mind which shows as much pity and sympathy as it does
detachment. There is a great deal of humor in Hardy too,
and a great deal of wit that edges into his dolorous pages.
Perhaps he might be best described as a great ironist so
acutely aware of life's incongruities that it doesn't seem to
him to make much difference whether one laughs or cries.

John Crowe Ransom

Spyglass

January 23, 1927

John Crowe Ransom's new book of poetry, *Two Gentle-men in Bonds,* has come from the press much earlier than was expected. It is on the bookstands now, and unless the proprietors have made unusually large orders, I daresay they will quickly find the need of replenishing their stock. The unexpected early appearance of the book does not permit a full comment to be made at this time, for Mr. Ransom's work is not of the sort that can be considered hastily. But in brief I may here record my impression that the new book shows that Mr. Ransom has refined and perfected his art into an instrument flexible and apt to all demands put on it, and that the application of this fine craftsmanship to his materials gives again, probably even more than in his first two books, a poetry satisfying in the clear, warm, and beautiful finality with which it touches its subjects. The verse is quiet, but it has a glow of deep fires within; the utterance is strange, but it represents a personal idiom that is inseparable from the art and that makes Mr. Ransom unique, not merely among American but among all poets. I make no apologies for appearing as an insistent advocate, and I herewith record my opinion that, of the contemporary American poets, Mr. Ransom is one of the few who will meet the ultimate tests.

Hart Crane's *White Buildings**
Extra Review
April 3, 1927

The best review of the poetry of Hart Crane would be
to give word for word the excellent study by Allen Tate
which stands as foreword to this strange, bewildering, and
in many ways impressive volume. Such a review might be
supplemented by the expository and laudatory remarks of
Waldo Frank in a recent issue of the *New Republic*, and,
even more pointedly, by the explanatory statements of Hart
Crane himself, made by way of reply to a criticism of
Harriet Monroe's in the October 1926 number of *Poetry:
A Magazine of Verse*. That a reviewer finds himself compelled to refer to such documents is, however, an implied
commentary on the work of Hart Crane, and signifies that
a critical approach is difficult.

I begin by taking some lines from Crane's "The Marriage
of Faustus and Helen," which has been praised by these
and other authorities as one of the important poems of this
generation:

> Capped arbiter of beauty in this street
> That narrows darkly into motor dawn,
> You, here beside me, delicate ambassador
> Of intricate slain numbers that arise
> In whispers, naked of steel; religious gunman!

The passage is unfairly torn from its context and is taken

* In his letter to Tate of March 21, 1927, Davidson says,
". . . here is a carbon of my review of Hart Crane. I wish it could
be more favorable, for I respect your judgment and a great deal of his
poetry. Nevertheless, I cannot get around an unpleasant effect that I
constantly get from his poetry. . . . Part of the unpleasantness comes, no
doubt, from the elements mentioned in the review; but there's something
else I just can't define. I just give up, gasping like a fish.
Remember, too, that this review was written for the *Tennessean*, not
the *New Republic*, etc., and forgive commonplaces. My congratulations
to Crane on the fine press he is getting. . . ."

practically at random, but it is typical and will serve as a
focus for discussion. The reader whose ear is trained for
poetry should here perceive at once a precise, almost stern,
beauty of words deliberately moulded into lines which
move with a slow dignity, jarred briefly by the entirely
contemporary and colloquial "gunman." The sound itself
pleases if the lines are properly intoned. But the meaning,
even with the context to help, eludes one in spite of the
extraordinary definiteness of the language. "Narrows
darkly" is perfectly comprehensible; "motor dawn" is more
difficult, but one can propose meanings; "intricate slain
numbers" and "whispers, naked of steel" are next to in-
soluble and is a gunman "religious"? There is evidently a
highly elliptical procedure which must be explained. I
believe that Mr. Crane deserves to have his case stated by
those who understand him best.

The poetry of Hart Crane, writes Mr. Tate, "is at once
contemporary and in the grand manner"; it deals "with the
complex urban civilization of his age: precision, abstrac-
tion, power." It is admittedly difficult, partly because we in
America are too accustomed to easy ways; we are not
prepared for a difficult poetry. His rhetoric "takes the
reader to Marlowe and the Elizabethans." He is indebted
also to Whitman and Melville, perhaps Laforgue, Rimbaud,
or such moderns as T. S. Eliot. Above all his method depends on "oblique presentation of theme"; and "the theme
. . . is formulated through a series of complex metaphors
which defy a paraphrasing of the sense into an equivalent
prose."

Mr. Crane himself, in the periodical I have referred to,
admits being elliptical and obscure. But he is deliberately not
ambitious for simplicity. Poetry is after all irrational and
antiscientific; the poet makes up his own logic as he goes.
Metaphor, on which poetry so largely depends, consists in
substituting for any given object some association or like-

ness which emotionally occurs, and this association or likeness becomes the symbol which the poet uses. Therefore, if
Blake can say "A sigh is a sword of an angel king," Crane
can write of the "unmangled target smile" of Dionysus,
for he is chiefly interested "in the so-called illogical im-
pingements of connotations of words on the consciousness."

This position is, I believe, quite unassailable, for it describes the typical procedure of all poets who have
depended on intensive symbolism for their effects rather
than on discursive declarations, rhythmically arranged, or
purely epical devices. The only question we can raise, and
it is a fundamental one, is: how far can the process of
telescoping metaphors be carried? Or, how far can Mr.
Crane favor his entirely personal verbal associations and
still achieve a poetical effect? It is Mr. Crane's application
of his theory that is assailable.

Addison, in one of the *Spectator* papers, pokes fun at
Ned Softly, the poet, who exclaimed in self-adulation
over a line he had written,

"For Ah! it wounds me like his dart. Pray how do you like that
ah! Doth it not make a pretty figure in that place?" cried Ned
Softly.

The "ah" meant something to poor Ned Softly; to him it
signified passion, the grand passion for it carried with it all
the associations of his amorous encounters. He made the
mistake of all versifiers who impregnate their verses with a
host of personal associations and read them into the lines
without getting them across to the reader. I fear that Mr.
Crane has often made the same mistake, though in no petty
way; if he has erred, he has erred ambitiously.

I might say also that the "contemporary" parts of his
poetry are often unabsorbed and jangle; that his meticulous
striving for precision, together with his crowding of
metaphors, makes his poetry stiff in texture; that his tone
is too often sticky and sepulchral.

Nevertheless, his phrases stay with me whether I understand them or not. Crane's poetry is masculine and bold and serious, and, with all its defects (as I see them) I prefer his poetry to that of the trivial soupy sycophants and pink-tea artists who monopolize the space given in most magazines to poetry. He is most successful, I think, in those poems where he is nearest to tradition: "Praise for an Urn," "Stark Major," and some parts of "Voyages." It is impossible to be indifferent to him, and he may well consider violent dislike in some cases a tribute, but I hope the future will find him gradually less severe in his individualism and more amenable toward an audience he ought to reach. It is a powerful poet who can write such lines as—

> Beyond siroccos harvesting
> The solstice thunders, crept away.
> Like a cliff swinging or a sail
> Flung into April's inmost day.

The Gumdrop School
Spyglass
July 31, 1927

There is nothing worse than a poetry magazine when it is puling, ignorant, and mistakenly zealous. Such a magazine is *The Journal of American Poetry*, published at Charlotte, N. C. The "preamble" to the first issue with some reason calls attention to the mistakes of the moderns—the class which it describes as the "blatant-ass-chorus and tin horn orchestra of the decadents." But what *The Journal of American Poetry* offers as a substitute is a worse decadence than the poetry of the experimentalists that it condemns.

For example, here is a quatrain from one of its contributions:

> Just a bunch of roses—and ('tis grandly true)
> Easter flowers give a purer, broader view;
> On this hallowed morn' our heavenward thoughts disclose
> Life and death to be as lovely as a rose.

Just a bunch of nice drooling sentiments dressed up in rhyme! *The Journal of American Poetry* belongs, evidently, to the Gumdrop School of Poetry. If any discredit is being brought on poetry, the gumdrop poets are more to blame than Maxwell Bodenheim and E. E. Cummings.

A prize of $500 with two additional prizes of $250 each have been offered for the best poems on the subject of Lindbergh and the Spirit of St. Louis. The contest, arranged by Mitchell Kennerly, will be judged by John Farrar, Christopher Morley, and Mr. Kennerly. The closing date was July 25, and so it is too late for me to render any exhortations to the competitors. What I am interested in is the judges. The erstwhile editor of *The Bookman* and the jovial conductor of "The Bowling Green" are most appropriately selected as judges for this highly trite and typically American proceeding. They, too, belong to the Gumdrop School of Poetry.

Josephine Pinckney, *Sea-Drinking Cities*

Extra Review
January 15, 1928

One of the chief centers of the poetic renaissance in the Southern states has been Charleston, where DuBose Heyward and others organized, shortly after the close of the World War, the Poetry Society of South Carolina, which surely surpasses all other organizations of its sort in the country in wise administration and active encouragement of poetic endeavor. One is inclined to think that there is something naturally poetical in the very air and whole environment of Charleston; it is a fair seed place for poets and writers in various fields, as witness the names of DuBose Heyward, Hervey Allen, Julia Peterkin, Beatrice Ravenel, Herbert Sass, Archibald Rutledge, all of whom have been associated either with Charleston or the Poetry Society of South Carolina.

And now comes a poet who, whether as poet in general or poet of Charleston in particular, promises to outdo her predecessors, or at least make them look very carefully to their laurels. Miss Pinckney's poems have a calm Southern repose, a luxuriance of phrase, a quiet humor controlling deep emotion—qualities which we should naturally expect to find in a Charleston, or a Southern poet, but which the unnatural self-consciousness of the times has often driven out. On the technical side Miss Pinckney is a modern; perhaps she has been guided a little too much by imagism, or whatever influence it is that makes her see things nearly always in pictorial terms, so that her poetry is at times not only in repose, but static. And there is the slight diffidence that one finds often in the moderns, the shrinking from direct utterance, the finical carefulness. But these faults (if they be faults) are not excessive and will no doubt be absorbed as her work grows and is unified. A poet's first

111

volume is necessarily somewhat a tentative thing.

What is important is that Miss Pinckney writes from the inner compulsion which only true poets feel. She writes from conviction, not because it is fashionable to write. And her conviction is not, like Mr. Wheelock's or Mr. T. S. Eliot's, a product of defeat rendering itself in melancholy beauty. Her glance goes out spontaneously to the physical and spiritual life of old Charleston and coastal South Carolina, the life whose ways she knows and has inherited. The world she reveals to us has little of the hauteur and aloofness which we outsiders have insisted on ascribing to Charlestonians. Indeed, Miss Pinckney generally becomes a little ironic, though she does not forget to be tender, when she touches the aristocrats, as in the picture of the three women who look out of windows on the sea, and

> They keep their glances poised to paralyze
> The passerby who happens to lift his eyes.

On the contrary, there is more of homeliness, more of the romance of the familiar, more of good humor and delight in rustic simplicity than a reader would guess. The Charleston of Miss Pinckney is a Charleston where streetcries float up onomatopoetically of honey and melons to sell; of the harbor where bells sound slow and far from the warships; the milkboat where bare feet scuff and "moon-bright cans" are unloaded in a lantern's light; of hot days, or warm nights when cattle stir in the meadows; of backyards where the iceman's tongs clink and

> The dogs augment their simple joys
> By biting the colored butcher boys.

Most of the joys here are, in very truth, the simple joys of an old, gracious life in an old beautiful city that has learned how to live. But there are other pictures, too. For instance, in the sketch "On the Shelf," we have the

pathetic presentation of Mr. Skirling, who lived in genteel
poverty, eking out his larder by selling now and then, with
regretful courage, a volume from his precious Abbotsford
edition of Walter Scott. And still he did not stint his guests:

> At dinner Mr. Skirling was expansive.
> He helped the joint, pressing a second slice
> Upon the relatives that came to stay,
> And stayed and stayed. It was the right tradition
> That his own blood should cling to him in need.

And there are the Misses Poar, who drive to church and
follow the clergyman conscientiously:

> Up to the moment when he prates
> Of the President of the United States;
> Then, knowing full well that Heaven can't
> Expect them to pray for General Grant.
> They bury their noses' patrician hook
> In dear Great-grand-papa's prayer book.
> Better to pray for the Restoration
> Than the overseer of a patchwork nation.

Miss Pinckney's lyric gift is great, her technical skill is
considerable, and she is almost invariably charming except
in some of the slighter poems where both thought and
style take a more or less conventional turn. But the longer
poems from which I have quoted are even more interesting,
for they suggest an expansiveness of mind and a far more
penetrating sympathy that indicate her capacity for working on larger designs than brief lyrics allow. At any rate,
Miss Pinckney's book is the most interesting first volume
that has come into my hands in a long time, and there is
little doubt in my mind that she is going to make (if indeed
she has not already made) a place for herself in American
poetry; for her poetry is comparable to the best that is
being written, whether by the younger generation or some
of the more well-established poets.

Carl Sandburg

Critic's Almanac
December 2, 1928

Carl Sandburg's *Good Morning, America* contains 162 poems written since 1922. It is regrettably necessary to say that there is little of the old Sandburg here. His vocabulary is as bold and diverse as ever; his imagination pours itself out profusely; there is always the interest of oddity and the interest of following a likable mind through its varied play of sympathies, hopes, and fears. But except in the rather Whitmanian title poem, which is a lengthy examination of American phenomena, there is very little actual poetry. We cannot quite go along with Sandburg when he wistfully chants, "Frogs of the early spring, frogs of the later days." Sandburg may see and feel the essential poetry of the frog, but he does not get it across. Frequently, like the later Vachel Lindsay, he babbles puerilities—

> Let me be your baby, south wind,
> Rock me, let me rock, rock me now . . .
> Comb my hair, west wind.
> Comb me with a cow lick.

There is a great deal of this sort of thing. In short, there are mannerisms, fancies, odd philosophizings that have a verbal punch but very little else. One is led to think that Sandburg is, after all, a poetic-minded, notionate, delightful fellow who is nevertheless not quite a poet.

I may be wrong. But while I maintain considerable respect for Carl Sandburg's general performance, it seems to me that in this book Carl Sandburg's special idiom of expression has failed him as a medium, and I think it has failed him because all along it was a prose idiom and not a poetry idiom. It does immensely well in *Rootabaga Stories,* which are delightful nonsense in story form, and it reappears successfully, though in a tempered form, in his

114

biography of Abraham Lincoln. In *Good Morning, America* it breaks down and the breakdown makes me doubt the validity of much of his previous poetry.

Elinor Wylie
Critic's Almanac
April 28, 1929

The day before she died, it happened that Elinor Wylie was arranging for publication a book of poems. This book now appears under the title *Angels and Earthly Creatures*. Everywhere it reads as if she had the taste of death already on her tongue, so that one is moved to wonder whether Elinor Wylie did not, like Shelley, foresee her fate. However that may be, there is little doubt that *Angels and Earthly Creatures* is her best book of poetry. It is more or less free from the finical toyings with words for their own sakes that had seemed at times to threaten her poetic art with decadence. This book has a sincere force, a humanity (if still shot through with fantasy and a tentative mysticism), and an open fervor that her poetry did not always have in the past. I am forced to confess myself a false prophet, for I remember that I once remarked that Elinor Wylie, if she had lived to be a centenarian, would have made no material advance in poetry.

What transformed her art, we can only speculate. Some of the poems seem to be highly autobiographical, and suggest a new, passionate experience that gave a fresh stimulus to poetic creation. Another thing is that her style, instead of becoming more modern and experimental, is more definitely shaped into traditional modes, flavoring strongly of the seventeenth century metaphysical poets and the Elizabethans—a tendency that her work had already shown.

There is even a little of Milton in the fine "Hymn to Earth." "This Corruptible" with its dialogue between Mind, Heart, Body and Spirit, reflects the method of John Donne and his followers. And the central feature of the whole book, a sonnet sequence entitled "One Person," fully illustrates the Elizabethan manner.

These sonnets are written in the "Italian" form, but with the idiom of Shakespeare. They celebrate the love of a woman for a man (reversing the conventional situation of the sixteenth century sonneteers), and are probably very strong examples of the turn that amorous poetry will take, now that women are writing more and more of it. They have a tenderness both fierce and sorrowful. Their mood is one of utter surrender, self-abasement, and idealistic worship. It is little short of startling, too, to find in them the exact manner, even to language and stock conventions, of the sixteenth century sonnet cycles: the compliments of the beloved, the dissection of the lover's intimate feelings, the half-veiled hints of the details of an "affair," the brooding over mortality, the elaborate conceits centered around mythological and chivalric lore—all are here, of course somewhat transformed by Elinor Wylie's characteristic style.

Phrases like "Time, who sucks the honey of our days"; "Had enriched my sight"; "To memorize the pure appointed task" are all Elizabethan. In its air of self-depreciation, in the very cadence and accent of the words, this sonnet is Elizabethan:

> The little beauty that I was allowed—
> The lips new-cut and coloured by my sire,
> The polished hair, the eyes' perceptive fire—
> Has never been enough to make me proud:
> For I have moved companioned by a cloud,

And lived indifferent to the blood's desire
Of temporal loveliness in vain attire:
My flesh was but a fresh-embroidered shroud.

Now do I grow indignant at the fate
Which made me so imperfect to compare
With your degree of noble and of fair;
Our elements are the farthest skies apart;
And I enjoin you, ere it is too late,
To stamp your superscription on my heart.

In a previous Romantic revival, poets went back, as Elinor Wylie did, to the fountains of inspiration of the sixteenth and seventeenth centuries. *Angels and Earthly Creatures* is another mark of the steady movement of our poetry toward refreshing itself from an old tradition.

The question of Elinor Wylie's greatness or non-greatness need hardly be discussed. It will finally settle itself. But we can observe that in a distinguished volume like this the satisfaction with the almost perfect art will outweigh the melancholy uneasiness that one feels over a somewhat fragmentary career, or the suspicion that one has of an attitude that is part pose and part an intense yet uncertain striving for some kind of human salvation. I should be loath to join with those who have adopted canonical enthusiasms and have spoken with bated breath of "Saint Elinor." A firm estimate of her work would probably show that it lacks the final touch that sets major above minor. Possibly Elinor Wylie was not a great enough person to be a really great poet. No matter—we can hardly ask for a better artistic performance than *Angels and Earthly Creatures*. Slight though its compass is, it will be for many tastes the book of poems of the year.

Critics and
Commentators

Harriet Monroe

Spyglass
August 1, 1926

"To have great poets there must be great audiences too,"
is the quotation from Whitman carried as a motto on
Harriet Monroe's *Poetry: A Magazine of Verse*, published
in Chicago, indeed founded and started there in 1912 with
the beginning of the so-called New Poetry Movement. In
Miss Monroe's behalf it must be said that she has worked
to create this "great audience" and has accomplished more,
possibly, in this direction than any other of the propa-
gandists for poetry, with the possible exception of Mr.
Louis Untermeyer. She has done American poetry a good
service because she had the foresight to establish her magazine at exactly the time when it was needed, and the courage to publish writers who needed an introduction to the
public. She has argued for poetry, lectured for it, and tried
to stimulate respect for it. She has also written some poetry,
a goodly selection from which you will find included in
her anthology, *The New Poetry*, just as you will find a
goodly selection from Mr. Untermeyer's poetry included
in his anthology, *Modern American Poetry*. Oh, well, fair
enough! We can forgive anthologists for including themselves if they will only include enough other people. And
here I do not have to discuss Miss Monroe as a poet.

It is her recently published book, *Poets and Their Art*,
that stands for the most important part of Miss Monroe's
career—that is to say, her function as editor of the first
magazine in the United States to be devoted entirely to
poetry and discussion of poetry. This book, consisting of
essays taken in large part from *Poetry's* editorial pages, is
not only, as she suggests, a record of *Poetry's* adventures,
of great names published and good causes sponsored. It is a

121

very illuminating picture of Miss Monroe. She reveals herself in all her vices and virtues even more clearly than she reveals the poets she discusses.

Do not misunderstand me. I am sure that these brief, charmingly written essays on Robinson, Pound, Sandburg, Amy Lowell and others, and the "Comments and Queries" part, which is more directly propagandist, and the arguments and speculations about prosody, free verse, etc., are just the thing for people who conceive of modern poetry as shocking, wicked, unintelligible. I heartily recommend Miss Monroe's book to all who have only a mild interest, or no interest at all, in poetry: it will start them thinking: it will tease them onward. And I wish that women's clubs, which are always glad to find good causes to work for, might be actively infected with Miss Monroe's enthusiasm for the advancement and understanding of poetry, in the same measure as they seem to have enthusiasm for painting, music and lecturers. For that matter, Rotarians, Exchangeites, Boosters and such earnest gentlemen with promoting capacities might profitably introduce themselves to Miss Monroe and seriously ponder her statement that the poet is "an advance agent of civilization." Considered in this light, Miss Monroe's book is a measure of the propagandizing service which she has done for the finest of the fine arts.

That service, however, lies pretty largely in the past. It is a book of memories, a backward glance to the stirring days of 1912 and thereabouts, when Harriet Monroe was energetically introducing us to newcomers who have since become leaders. Harriet Monroe is still apparently living in that past, and her magazine is running by sheer momentum only. One finds news, gossip, reviews in *Poetry* these days, but very few good poems. Miss Monroe is not now "discovering" Lindsays, Sandburgs, and Masterses of a new day. Her magazine is diluted with fripperies, minor wails, schoolgirlish platitudes. It is decaying.

Another disappointing fact is that Miss Monroe, in spite of honesty, diligence, and independence of mind, is not really a critic. Other than her vague but determined defense of free verse, her somewhat opportunist championing of poetry as a factor in the national life, what claims can she make to the title of critic? It will be impossible to discover in her book any body of principles such as we might have expected her to be maturing in her fourteen years' experience as editor and student of poetry. Compare her book, for instance, with critical volumes like T. S. Eliot's *The Sacred Wood* or even Conrad Aiken's *Skepticisms*, which is mainly a book of reviews. These volumes have a solidity and purpose which Miss Monroe's does not possess.

Delightful as these essays often are, they rarely get down to bedrock. They play earnestly over the surface of poetry. They introduce us with a pleasant feminine urbanity to a series of notables, breathing recollections, recording tilts and encounters, volleying opinions and dogmatic preferences which have little systematic dogma to uphold them. They represent crusades rather than analyses. They show a fondness for neatly turned phrases which have more of the flavor of the tea-table than of the critic's study. I note, in the essay on Robinson, references to the "meaty richness" of Robinson's produce, "the exquisitely tender and beautiful 'Mr. Flood's Party'" (Miss Monroe likes the word "exquisite"). One of Pound's poems has "the fragile loveliness of old Venetian glass." Lindsay's "Chinese Nightingale" has "lines which entrap the imagination." Edgar Lee Masters has "a big-hearted wistful sympathy" with God's creatures. Frost's "The Hill Wife" has an "exquisitely delicate pathos." Millay's lyrics are "ineffably lovely." And so on! Furthermore, the volume is notable for its exclusions as well as its inclusions. Miss Monroe has space for the fifth-rate Marjorie Allen Seiffert and a pack of minor feminine singers, but nothing at all to say for Conrad

Aiken, E. E. Cummings, John Crowe Ransom, Louis Untermeyer, John G. Neihardt, Robinson Jeffers, and William Ellery Leonard. Elinor Wylie gets only a narrow corner in Miss Monroe's gallery of women poets, and T. S. Eliot, whose "Waste Land" has had a greater influence, perhaps, than any other poem of the last five years, is strangely yoked in discussion with Lew Sarett, who has written some charming but mild lyrics about the Indians. In short, Miss Monroe has fought for poetry nobly but blindly. She has wanted to be a general, but her strategical capacities are thin. She claims to be the friend of poetry and of poets, but has little of real importance to say to them. She is an enterprising editor who by courage and a happy combination of circumstances was able to launch a much-needed and, in the beginning, a notable magazine; but time has shown in her and in her followers of the Chicago group grave weaknesses which deny her claims to leadership in the field of poetry.

Without meaning to imply disparagement, I wish to record my belief that Miss Monroe has essentially the club-woman mind. This is, up to a certain limit, a very fine thing, and we may congratulate ourselves that it is firmly woven into the social fabric of America and may recognize in it one of the important elements of cultural progress. It signifies an earnest public spiritedness, an active and real interest in art, intellectual curiosity, zeal for "the good life." But in its dealings with literature, especially when it sits in judgment and proposes to make itself into a critical force the limits of its seriousness are evident. Keen for momentary sensations, quick to react to whatever is invitingly new, it seldom displays any real assimilative power, because the arts to it are a delightful game, intoxicating interludes in the serious business of life, entertainment rather than occupation. Its culture is a matter of additions, of acquaintances made and relinquished, of "keeping up."

It wants to be at the focus of excitement. It is too much content with surfaces, and does not take time to grow from within, to absorb and systematize ideas, to establish its culture firmly as it goes. No wonder that the men have grown to conceive of art, particularly poetry, as an un-masculine and frivolous matter, and have invented the bluff jocosities of luncheon clubs as a fortification to masculinity, or discovered the term "high-brow" as the pink-tea epithet best applicable to the traitors of their sex who surrendered to a bogus intellectualism, vaguely connected in their masculine-minds with the purely decorative pursuits of women.

Miss Monroe's book is, like a clubwoman's diary, too much a record of sensation. It might be entitled *Poets Whom I Have Met*, for it is the zest of her editorial adventures that seems to underlie her reactions and estimates. And I am not without some suspicion that, if American poetry for the moment shows an inclination to languish, and if the great poetic revival in which Miss Monroe participated seems to falter when it should be at its climax, Miss Monroe and those who have followed similar methods are partly to blame. They have made much of false issues, and now are without issues. They have been concerned with sensations rather than ideas, and are now jaded prophets, without a cause. They have arrogated to themselves power and dictatorial robes, and now, bereft of authority, have only the illusion of past triumphs to clothe their nakedness. I would not take away from Miss Monroe one iota of the credit that is due her as a leader, but it is time to recognize that leadership has passed or ought to pass into other hands. Her magazine should either be re-vitalized or it should be discontinued.

H. L. Mencken

Extra Review
December 12, 1926

When I had finished H. L. Mencken's new book, *Notes on Democracy*, I looked out of the window with a sort of halfway vague expectation that I would find tottering buildings, rows of groveling sinners, and other Judgment Day effects. But nothing had happened. All the inhabitants of the Mencken universe—the Boobs, the Morons, and the Yokels—were calmly and even gaily going about their business, totally unaware of large volcanic disturbances in the region of New York. Streetcars were running. A new building was going up across the street. The bricklayers' cars were parked at the curb. A billboard announced that Chesterfields satisfy. The clouds were ambling northward in a gentle southern sky. All was as usual. There were no signs of crumbling civilization, or even of a penitent civilization.

After all, I thought, until Mr. Mencken convinces the Morons that they are Morons and should hence be submissive, how is he going to do the world much good? And since the Morons naturally haven't gumption enough to read his books, much less understand them, how is the convincing to be accomplished? Perhaps, however, he has no persuasive intentions. Let me try to understand Mr. Mencken, not to worship him or abuse him. After just consideration, I arrive at two possible views of his activity, as illustrated especially in his recent book. In one view he appears as a social philosopher or critic indulging in a rather destructive analysis but, unlike the giddy reformers, proposing no panaceas; and in this view he must be taken seriously. The other view puts him up as a gargantuan humorist with an immense capacity for invective and ridicule; and this view requires him to be enjoyed for his own sake, like any other writer who knows the pyrotechnic possibilities of language.

Taking first the serious view, I must offer the opinion that in *Notes on Democracy* Mr. Mencken deals with the weightiest subject he has yet approached. And, although the book is to a certain extent a restatement of his now familiar ideas, it is, on the whole, new material. He divides his *Notes* into three principal sections: "Democratic Man," "The Democratic State," "Democracy and Liberty." There is also a "Coda," in which, surveying the general destruction, he disclaims any knowledge of the future and declares that he enjoys democracy immensely because "it is incomparably idiotic, and hence incomparably amusing." The treatment of these various topics is not very systematic. Each Note is of course a denunciation; but each denunciation is a separate volcano, erupting lava like its neighbors, but disposed and erected by whim rather than geometry or logic. There is some overlapping and likewise some contradiction, as is usual in Mr. Mencken's writings. But there is no carefully symmetrical arrangement, no neatly marching parade of thesis—data—proof—conclusion.

Mr. Mencken sets up in his first section the idea that democratic man, considered in the mass, is a congenital moron incapable of an intelligent act. He admits that there are a few superior beings, but most minds are capable only "of a sort of insensate sweating, like a kidney." This view of the mob he bolsters up with the intelligence tests, which he sees as outlining intellectual levels beyond which no advance can be made. Therefore education offers no hope, because the Moron mob, which has a low "I.Q.," cannot be educated. Thus he knocks over the foundation of democratic theory which attributes some sort of mysterious (and Mencken would say, bogus) wisdom to the masses and exalts the Will of the People. The Will of the People, in his opinion, signifies simply the triumph of inferiority. And, since the mob is animated only by the savage motives of fear and envy, a government based on intelligence becomes an impossibility, for the masses are so stupid that they will oppose, and always have opposed, even sensible efforts to better their lumpish and besotted condition.

Furthermore, the democratic state, in Mr. Mencken's survey, becomes a travesty, simply because it is so thoroughly and nauseously democratic. The will of the people, if exerted, can accomplish any fool thing. The democratic mob "could extend the term of the president to life, or they could reduce it to one year, or even to one day. They could provide that he must shave his head, or that he must sleep in his underclothes." Politics, instead of a science, becomes a "combat between jackals and jackasses." Only demagogues can rule. Gentlemen stay out of politics. Instead we have a Harding, whose "notion of a good time was to refresh himself in the manner of a small-town Elk," or a Coolidge, of whom Mr. Mencken says: "There is no evidence that he is acquainted with a single intelligent man." The typical senator is "simply a party hack. . . . His backbone has a sweet resiliency. . . . it is quite impossible to forecast his action, even on a matter of the highest principle, without knowing what rewards are offered by the rival sides." Bribery and corruption are the order of the day. Public servants become cowards.

And then the fair principle of liberty, what of that? Democratic man, says Mr. Mencken, doesn't want it. He wants only safety and peace: "The peace of a trusty in a well-managed penitentiary." He wants laws, and especially laws that protect him against himself. Democracy "kills the thing it loves." It applauds mediocrity and pulls down superiority. Therefore puritanism is a natural accompaniment of democracy. For the puritan wants (1) "to punish the other fellow for having a better time"; (2) "to bring the other fellow down to his own unhappy level." It is typical of democracy that "Every district attorney goes to his knees each night to ask God to deliver a Thaw or a Fatty Arbuckle into his hands"—all because the mob delights in seeing rich persons browbeaten.

Thus Mencken! I have quoted freely but not as freely as I would like to, for every page is thickly sown with verbal torpedoes, exciting for their explosive vehemence, however questionable their direction and effect. But how shall Mr. Mencken's criticism of democracy be criticized? Mr. Mencken, who uses the South as the butt of his jokes and represents it as totally intolerant, would perhaps think that I would be in danger of assassination if I ventured to express any agreement with his ideas. But I do so venture, with a feeling of complete safety. The truth is that most of his excoriation of democracy is old stuff—at least as old as Thomas Carlyle, who also asserted that democracy sabotaged the superior man. Even the most ardent democrats must admit—and can admit with a tolerant smile—the bulk of Mr. Mencken's charges as to democracy's shortcomings. Furthermore, the influence Mr. Mencken wields and the whole secret of his method lie in the fact that he turbulently overstates what everybody knows. Nowhere, except in political editorials and the platitudes of orators, both of which are pretty generally received with skepticism, will you find the view that our present democracy is the absolute "summum bonum." Mr. Mencken's criticisms of democracy are paralleled by the jokes of Will Rogers, the bitingly satirical comic strips, and vaudeville patter, all of which we absorb with enormous gusto. Andy Gump's political campaign went over with a bang; but it was in its implication as destructively critical as *Notes on Democracy*. Goldberg's boobs are as savagely treated as Mencken's boobs. But this is true, also, that Mr. Mencken exceeds other critics in his ferocity and unscrupulousness. His ex-

aggerations are not simply exaggerations; they are often
studied distortions at plain variance with the truth; in fact,
Mr. Mencken, who is as poetic as a tale-bearing child, cannot always be trusted to give the correct facts. In spite of
his really powerful intellectual equipment, he often draws
on himself the just charge of malice because he is either too
lazy or too prejudiced to separate truth from falsehood.

His criticism of democracy is, of course, full of holes and
non sequiturs. We have not merely to make the charge
that Mr. Mencken views democracy everywhere at its
worst. His major premise, based on modern biology, be-
havioristic psychology, and the like, serves his purpose,
but is shaky in its claim that inferior men can never become
superior men. Mr. Mencken admits that some men are superior; he does not admit that the class can be enlarged; the
best democratic theory might say that it could be. Furthermore, though Mr. Mencken makes much of the gullibility
of the mob, he refuses to admit that superior men can do
the gulling; and though he is raucously tolerant of biological evolution, he is quite intolerant of the idea of political
evolution. In fact, his opinions drive him, as he is frank
enough to admit, directly toward anarchy; and in essence,
we are forced to conclude that Mr. Mencken is sorry he
was born, and that life offers him no pleasure except an
occasional tickling, a sensual excitement, or sardonic laughter at the ridiculousness of the world. Even so, though Mr.
Mencken may be sorry he was born, it is fortunate that he
was born in the United States, which, with England, is the
only country democratic enough to permit a confirmed
and lowly misanthrope to rise to his present position of
honor, wealth, and power, or to tolerate his persistent
rowdyism after he has arrived.

So, Mencken, the destroyer, necessary as he may be in
his role as an occasional stimulant or a gadfly, is not to be

trusted as a purveyor of ideas. Mencken as humorist is another thing. Others may imitate, but none can approach the vivacity and brilliance of his style: the sentences that crack like a whip, the phrases that fall and rebound like Thor's hammer, the surly laughter that revels in well-seasoned colloquialisms, ridiculous incongruities, sudden and vulgar paradoxes. Read Mr. Mencken for his ideas, and you will only hug the viper of melancholy to your bosom. Read him as you would read Mark Twain, you will not only escape the virus, but you will have a rare, indeed a unique, entertainment. You will have also the democratic (according to Mencken) pleasure of seeing the mighty ones biffed soundly; and you will only spoil the joke if you get angry because you are biffed yourself.

Two Professors

Spyglass
June 19, 1927

Two college professors, one from the East, the other from the West, have labored and brought forth capacious volumes, the produce of years of research. Vernon Lewis Parrington, professor of English in the University of Washington (in the state of that name), gives us *Main Currents in American Thought*. John Livingston Lowes of Harvard, also a professor of English, after eight years of super-detective work, publishes *The Road to Xanadu*. The contrast between these two books, if not between these two men, is precisely the contrast between the living and the dead. Professor Parrington's work, which has already reached two volumes and will run into a third, is a re-examination of the field of American literature for those ideas that are distinctly American; it is a definition of our civilization in terms of literature. Professor Lowes's book, brilliant and suave though it is, reduces at last to that driest phase of scholarship, "source work"; it is an examination of the sources, chiefly literary, from which Coleridge got the combination of materials found in "The Ancient Mariner" and "Kubla Khan."

The first two volumes of Professor Parrington's fruitful study are entitled, respectively, *The Colonial Mind* and *The Romantic Revolution in America*. They cover the periods of our national development from 1620 to 1800, and from 1800 to 1860. Volume III, yet to be published, will deal with "the beginnings of criticism of the regnant middle class, and the several movements of criticism inspired by its reputed shortcomings"—that is to say, the period of our great industrial development up to the present. The author's general purpose deserves to be stated in his own words,

to give some account of the genesis and development in American letters of certain germinal ideas that have come to be reckoned traditionally American—how they came into being, how they were opposed, and what influence they have exerted in determining the form and scope of our characteristic ideals and institutions . . . I have chosen to follow the broad path of our political, economic and social development, rather than the narrower belletristic, and the main divisions of the study have been fixed by forces that are anterior to literary schools and movements, creating the body of ideas from which literary culture eventually springs.

Such a program is one of the broadest, the most intelligent, the most ambitious, and I think the most valuable and successful that a professor of English has yet carried out in this country, where professors have often deserved the scoldings that such critics as Mencken have given them.

Professor Parrington's viewpoint and procedure remove him from the ranks of those scholars who, following the German ideal still dominant in our universities, dwell among literary and biographical trifles, practicing the pseudo-scientific and microscopic methods of which Professor Lowes's book is an inflated example. Nor is Professor Parrington the strict aesthete who is concerned with no values but artistic values. He commands the technical methods of both these types, but he goes aside from them to the more general viewpoint of the social historian. In this moment when, assailed by evils and confusions, we are making the attempt to understand ourselves, Professor Parrington's book comes as a judicial, clarifying force. He shows us what the diverse factors of our Americanism have been and are; he comforts us to withstand the claims of the unhealthy Waldo Franks and blatant liberators of the *Masses* crowd, as well as the equally blatant and shallow outcries of Judge Gary, *The Saturday Evening Post,* and the regular 100-percenters. Between these two extremes is the America of our real tradition, which is convincingly discovered to us in Professor Parrington's two volumes.

Even a general outline of the book is difficult to give and does little justice to the thoroughness and wisdom with which the author has gone about his job. To define the Puritan heritage, he goes into English backgrounds. He shows the mingling of economic necessity with theocratic idealism which characterized New England society, distinguishes between Puritan and Yankee, and deprecates the triumph of Calvinistic over Lutheran doctrine which resulted in blocking liberalism. He hails Roger Williams as "a humane and liberal spirit . . . groping for a social order more generous than any theocracy." He deals harshly with the Mather dynasty. And after defining Puritanism far more nearly adequately than I have yet seen it defined, he goes on to the later developments that preceded the rise of Jeffersonian doctrine: Benjamin Franklin, Samuel Adams, Hamilton and the Federalists.

But it is the second volume which is of peculiar interest to Southerners. At this moment when industrialism is sweeping down upon them, and Northern capital is resuming the process of conquest which Grant and Sherman never, thank Heaven, fully completed, Southerners need to examine their great heritage before they commit themselves beyond retraction to the processes of the machine age.* Professor Parrington has defined this heritage more sympathetically and fully than any other student of literature and society that I know. The aristocratic tradition of the Old Dominion, he shows, developed not because Virginia was exclusively populated with Cavalier stock, but because the Cavalier spirit took dominant possession of the middle-class, originally rather mercantile society. Virginia tradition animated Kentucky and Tennessee in their establishment; Alabama and Mississippi were "the intellectual heirs of South Carolina." The tendencies which finally disrupted the South came from the conflicting schools of thought represented by Jefferson and Calhoun, the former representing "equalitarian idealism," the latter a Greek-like conception of society based on economic realism. Professor Parrington possibly insists too much on the South's committal to slavery as "an incubus certain to alienate the liberalism of the North," but his distinction between the two schools of thought that prevailed in the South is far-reaching and well-sustained.

In relation to these broad analyses are fitted studies of individual thinkers and writers. John Taylor, an almost forgotten "philosopher and statesman of agrarianism," is resurrected from an undeserved oblivion. John Marshall is sub-

---

* Such statements are straws in the wind. *I'll Take My Stand* was published three years later.

jected to some rather stern searching; it was a contradiction that Virginia should furnish a man

to save the day for the Hamiltonians, erecting the old federalism into the law of the land. . . .

. . . .

Of social and humanitarian interests he (Marshall) was utterly devoid. One might as well look for the sap of idealism in a last year's stump as in John Marshall.

Edgar Allan Poe is considered but briefly in this book, for "aside from his art he had no philosophy and no programs and causes." Of Calhoun, this is said:

Whatever road one travels one comes at last upon the austere figure of Calhoun, commanding every highway of the Southern mind.

He points out that Calhoun wished to set up a kind of Greek democracy (including a beneficent slavery) over against the Northern system of wage labor. And now,

What Calhoun so greatly feared has come about. He erected a last barrier . . . against a universal cash register valuation of life; and the barrier was blown to pieces by the guns of the civil war.

One of the best studies is that of William Gilmore Simms, who in Parrington's view was undone by the aristocratic Charleston society that he worshipped.

The volume proceeds through the agrarian liberalism that marked the rise of the West, and then goes on to the

Knickerbocker romantics and the building of the New England school with its transcendentalists and brahmins.

I realize that I can give no adequate idea of the particulars of the book, and perforce return to generalities. Professor Parrington's style is not, except in flashes here and there, exceptionally brilliant from a literary standpoint. Yet it is adequate to his critical and expository purpose. He knows the art of compression; he can sum up a man or a cause with a packed, significant brevity that suggests the wide areas he has covered and the profound depths he has plumbed in making these coherent studies. This book will be dull to the unserious mind; but no American whose devotion goes beyond flag-saluting will find it so; and those who wish to be fully armed against the Menckens, the Oswald Garrison Villards, the Sinclair Lewises, and other questioners and malcontents will find in this book—with the accompanying studies to which it leads—the only sort of ammunition by which it is possible to prevail.

As to Professor Lowes's book, it is the polished acme, the absolute *summum bonum* and topmost peak of the scholarship to which English teachers are urged professionally to subscribe. Professor Lowes does more brilliantly, more capably, more interestingly than most other professors the minute jobs to which the pages of the *Publications of the Modern Language Association* are devoted; he makes a dull business read like a charming adventure. Starting with Coleridge's notebook he hunts down all the books that Coleridge read or might have read, and from ancient navigators, pseudo scientists, obscure and rare philosophers, and oddity-mongers reconstructs the paths Coleridge's mind followed in seeking, finding, and bringing together heterogeneous matters into "The Ancient Mariner," till they became simply and marvelously one. He allows himself to believe that in so doing he has plotted the course of the poetic mind, but he has in reality advanced our knowledge very little, if any. He has proved that Coleridge read many books, that Coleridge had a fine memory, that all was grist to Coleridge's mill—and has proved practically nothing else, except the laudable and perhaps foregone conclusion that opium had little to do with the creation of "The Ancient Mariner." His concluding chapter is an almost defensive argument that what he reveals is worth knowing and what he does is worth doing because it is done scientifically and science seeks the truth.

But this reasoning surely is delusion; it is the bankruptcy of scholarship; it is pedantry. To science, indeed, no fact

is unimportant, since science aims at composing the world
for practical ends. There is no practical end in Professor
Lowes's studies; there is no aesthetic end, for he takes the
"quality" of Coleridge's art for granted. He cannot make
another Coleridge; he cannot make us like or understand
Coleridge's poetry, as poetry, any better by such means.
What he does is exactly paralleled by Manly's *Some New
Light on Chaucer*, which attempts to show that the persons
of Chaucer's tales were drawn from real life, or the detec-
tive work of some other scholar (I have forgotten who)
that established the facts in the case of Christopher Marlowe, stabbed in a tavern brawl. There was a day when
learning was important in itself, because men just previously
had been allowed to know very little. Nowadays learning
is dignified and good up to a certain point. After that it
merely clogs the wheels, unless it assists one to move toward
practical, aesthetic, or philosophical ends. *The Road to
Xanadu* would have been magnificent in Renaissance days;
in modern America it is hopeless anachronism.

Two Critics

Critic's Almanac
June 23, 1929

Mr. Henry Seidel Canby and Mr. T. S. Eliot issue their
criticisms from the opposite sides of the Atlantic. That is
not the only reason, some knowing ones would say, for not
speaking of these two critics in the same breath, the intima-
tion being that Mr. Eliot, as Priest of the Sacred Wood,
should not be sullied by the briefest association with such
a journalist-critic as Mr. Canby. To tell the truth, I am a
little abashed myself at intruding into the Presence without

having first washed my feet of vulgar Tennessee dust and tendered a burnt offering—perhaps consisting of Mr. Canby himself. Rashly I would insist that the separate residence of Mr. Canby and Mr. Eliot is the point at which discussion of their most recent critical productions begins. I refer to *American Estimates,* by Mr. Canby and *For Lancelot Andrewes,* by Mr. Eliot.

Obviously, Mr. Canby is one of us. Like all good Americans, he is more concerned with the day's work than with eternal principles, and in that fact is his great usefulness. He writes easily and with generous insight about the books and the tendencies that the American audience is interested in; an editorial estimate when Hardy or Amy Lowell passes away; Mr. Cabell's romantic ironies about sex; Mr. Lewis's excellent reporting; the "gyring and gimbling" of Joyce and Stein; standardizing and cosmopolitanizing tendencies; occasionally the elder Americans—Thoreau, Emerson, Henry James—when they make current appearances. His temper is catholic and perceptive. When a good new writer emerges, Mr. Canby is quick enough to recognize and assist his emergence with sympathetic expository reviews that clear the way for public appreciation.

Probably there is no critic in the country who can beat Mr. Canby at the hard task of presenting a book appreciatively. Aside from this function, which is no mean one, he is often shrewd and just in his observation of tendencies:

A hundred critics shouting "Down with Babbitt" are not worth one poem, one novel, one play, which represents all that Babbitt is not but may very possibly desire to be.

. . . .

Criticism, which is always written for the cultivated, is shot through today with capital *I*'s.

. . . .

There is only one theme with blood and life in it for literature in our century. . . . Reduced to lowest terms, it is the effect of machinery on man.

Like Mr. Mencken, he sees the crass folly of many American phenomena, but he does not share Mr. Mencken's jocose pessimism. If Mr. Canby has a central doctrine, it is a quiet faith in the ability of American genius to find the right path finally. His sensitiveness to the better side of modern American literature is a quality that we rejoice to discover in the editor of the *Saturday Review*, our only periodical devoted wholly to criticism. It makes up, in great part, for a certain lack of savor in his writing, and we should be glad that Mr. Canby has not, like some of his academic contemporaries—Irving Babbitt and Paul Elmer More, for instance—retired discreetly behind the scenes. In some of his essays he has taken pains to define the paths of older American literary tradition that a contemporary writer may profitably follow up. He is not overly impressed by the tendency of some of our writers to adopt foreign modes:

Our young writers are going to Paris and London as never before. They will find nothing being written there more vital than what we are producing here. They will find less inventiveness in technique, a narrower range of literary subjects, and in style precisely those results of a long and homogeneous culture, which it is most dangerous for an outsider to imitate.

It is natural that the criticism of Mr. Canby should be indicted for its journalistic quality. It has the extemporaneousness, the lack of finality, that is inherent in its origin. To be an editor and a chairman of a book club at the same time obviously injures Mr. Canby's work as a critic; his leadership will express itself in deeds more often than in words, perhaps not always fortunately. He has his blind spots. One feels that he has been excessively enthusiastic about some good but not first-rate authors. But these defects are incidental, one supposes, to the position that he fills; an editor and a chairman of a book club is bound to make more mistakes than a severely detached critic. At least he is with us and of us. He is in the arena, giving and taking blows; he is mixing with events, not sulking in a corner.

And Mr. T. S. Eliot is far, far away, not only in space, but in time. He is an anglicized American, who now definitely describes himself as "classicist in literature, royalist in politics, and anglo-catholic in religion." Somehow one gathers that he is not writing for us hungry sheep, swollen with the wind of temporal doctrines, but for posterity. With troubled heart, one surmises that Mr. Eliot would regard the possibility of writing on Sinclair Lewis with exactly the same revulsion that he would contemplate a visit to his mother country. The Sacred Wood of literary tradition that Mr. Eliot explores critically is a carefully picketed area, rarely extending beyond the seventeenth century. His new book, the third critical volume he has published, consists of eight rather brief essays: Lancelot Andrewes, John Bramhall, Niccolo Machiavelli, Francis Herbert Bradley, Baudelaire in Our Time, Thomas Middleton, A Note on Richard Crashaw, The Humanism of Irving Babbitt. . . .

Mr. Eliot's essays are built on the presumption that they are to be read by people of sound and extensive learning. Unless one has this learning, he is sure to be ill at ease, and he will not appreciate their remarkable degree of lucid concentration. For instance, I was at a stand in reading the essay on the great churchman, Lancelot Andrewes, since my ecclesiastical education is poor: I know little about the sermons of Hooker, Taylor, Donne and even less about the inside history of the Church of England. The best I could do was to see that Mr. Eliot's prose quotations from Andrewes have the merit that he claims. I was even worse off with John Bramhall, and almost as bad off with Machiavelli and Bradley.

Furthermore, I am much intimidated by Mr. Eliot's impressive habit of referring to authors quite casually, as with the presumption that any decent person knows them by heart, when in fact I do not know them at all or never heard of them. It is terrifying to be referred to Mario Praz, Gentillet and Dr. Sparrow-Simpson with a passing wave of the hand. My own confusion and ignorance, not Mr. Eliot's learning, are blameworthy. If objection is to be made, it must be to Mr. Eliot's pontifical air. A chilly hauteur is part of his manner; one suspects it to be the psychological defense of a lonely heart. At any rate one feels icily re-pelled, put in one's proper uncouth place; it is the same as being viewed through a monocle.

But taking this all in good part and, like an idiotic American, refusing to be snubbed, one sees the drift of Mr. Eliot's criticism and grants its great distinction—even its present importance if it can cross the Atlantic and get farther inland than New York City. Mr. Eliot promises us three more volumes, which, if we are patient, will in time explain his position fully. The most interesting point to me in his recent critical doctrine is that Mr. Eliot, a self-styled "classicist" in literature—elsewhere loosely called an "in-tellectual," a "radical," and whatnot—has taken a religious turn. Those who will reread "The Waste Land" in con-nection with the new volume will see that Mr. Eliot has been heading toward religion all the time. The poem was not only an expression of modern despair, but a reproach of modern irreligion. And now Mr. Eliot finds the weak point in Mr. Irving Babbitt's proposal of humanism as the chief element of salvation. Humanism without religion is, to his notion, sterile, and humanism itself cannot be a religion. "It is doubtful whether civilization can endure without religion, and religion without a church."

This particular essay sheds a backward light, not only on the other essays in the book, but also on Mr. Eliot's studies in the seventeenth century metaphysical poets. In fact, it illuminates a great deal that seemed obscure in Mr. Eliot's writing heretofore. It provides a central point from which to regard Eliot *in toto*, and it shows what he can do when he forsakes the safe ground of the past and enters the debatable ground of contemporary thinking. It is a pleasure to see the thoroughness with which Mr. Eliot exposes the shallowness of Arthur Symons's approach to Baudelaire, and one is stimulated with a new desire to study the late Elizabethans when one has read his essay on Middleton; but the essay on Irving Babbitt is, for contemporary purposes, worth dozens of the other sort.

We can but lament that the case of Canby and Eliot shows one of the common ills of our time: the impossibility of all-round-ness anywhere. Neither Mr. Canby nor Mr. Eliot carries out Arnold's neat idea of the critic as a sort of John the Baptist preparing society to receive the Word. Editor-Chairman Canby is simply too busy to develop Critic Canby into an effective leader; a lively interest in contemporary literature somehow doesn't go along with thoroughness and finish—and Mr. Canby suffers less than many others. On the other hand, thoroughness and finish seem to have an affinity for London fog. Great learning engenders trepidation, and the world slides buoyantly hellward while Mr. Eliot is germinating foolproof ideas for a posterity utterly gone to the devil. We may wish that Mr. Canby would be more deliberate; even more heartily we could wish that Mr. Eliot could be more expansive. I can think of no better solution than to invite him to come over and enjoy himself for a change.*

* Eliot came back the first time in eighteen years when he taught at Harvard during 1932 and 1933.

Society and the Arts

Notes*

Spyglass

November 30, 1924

First of all this week, let it be known that we do positively know how to spell the name of Max Beerbohm, though those admirable persons, the printers, recently made us appear to spell it with an "n." So now that's off the conscience, and it will be easier to write this column. This is the way we feel like doing it:

1. Arnold Bennett has a new novel.
2. John Galsworthy has a new novel.
3. Hugh Walpole has a new novel.
4. John Masefield has a new novel.
5. Michael Arlen has a new novel.
6. Mary Johnston has a new novel.
7. James Stephens has a new novel.
8. May Sinclair has a new novel.
9. Ben Hecht has a new novel.
10. Selma Lagerlof has a new novel.
11. Thomas Nelson Page has a new novel.
12. Ethel Dell has a new novel.
13. Stewart Edward White has a new novel.
14. Rafael Sabatini has a new novel.
15. Thomas Dixon has a new novel.
16. Joseph Hergesheimer has a new novel.
17. All God's chillun got a new novel.
18. H. G. Wells got a new novel? No, not this time!

In other words, the above might be taken as a chart of a Literary Editor's brain after receiving his morning mail from the publishers. Why do all these old boys and all these old ladies keep on writing novels, anyway? Why don't they

* This selection is characteristic of many early *Spyglass* columns in variety of subject matter and in tone.

quit and let somebody else have a go? Do they set a goal, you suppose, and say to themselves: "Well, when I get up to thirty-seven I'll quit"? And then, when they get to thirty-seven, they say, "Well, I'll try one more, just for luck, to make the score even." And so they go, on and on, till the brain reels. In our present mood, it gives us heartache to think how they keep on writing and writing. At this time, we can think of two facts of far more interesting nature to us, at least. Thus we state them:

1. We have a new cook!
2. We have a new cook!

Thus having shifted the universe into a new equilibrium, Atlas may heave a sigh of deep self-satisfaction. But after all, it is necessary to recognize the personal construction of the universe just specified. After all, there are other people who have other cooks, or do not have them. With a stupendous effort at magnanimity, we turn from beatific contemplation of our own new universe, revolving about its new gastronomical center on its new digestive orbit, and view this American and Tennessean and Nashvillian world, where a great deal is happening too. For instance:

1. Stanley Johnson's novel, *The Professor*, is scheduled for early publication by Harcourt, Brace and Company, of New York.

2. John Crowe Ransom's third volume of poems, *Grace Before Meat*, has just been issued by the Hogarth Press, London, England, with an introduction by Robert Graves.

It is naturally a peculiar happiness to herald the forthcoming publication of Mr. Johnson's novel. We daresay that no novelist in this country has made a more painstaking study of the art of fiction than Mr. Johnson. He brings to his writing a preparatory scholarship that is as desirable among Americans as it is often lacking. And we shall look forward to the issuance of his volume with more than usual anticipation. The title has ominous sound to these alas professorial ears. If we wore horn-rimmed glasses, we should polish them, and look again. But there it indubitably is: *The Professor.**

John Crowe Ransom's third volume is his third, of course, only in the matter of chronology. It is a collection of twenty poems from his first volume, *Poems About God*, and his recently published *Chills and Fever*, which is receiving fine press notices everywhere. The selection of the poems was made by the English poet Robert Graves, who sponsored the publication of the book, and who writes an introduction that should make the tardy American critics sit up and take notice. Mr. Graves relates how he came across Mr. Ransom's *Poems About God* and became greatly interested in it. His inquiries among the so-called critical authorities of American poetry gave him no information. He determined "that the best thing to do was to publish a selection from *Poems About God* and from Ransom's later work, in England, hoping for the usual repercussion in America." Upon the solicitation of Mr. Graves and T. S. Eliot, the publication was undertaken by the Hogarth Press.

In his critical discussion of Mr. Ransom's poetry, Graves finds that Robert Frost is the only American poet with whom Mr. Ransom has "the least discoverable affinity." He furthermore states that Mr. Ransom "is doing for his own state what Frost has done for New England, Vachel Lindsay for his Middle West, and Carl Sandburg for Chicago," and that "such poets are the forerunners of a national American school that will one day produce a synthesis of all regional contributions." We agree with the important rank among American poets that Mr. Graves as-

* The novel, which is rather poor, attained some notoriety because its chief character was seemingly a composite of various local notables. Johnson, an original member of the Fugitive group and instructor of English at Vanderbilt, resigned from the English faculty before his novel came out.

signs to Mr. Ransom. Nevertheless, we do not discover that he has any likeness to Robert Frost (he seems, in fact, more like Edmund Spenser); and above all we do not see, as Mr. Graves claims, that he is a sectional voice, as the poets above named are sectional voices. We are sorry to disagree with so excellent a critic as Mr. Graves, but perhaps in this case he has made a long-distance interpretation not in accordance with the facts. Anyway, it's a splendid and glorious introduction, and a splendid volume.

Note

Spyglass
July 5, 1925

Mr. and Mrs. Alfred Knopf have sailed for Europe to look for more foreign authors to publish in America. They have been invited by Ladislas Reymont, author of *The Peasants*, to visit him at his estate in Poland. While there, they hope to meet two other important Polish authors, whose names the reading public will never forget—Przybyschzewski and Zeromski. Zeromski doesn't interest me, I must confess; his name is too colorless. But Przybyschzewski!

Notes: Sex in Literature, Poetry Magazines
Spyglass
March 28, 1926

Reading realistic and satirical novels, poring over realistic and satirical biographies, absorbing psychoanalysis applied to literature—that's not much of a recreation for spring-time, with Nashville just beginning to cast off its smoke-screen, and with multicolored rayon silks flashing (at bargain prices) in department store windows. What's the matter with all these fellows who write fiction and biography and criticism? Are they sick? Have they merely drunk too much bootleg liquor? Are the George F. Babbitts intruding too raucously into their lonely lives? All of that, probably, and more besides!

Then here's somebody named Ann Heritage (a suspicious name) writing Edwin Valentine Mitchell's "Booknotes":

People say, "What does make a best-seller?" The answer in nine cases out of ten, is "Sex."

It is probable that but for the story of Eden, we should never have had best sellers, for the best seller is the literature of the fall.

This same Ann Heritage lists a few best-selling novelists who best-sell sex stories: that is, E. M. Dell, Mrs. Barclay, Michael Arlen, Gilbert Frankau, Somerset Maugham, Joseph Hergesheimer, Margaret Kennedy, A. S. M. Hutchinson, D. H. Lawrence. Of course, in many of these, the sex theme is disguised or mixed with other ingredients. But it's there.

Depressing reflections, these! Yet equally depressing is the contrary reflection that very many of the so-called "healthy" books are tame and ordinary affairs, very tepid, often silly. After all, D. H. Lawrence is to be preferred to Harold Bell Wright, Robinson Jeffers to Edwin Markham, Eugene O'Neill to the unremembered author of *Lightnin'*.

149

If we have to choose between the bad boys of contemporary literature and the sweetly sane apostles of the uplift, we are likely to choose the bad boys, who are at least intelligent and unafraid.

Too bad that it is necessary to choose! All the worse, also, when one chooses with considerable irritation, such as I have felt in going over certain recent books, for instance, Joseph Wood Krutch's new biographical study of Edgar Allan Poe, which coldly demonstrates that Poe was actually a madman, burdened with unmentionable psychological complexes, and that all his work derives itself from pathological conditions; or William Faulkner's brilliant new novel, *Soldier's Pay*, a book done in the modern style, containing postwar people writhing in various attitudes of disillusionment; or D. H. Lawrence's *The Plumed Serpent*, with its fierce disgust at modern civilization and its defiant exaltation of the primitive impulses; or T. S. Stribling's *Teeftallow*, which I have not yet read, but which reviews seem to indicate as another bitter dart, puncturing indifferent Tennessee; or Alfred Kreymborg's *Scarlet and Mellow*, which is merely odd poetry, with all sorts of hidden sniggers; or William Ellery Leonard's *Two Lives*, a poem of insanity and tragic love. The list might be lengthened immensely. . . .

To turn to matters a little less unpleasant, I summon up a feeble inquiry as to what has become of all the Southern magazines that were flourishing bravely at this time a year ago. *The Fugitive*, of course, perished by *felo de se*; it could have continued, but no single member of the group of publishers was willing to be hitched to the editorial oxcart. Besides, what was the use of publishing a magazine for a practically nonexistent audience? But, if rumors are correct, *The Fugitive* is not the only Southern casualty. *The Nomad*, I believe, gave up the ghost long ago. Both *The Southwest Review* and *The Reviewer* are in difficulties, it is said. *The Buccaneer* has been discontinued. *The Double Dealer* comes forth at dubious intervals with a vague show of courage. The Little Magazines of the South are rapidly becoming the Little Magazines of yesteryear. What is the reason? It is possible to guess. They do not perish for lack of writers, certainly; there are more and more writers, and good ones, every year. But I daresay that their situation often reflects the situation in which the Fugitives found themselves—namely they confront barren rewards or a lack of rewards in attempting to publish a magazine in the South over a period of years. The publication of a Little Magazine such as *The Fugitive* is an inspiring enterprise, for a while; finally one decides it is better to quit than to agonize.

By contrast, observe Harriet Monroe's *Poetry: A Magazine of Verse*, which runs on and on forever, in Chicago, publishing bundles of verse, good, bad, and indifferent, every month in the year, together with book reviews, critical discussions, poetry news, and so on. What keeps it going? Look into the March number. Turn to the back of the magazine, where are listed the subscribers to the "Fund," which, no doubt, not only supports the magazine but also Miss Harriet Monroe, as is quite proper. Observe on that list of names such people as the following: Mr. Charles G. Dawes, Mr. Charles Deering, Mrs. Frank C. Lowder, Mrs. Julius Rosenwald, Mr. Charles H. Swift, Mrs. Rockefeller McCormick, Senator James D. Phelan, Mrs. Robert N. Montgomery, Mr. Ira Nelson Morris. It is therefore possible to reflect that when Southern wealth supports Southern magazines, then Southern magazines will flourish.

But weeds grow where nothing else will. That is to say, *Poetic Thrills*, of which I lately gave some report in this column, has not been discontinued. Here is the spring number, with a bold slogan at the top of the title page, namely,

"A Journal of Verse with National Scope and International Hope." The editor, Gertrude Perry West, prints one of her own poems, with the following interpretative comment:

We wish to remind the reader that "Teen Days" is not a personal poem, but is one that applies to any girl in love for the first time, from a princess to a milkmaid. Some of the scenes we have builded are classic, while some are provincial and epical. As this was the poem most quoted when we were nominated to a place in the "Hall of Fame for Originalism," which is Statuary Hall, or the National Hall of Fame, at Washington, D. C., we suppose it, with its "wonderful creative imagination," was the poem most instrumental in having this "greatest honor" bestowed upon us. And with the humble gratitude of a Carolinian we will quote a few stanzas as the beginning of the poem serially in *Poetic Thrills.*

Yes, there's no doubt that Gertrude Perry West belongs in the National Hall of Fame, that is to say, the Hall of Fame for Originals, or Statuary Hall, located in Washington, D. C.—she belongs there, together with J. Gordon Coogler and the Sweet Singer of Michigan. As evidence, we quote a few lines from this remarkable poem:

> If I were a border shepherdess,
> And a wounded lamb were you,
> I would take you up and fondle you—
> I would lay your head upon my breast;
> Your fright'n'd heartbeats growing less;
> And there you'd find a bed of rest,
> Where my heart for you beat true.

Notes: Zona Gale, Censorship

Spyglass
February 6, 1927

Getting slowly, almost feebly, under way in Zona Gale's new novel, *Preface to Life*, I thought: "Well, here is another Middle Western novel . . . the dull life of little towns, especially such as are named Pauguette, Illinois . . . the wistful young man who wants to escape and can't . . . the rich young lady who wants to escape and does . . . the people, all foiled, browbeaten by dullness, eating their bread-and-butter in a sickly discontent, and nobody coming to any good end." Zona Gale's book is all of that, and happily it is more, especially in the latter third, which is the only part worth reading and which is as near to being fine art as anything written in America these days. The preceding two parts can only be justified as perhaps a necessary preliminary to the third part.

Here we have the ambitious young man who, somewhere in the early 1900's, decides to flee the parental nest. But Pauguette, Illinois, lays pudgy hands on him and pulls him back. All in a breath, almost, he falls in love with two young women, marries one, and reluctantly settles down to carry on his father's lumber business. His father has meanwhile died of an apoplectic stroke induced partly by the young man's refusal to enter the said lumber business. A tender conscience, propinquity of a marriageable girl, family pressure do their work. The young man settles down to a dull existence—dull and prosperous—while the girl he really loved travels in Europe and sends him an occasional letter which he conceals in a sacred drawer of his desk. There follows, after a period of outward reconcilement, a highly developed case of maladjustment. In 1925 the young man, now the benignant grayheaded father of incomprehensible children, finds a peculiar escape from his maladjustment.

153

There comes on him now a strange faculty of vision, a sort of exaltation in which he sees the world in a totally new guise; all things are, by an exercise of his will, transfigured into shining forms which partake of the external movement of the world; they become timeless; their awkward external shapes merge into a reality which he finds indescribable, bringing with it a sense of the infinite flux and stir and change of the universe. He has no words for this new conception, which the author states for him (when she outlines what he sees) in passages of wonderful prose unexcelled in their clarity and beauty. And because he has no words, and because other people are dull and unappreciative, he becomes for them a madman, a mere pathological case, to be pitied, humored, and whispered about. The end of course is tragedy, none the less poignant and human for the floating veil of introspection flung over it, sometimes Poe-like and macabre, sometimes charged with the fierce bright energy of a Blake.

The effect of the book is that of a dream brooded over and remembered, and its strangeness is increased by the device the author has employed of ignoring conventional paragraph divisions and letting conversation, action, introspection run in a smooth undisturbed stream. So *Preface to Life* is not after all, in spite of its early flat passages, just another Middle Western novel. It is a fresh and powerful conception, magnificently executed, and defective perhaps only in its proportions. The book leaves one dizzy; but there is page after page of prose which demands to be read again and again.

A correspondent from Tennessee sends a copy of Henry Bellamann's *Petenera's Daughter* with the request that I deliver an opinion. "If a spade must be called a spade," she writes, "why do the modern fictionists always select unclean spades?" Mr. Bellamann is, according to her professed personal knowledge, a "charming and cultured man." And since he is "charming and cultured," she is shocked that he could write such a book.

Such a reaction I can understand because there are still many people, as George Moore points out, who indulge the fallacious belief that morality depends upon literature. But such a reaction I certainly cannot approve. *Petenera's Daughter* is the simple tale, told without affectation and with not a single wicked smirk, of a Dutch farmer boy in Missouri who was quite ignorant of life, and of a girl who was quite as ignorant as he. It is true that the love affair of this naive couple resulted in an illegitimate child, that the young man during his futile effort to escape visited certain unmentionable streets in St. Louis; but what of it? These matters are not dragged in. They form an integral part of the story, and the story presents, in honest and often dull entirety, life in Missouri which biologically resembles life elsewhere on the globe. And the story is told well, fairly well, at least; it certainly has no sinister purpose; indeed it seemed to me rather more "healthy" and "wholesome" than the average Middle Western novel; it has vigor and sanity. I fail to see that it is shocking.

If *Petenera's Daughter* is shocking, what about Shakespeare's *Othello*, the *Merry Wives of Windsor* and the songs of brokenhearted Ophelia? What about *Don Quixote*, *Tess of the D'Urbervilles*, *Tom Jones*, many of the poems of Swinburne, some of the tales of Chaucer, various parts of Homer and Virgil and a great part of the Greek dramatists? What about *The Scarlet Letter* of Hawthorne and the *Agamemnon* of Aeschylus, both of which are concerned with adultery? What about the various passages in Chronicles, Deuteronomy, etc.? There is, indeed, no end of these perfectly obvious retorts, on which I might as well expend some space, since there may be still a few readers who go around looking for a chance to be shocked.

To say that specific parts of a modern work are shocking

or immoral is to invite an infinite series of parallels from the masterpieces which everybody is at least supposed to read and which a countless number of people have read without becoming corrupted, much less shocked. How in the world can we ask an artist who deals with life to refrain from using any feature or features of life he pleases? We can praise or condemn him only by what he does with his materials, by the final impression he leaves on us, by the total meaning, beauty, sincerity of his work. Will my correspondent reject *Paradise Lost* because of the "objectionable" scenes in the Garden of Eden? I hope not, for Milton's intention was certainly moral enough, and besides, *Paradise Lost* is to be judged as literature. Pornography is another thing. As George Moore shows in his *Avowals*, it is not literature at all, but merely an article of trade, openly and professedly (or sometimes under a thin disguise) soliciting the attention of the prurient, who always know where to look and would seldom make the bad (for them) bargain of picking up a serious masterpiece. There is also perhaps a doubtful class of literature where the balance wavers; such books resemble literature in outward seeming, but one feels in them a little too much of a smirk, an artificial sophistication, or something plainly morbid and perverse. A recent example might be Frances Newman's *The Hard-Boiled Virgin*. But even here I should hesitate to draw the line. I should certainly oppose censorship.

Censorship, indeed, as I have before now said, gets nowhere, because nobody can decide with any sort of accuracy what really ought to be censored. In George Moore's *Avowals* the whole matter is discussed at great length and with much good sense; I recommend this book, pages 120 to 139, to my correspondent and other interested persons. As the witty Irishman shows, censorship reduces itself to absurdity, especially when it comes to libraries and to Bowdlerized versions of literature. There are still libraries in this country, I have heard, where Cabell, Dreiser, and Hardy are not admitted, or else are given seats on the back shelves where they can be doled out only to qualified persons bent on some scholarly or educational enterprise. But how is this, George Moore asks, that if books will corrupt people at all, they will not corrupt educated and scholarly people? And do not the highbrows deserve protection as much as the little boys and girls? And imagine the

amusing scene of a librarian questioning a girl as to her age and education she has received, and looking into her face, trying to determine from the profile as well as from the full face whether she is qualified to read Sterne in an unexpurgated version and putting the same questions to a boy who saunters up to the same counter. Are the boy and girl to be called upon to affirm upon oath that they are not actuated by desire to read spicy passages, but are merely anxious to acquaint themselves with literature of a certain period?

Indeed, it is a quite impossible problem. I must confess to a great unwillingness to pass judgment in such matters, and I certainly know no person I would trust as a literary censor, although I can think of many whose opinion I would think good in purely artistic concerns. The only safeguard is good taste, and perhaps even good taste is variable and not easily capable of definition. But certainly this is true: the cheap book, the false book, the insincere book eventually fails and dies of its own literary defects. And if a so-called "off-color" or "shocking" book survives the process of centuries, you may be sure it has some of the qualities of genuine art.

But I fear I have said too much. I can hear the legions of Sumner and the various protective associations shouting angrily at my heels. Lest I be thought a friend of vice, let me record that I am no particular advocate of those moderns who are inordinately obsessed with sex; and even the amours of the Cabellian heroes weary me a little, and Carl Van Vechten often makes me more than a little sick. But even here it is a matter of tedium mainly. The insistence on uncouth themes merely becomes boresome. I still maintain that it does not corrupt unless stories about murder and theft drive people to commit murder and theft. And, far from vice being aided, virtue was never so well served as in the novels of the moderns, where sex becomes a platitude, immorality simply dull, and all unmentionable things so trite as to produce yawning and heaviness of the eyelids.

Old Songs
Critic's Almanac
May 27, 1928

If a prognostication had to be made—as the heading of of this column invites—about the immediate future direction of contemporary literature, I should not be loath to declare that twin schools of realism and protest have passed their climax. The signs of the literary zodiac point again to romanticism, and one of the strongest omens is the new interest in folk song of all sorts, gathered from mountain and plain, forest and sea. We should not bother too much about the famous "lost generation" of younger writers who have fed deep on despair and show the effect of their diet. So long as folk songs are gathered and studied—still better, if they are also sung—there will be one core of health in the unhealthiness of the times. It was not literary censorship, nor yet literary criticism, that put an end to eighteenth century smartness; it was Percy's *Reliques of Ancient English Poetry*, which now has a number of twentieth century descendants.

One of the latest of these is W. Roy Mackenzie's *Ballads and Sea Songs from Nova Scotia,* published by the Harvard University Press, which, by the way, seems to take a special interest and pride in putting out collections of this type. And if you ask me what interest a Southern audience can possibly have in the ballads and sea songs of Nova Scotia, my answer is ready; it is, first, the interest we all ought to have in the genuine primitive elements of any literary tradition, whether English, Irish, Scotch, or Nova Scotian; and, second, it is that the tradition of the Nova Scotia songs is also pretty largely ours. Nor do I except from this even the sea songs, which Mr. Mackenzie justly notes as forming so large a part of his collection. A great many students of American balladry have observed that the songs of the Southern mountaineers include many references to the sea, not unnatural references, either, since they only demonstrate that after some hundreds of years our mountain folk still preserve these stubborn traces of their seafaring ancestors. The song which Mr. Mackenzie records as "The Single Sailor" I have heard under another title and in a slightly different version. I was brought up to know it as the song of the "Fair, Pretty Lady," and I note that Mr. Mackenzie records, as one title variant "A Pretty, Fair Maiden."

In Mrs. Ethel Park Richardson's collection of *American Mountain Songs* will be found the tragic story of Willie, who "got drownded in the deep, blue sea." And so on! I ran across with pleasure in Mr. Mackenzie's book such old favorites as "The Quaker's Wooing," "When I Was Single," "Barbara Allan," and the like. Here are also many of the familiar deep-sea chanteys (or "shanties," as this book has it), a goodly group of very ancient ballads like "Young Beichan," many old nursery songs, sentimental and heroic broadsides, and others of lesser note. It was amusing to discover a song entitled "Dixie's Isle," and still another called "The Sunny South," which carried peculiar associations in the lines

> Time points the way when this
>   conflict will be over,
> When from Yankees and Fenians
>   our country will be free.

Mr. Mackenzie's lengthy preface explains his grouping and discusses the various types of songs at considerable length. One moot point he makes pretty clear. That is the arguable question of just how the chanteys were really sung. In the first place, whatever divergencies of practice there may have been, the old sailors whom this collector interviewed agreed that the chanteys were esteemed to be of real value in lightening labor and "giving the crew a sense of unity and fellowship." Furthermore, there probably was not communal composition in the sense that any member of the group who was pulling on a rope might add a line to the song. The chantey was led by a chantey-singer, chosen for his special ability. The chanteyman led with the verse, which he might make up, if his fancy prompted him and the crew joined in on the chorus, which seems to have been the fixed part of the composition. Mr. Mackenzie's very full account of the ritual of chantey singing is the most valuable part of his very interesting introduction, and I wish that I had space to quote from it.

But I cannot. I pass the word along that here is a fine collection of 162 miscellaneous songs and ballads, current in Nova Scotia, and return to my meditations on general themes—wishing, however, that collectors of such things as songs would put the melodies along with the songs themselves, and not in the back of the book. And what are my meditations about, you ask? Why simply that there is still a tremendous store of folk songs in this section of the South, uncollected still, and soon to be forgotten unless some good spirits get to work with all diligence. Let us not wait for the civilizing influence of jazz and music memory contests to make our treasurers of these old, rude, virile songs ashamed of their heritage. Every Southern university ought to have at least one faculty member who would make it his chief interest to collect such things. And, furthermore, they ought to be not only collected and put in books to stand on library shelves. They ought to be sung by concert singers, school children, choruses. They ought to be known and loved, in their traditional melodies. Why do we need to give all our favor to the "Song of the Volga Boatmen" and "O Sole Mio," when we have good folk songs of our own right near us? If we neglect them, we are a contrary and heedless generation.

Crippled Caravan

Critic's Almanac
November 11, 1928

The book I have been attempting to read is not a child's book,* nor is it fit for children, but it has a great deal of childishness about it. I refer to *The Second American Caravan*. The correct adjective to apply to it is, I think, "puerile." Most of its sixty contributors might easily be catalogued, from their showing here, as perverse imps, telling dirty stories in a frowzy backyard—crude imps with unformed minds, imps without prankishness or dignity, imps with a dull, insistent way of exposing their own hurts.

One of the first offerings, a fragment of a novel by Jonathan Leonard, tells a drab, unintelligible story of a

* This is the last part of a Children's Book Week column.

wounded philosopher who blows out his brains, ejaculating "Perhaps this is the most foolish thing I ever did." Wallace Gould, in awkward long-line verses, warms over Aeschylus, Euripides, and other Greeks. Sherwood Anderson writes vaguely of a suspicious husband who says over and over to his wife, "What are you doing, my dear?" And she answers, "I am taking a bath." Lewis Mumford, one of the honorable editors, offers a condensed novel, chapters written paragraph length, concerning the foolish amours and trivial philosophizings of one Bernard. Margery Latimer, Evelyn Scott, H. D., Frances Gregg, Joseph Vogel, Nathan Asch, and others contribute various bits of undistinguished prose. There are two or three critical essays, not very astonishing. A particularly dull and mean novel is offered by one John Herrman: it is a combination of the worst of Gertrude Stein, Ruth Suckow, Ernest Hemingway and such folks. Waldo Frank contributes a play, and so on.

I used to be inclined to defend modern literature against the charge of "unhealthiness" brought by the conservatives, mainly because it seemed that, if a piece of writing were honest and artistic, the particular subject matter was unimportant. But a seduction on every page or so gets to be tiresome. The physical details of the love affairs of fools and wastrels soon cease to be attractive. The psychology of imminent motherhood, the insistent return at every opportunity to the sex motif, the maundering rambles into Kraft-Ebing—all this is a duller pattern of conventions than the Romanticists or the Victorians ever affected.

Furthermore, most of the contributors lack style, lack ideas, lack even common sense. And although the editors cheerfully declare that they are "as hospitable to the America of Poe as to the America of Whitman, to the America of Dickinson, Melville, or T. S. Eliot as to that of Sandburg, Dewey, and Sherwood Anderson," their declaration has little weight when put against the evidence they themselves present. Their collection is a "caravan" of cripples. Worse, to change the figure, it is a chamber of horrors, a faintly glowing waxworks representing the professional Greenwich Village type rather than America as a whole.

The editors further intimate that their purpose has some connection with the growth and "health" of our literature. The whole subject, after going through this volume, becomes distasteful. If American literature is to be saved by any such means, honest literary critics are wasting their time. They had better hire out to Henry Ford, who at least can give a man clean work. There could not be a worse indictment made against the good sense and good taste of the editors—Kreymborg, Mumford, Rosenfeld—than the collection of material they have deliberately chosen to represent the supposed "growth" of American literature.

The sole exception that I can make is in favor of the poets. John Gould Fletcher, Robert Frost, and Mr. Kreymborg himself seem in their offerings to be apart from the general trend of the book. And two young Southern contributors, Robert Penn Warren of Kentucky and Saville Clark of Mississippi, though somewhat touched by the general fever of despair, present bold and original poetry.

Book Clubs*

Critic's Almanac
November 18, 1928

The Book-of-the-Month Club and the Literary Guild
have got their start as book-selling schemes and are waxing
apace. Now comes a third organization which is of a more
persuasive and perhaps a more sensible character than either
of its predecessors. The Book League of America, whose
general offices are at 80 Fifth Avenue, New York, an-
nounces the poet Edwin Arlington Robinson as the head
of its editorial board, with Van Wyck Brooks, Hamilton
Holt, Gamaliel Bradford, and Edwin E. Slosson as col-
leagues, Frank L. Polk as advisory editor and Isaac Don
Levine as managing editor. The plan of the Book League
is to offer, for a subscription price of $18 a year, twelve
new books, chosen by its editors from current publication,
and twelve old books, chosen from the general ranks of
the classics and of late successes. The twelve new books
will be published, one complete book per month, in the
Book League Monthly, which has the form of a magazine
and has the further attraction of containing, first, an intro-
ductory discussion of the book published, written by a
competent authority; second, literary articles and essays,
reviews of current books, news and comment; third, a
"review of reviews" consisting of quotations from critics'
remarks in other periodicals; fourth, a readers' own department. The other twelve books, the standard ones, will be
published in a good library edition and will be selected by
the subscriber from a list tendered him.

* In a letter to Tate, February 23, 1927, Davidson said, "I wish you'd
tell me HOW the Nation's prize poem is chosen. Also what's behind
this Literary Guild, presided over by that sweet-toothed Carl V. D.? As
a Southerner, egad, and a gentleman (I hope) of independent mind, I
hate these cliques and Star Chambers. So far as my critical word goes
. . . I propose to fight 'em like hell."

BOOK CLUB SUBSCRIBER

"How would you like to read a book personally selected for you by Ruddy Valee or Cara Bow?" reads the circular; and Mrs. Dribble thinks that would be just fine. she is filling in the coupon. "Every fortnight a committee of eminent judges select for you the most noteworthy current volume." it is just like having a group of celebrities such as Tom Mix, Bruce Barton, Will Rogers, Rudy Vallee, Al Capone, etc., guide you as to reading matter. "Of course," the appeal later explains, "these people do not actually select your book for you, but the book you will receive is precisely the one they would select for you if they did select your book." The volume the happy subscribers will receive upon mailing the coupon is the biography of a quaint old human derelict, a trader in rat skins, whom Mrs. Mathilda Looney discovered upon her back porch casting an appraising eye at her pet Mexican chihuahua. Mrs. Dribble is all a-thrill.—G. W.

These drawings are from a series contributed to the book page during 1930 by Carlos Bissell (Gaston Werm), a member of the *Tennessean* staff.

A GOOD VICTORIAN.

Mrs. Nastanice is a relic of the Victorian Era camping out in the Twentieth Century. So ardent is her love for decent literature that she must needs read all the indecent books that come her way, the better to compare them and condemn with righteous indignation. Mrs. Nastanice is the mother of a slightly mannish daughter who clutters up the house with literary blasphemies of Gertrude Stein, James Joyce, Schopenhauer, Nietzche, Anatole France, and James Branch Cabell. At present Mrs. Nastanice is perusing France's "The Red Lily," in which the almost naive disregard of the seventh commandment boils her blood. She worries considerably about the world going to the dogs—which, of course, is more than likely to happen.— G. W.

Certain merits of the scheme are at once obvious. First of all, to the average citizen, is the money-saving feature. Twenty-four books a year for $18!—it is a wonder Haldeman-Julius overlooked this sort of bargain appeal. Then one not only gets his twenty-four books; one "keeps up" with the literary procession by conning the *Book League Monthly's* own reviews, and one has his critical appreciation of a particular month's masterpiece done for him by an expert, thus avoiding needless agitations and perplexities of mind. In truth, it is the last word in the diffusion of culture, American style. Furthermore, the editorial board are engaging gentlemen. We observe with satisfaction that they have little or no connection with the literary cliques that we suspicious outlanders sniff on every New York wind. They are a wholesome lot, a judiciously mixed representation of poetry, criticism, journalism, biography, science, and politics, so far as their accomplishments go. There is no reason why they shouldn't be sensible. And the first issue of the *Book League Monthly* is well printed and well planned; it quite reconciles one to the idea of having the "book-of-the-month" in a paper binding. Finally, the first book selection (which, however, was made prior to the organization of the editorial board), stirs the cerebral centers immensely; it is Matthew Josephson's powerful study *Zola and His Time*, which seems, as far as I have gone in it, to be a biography of unusual merit.

So much in behalf of, now what against the Book League scheme? The old proud urge of individualism refuses, after all, to surrender utterly to these seductive arguments and these reputable persons. Grant that, as the *Book League Monthly* declares, American criticism is practically bankrupt in leadership and offers no practical guidance to a public wandering bewilderedly among thousands of books, book blurbs, and book reviews. Still I do not believe that any of the book-a-month schemes, including this latest, affords the right remedy. Their virtue is that they substitute a fairly well guaranteed satisfaction for a problematical adventure in book buying, and, from a purely commercial point of view, they thus offer great advantages. And I do not particularly blame a hundred thousand harassed readers (say there is such a subscription list) for wanting to turn their book buying over to a set of supposedly authenticated agents, if they feel that way about the matter. But Gentle Reader, have a care. If you join any of these schemes, you are substituting the judgment of a small group of minds for your own judgment, for the general judgment of the literary world, for the principle of freedom of taste; and you are submitting to their judgment not once, or now and then, but twelve times a year for as many years as you subscribe.

Furthermore, the power that these organizations wield, beneficent as it may be in some respects, may easily be dangerous in its influence on authors and publishers. An organization that can buy and sell a hundred thousand copies of a book, safely guaranteed in advance, has no small favors to dispense. It can make Mr. X, the author, prosperous and famous, and tell Mr. Y, who may be equally deserving, to go hang himself in the garret. It can receive to its bosom the firm of A. & B., who publish nice books, and relegate to outer darkness and to the risky competitions of free trade the equally nice books of Messrs. C. & D. In short, these schemes, beautiful as they seem, are the final and characteristically American step in the commercialization of art. If they continue to wax and multiply, they mean also the extinction of the critic as an artistic force and the conversion of him into a combination of schoolmaster and buying agent. That, indeed, is just what some of the prominent critics have already become. Yet maybe, for all I know, it is a good thing. Some good people have always wondered what a critic is for, anyway. And the American

public, in its commercial-mindedness, might well have leave
to marvel that we should have critics of literature, of drama,
of music, of painting, who write solemn, high-minded reviews thereon, when articles of commerce, like soup, furniture, automobiles, patent medicine, and toothpaste have to
depend, for the dissemination of their virtues, on the mere
power of advertising.

Notes: Reviewing, Thornton Wilder, Elinor Wylie

Critic's Almanac
January 13, 1929

In a recent issue of "The Atlantic Bookshelf," Harry
Hansen defends the journalistic review. Newspaper reviewing, he points out, cannot be just like reviewing by the
academicians of scholarly circles or of the high-minded
New Republic group. It has to meet certain everyday and
fairly commonplace needs.

> There are many times [he says] when it is much more important
> for me to announce a new book, and tell the reader just what he
> is like to find in it, than it is to turn the book over to an authority
> in etymology, Freudism, the mating habits of the Cro-Magnons, or
> marine life six fathoms down in the Caribbean.

Very true, Mr. Hansen. But in considering books as news,
after the delightful principle of Mr. Canby in the *Saturday
Review* and Mr. Hansen in *The World*, literary editors
encounter a greater danger than the expert dullness of the
academicians. It is the danger of not being selective. It is
the danger of pleasantly inclining to every wind that blows,
and thus of aiding and abetting the mass movements of
popular favor, which centers on this or that book, very

often without any reason at all other than the fact that the book is being talked about.

I am surprised to find that Mr. Hansen immediately contradicts the point of view I have outlined above by saying:

But I believe America is unique in having an audience which still allows itself to be imposed on in the matter of literary sophistication. For instance, one meets again and again readers who are struggling with a book, which has attained distinction and become a best seller, and yet completely baffles them. This is true no less of *The Bridge of San Luis Rey* than it was of *Main Street*. Why do these readers read books for which they have no appetite? Because they are trained to the American practice of regarding quantity as more important than quality, and doing what the greatest number of people do. If fifty thousand people have read Wilder, they must follow suit and read Wilder, when they ought to be reading J. S. Fletcher.

But it was not the academicians, certainly, and I doubt whether it was the *New Republic* group, that made Wilder popular. It was Mr. Hansen and the newspaper critics. It was the publication of "best-seller" lists.* It was high-power advertising, both of obvious and of subtle sorts. It was the abasement of most of the literary editors in the country before the person of Mr. Wilder, as the newest literary god of all the literary gods due special worship.

The Bridge of San Luis Rey is not an undeserving book. But I can hardly believe, as William Lyon Phelps recently quoted Barrie as saying, that the popularity of the book is a tribute to the intelligence of the American public. It deserved the same sort of audience, say, that such special sorts of books as *Jennifer Lorn, Jurgen, Lady into Fox, The Closed Garden* deserved and got—but it must have been a considerable, though a pleasant and puzzling, surprise to Mr. Wilder to have his book sell by the hundreds of thousands. I wonder how many of the great number of

---

* Davidson never published a best-seller list and often decried the practice.

readers of *The Bridge* were actually entertained by the dull and complicated episode of the supposedly witty, letter-writing lady who had a daughter in Spain? And how many, if they comprehend the philosophy of the book, enjoy the impression it gives of the cold futility of life and of the difficulty of striking a balance between good and evil?

The mention of *Jennifer Lorn* recalls to my mind the unfortunate death recently of Elinor Wylie. Here again is a case where popularity far outran genuine appreciation. As the *Saturday Review* very fittingly notes, Elinor Wylie was among the first poets of this generation to rebel against the rebellion of the Imagists and Vers Librists. Her poetry is of a most careful and deliberate sort, superconscious in the niceties of art, yet withal rather severe and often difficult. The forms she chose to use were traditional, but she turned them to new effects, using a rich and fastidious vocabulary and making the utmost use of specific images and metaphors, as well as unusual rhyme and sound features. The general result is of a cold delicacy, a restrained hard passionateness, a rather tense and intellectualized beauty. The tone of her verse is skeptical and tragical. It is never of the sort that one would put into schoolbooks for children to read. It is always a poetry for very mature people a bit sated with whatever is simple and easy and grand.

In her prose she seemed to write with less restraint. But *Jennifer Lorn, The Orphan Angel,* and *The Venetian Glass Nephew* again are for fastidious and perhaps for overrefined tempers. It is hard to see how they can ever delight a great number of people, although the bright play of fantasy in them and the continual flash of her beautiful prose secure their place as literature of a peculiar kind, belonging to no age, climate, race, or nation. Indeed they are as non-human as music, and make just about the same sort of appeal to readers as Debussy's sweet complications of harmony and melody or his pretentious simplicities make to hearers.

The Amateur Spirit in Music

Critic's Almanac
January 27, 1929

Mr. Daniel Gregory Mason's book of essays grouped under the title *The Dilemma of American Music* contains much that is of interest to musicians primarily. The several studies of Beethoven, Vincent d'Indy and Stravinsky, the decidedly technical essays on rhythm, "The Tyranny of the Bar-Line" and the like are of this sort, although they are far from being out of the range of the cultivated person who takes a general interest in the fine arts. But the five or six leading essays of the book are addressed quite deliberately "to that large body of intelligent listeners— neither 'high-brows' nor 'low-brows,' but plain men and women—who must contribute their active cooperation to our American musical art if it is really to live." To these people Mr. Mason has something very important to say, and, for my part, I think that the most devoted musicians, professional or amateur, will not do well to ignore his remarks.

In the title essay of the book Mr. Mason observes with some discontent and fear that we have no single musical tradition in America, rather a mixture of several traditions, beginning with German romanticism, and varied by involved strains coming successively from France, Russia, Spain, Scandinavia, England, and so on down to the wildest modernists of all countries. The effect upon American music in a creative sense has been bewildering. We have swallowed without digesting; American music from 1914 to 1928, in fact, is a "Music of Indigestion," and we have become "polyglot parrots." So the question is, whither are we heading? Are we going to be altogether cosmopolitan, or are we to develop some kind of particularized national music, after the assimilative process has at last been agonizingly completed? To such questions Mr. Mason makes perhaps a too-easy answer. He proposes an equivocal sort of "elastic eclecticism" in an apparently vague hope that we shall arrive somewhere even though we do not know our destination. This, he thinks, is the only proper guard against a nationalism that would limit American composers to exploitation of native themes—such as the Amerindian, the Negro, the old heritage of transported British folk melody—all in his opinion too narrow a scope for broad and diverse America.

It is hard to take much comfort from such an outlook. But this half-doubting hope is more than balanced by points that Mr. Mason makes in the essays following, notably in "Music and the Plain Man," "Our Orchestras and Our Money's Worth," "The Depreciation of Music," and "Stravinsky as a Symptom." In brief, his contentions are that we are becoming enormous consumers of music or "appreciators" of it, but we are less than ever actual participators in music; that we are hiring our music to be done for us, on the typical American principle that "culture" can be bought and so, by relying passively on musical experts, we have quite lost the good "amateur spirit," without which music cannot truly flourish.

Furthermore, even our vast endowments of orchestras and our princely fees to noted artists simply result in befoolment and cheating. The expensive imported conductors, as an analysis of their programs shows, give us the same fodder year in and year out, filling their repertoires with "stand-bys" and "war horses" for the sake of sure-fire effects and box-office receipts, and we make no broad acquaintance with the diverse field of musical composition. American composers, too, are treated with utter contempt and are allowed no fair chance on the programs. Yet surely we are as much entitled to hear them as to hear European mediocrities. And how shall American music begin to grow unless it gets a public hearing? Finally, Mr. Mason denounces modern music generally as a symptom of boredom and a reversion to primitive sloth, recalling De Reszke's remark, "Debussy is all right for bored people, but I am not bored." Stravinsky is but a sophisticated elaboration of jazz; his melodies are "just the jazz tunes over again more strangely and handsomely dressed." Jazz is pure sensationalism, "the doggerel of music . . . the sing-song the school boy repeats mechanically before he becomes sensitive to refined cadence."

What explosion of pros and cons Mr. Mason's remarks may excite in the musical world I do not know. Speaking as a layman, and addressing a public that has suffered under the conditions that Mr. Mason outlines—though with a silent and timid suffering, fearful to express its unauthoritarian disgust and boredom in the face of the solemn pronouncements of the Moguls of Music—speaking thus, I should venture the firm opinion that Mr. Mason is most terrifically right. No matter how much we spend on music, no matter how many concerts we take in, no matter how sweetly we dote on musical education, we are still a nation of musical dubs if we allow the amateur spirit to languish. The lack of the amateur spirit in music is, I take it, the most essential point in Mr. Mason's criticisms. The amateur spirit is, indeed, the most important thing in music.

But what heresy am I speaking? We have all been taught and have dutifully believed that the *summum bonum* of achievement in musical art and appreciation is a well-gloved and stiff-shirted audience sitting in beautiful passivity while a master performer spins out a Bach fugue with absolute precision, or while a master orchestra plays Beethoven's Fifth Symphony. To listen to Kreisler's "tone" and speak glibly of it; to mob the door when Paderewski is announced at the local auditorium; to promote a Grand Opera season

—all that, we have been told, is musical culture and indicates a laudable advance from some previous condition of barbarism. Is a young lady musically gifted and ambitious? Then she must study laboriously for dozens of years under "masters," paying unbelievable fees for the privilege, and at last, perhaps—very much perhaps—she, too, may emerge before just such a passive and proper audience as I have indicated. Is it discovered that a young man has a good tenor or bass voice? Why, then, nothing will do but that he must go to the Metropolitan, where he will encounter an audience even more impeccably gloved and shirt-fronted and still more beautifully passive than anywhere else. That is our ideal, it seems. But I say that this ideal, so far as it is prevalent as the major ideal in music is nothing more than nonsense, a sin and a shame.

We have put all the emphasis on performance. We have missed and are still missing the sweet and saving joy of participation. The ideal of expert performance—of perfect artistry in technical execution—is, in so far as it is our main preoccupation, a curse and a hindrance in the development of a true musical culture in America. It is all right, it is good, to be a good listener. It is still better to be a participator, even though an imperfect, nay, a stumbling performer. To be musical does not mean to listen well, or is not merely that. To be musical in the most enjoyable and the finest sense means to play or sing music. Through this route and this only can we achieve the most desirable kind of musical "culture" in America. Not to train a few lonely individual performers of inapproachable expertness, but to develop large numbers of decent, intelligent participators in music ought to be the norm of musical education, public and individual.

How absurd the present ideal is will be seen when we compare musical education with every other sort of education. Suppose courses in English literature were devised with the major end of developing great poets or essayists or novelists, or phenomenal declaimers of poetry, or actors of drama!

Even if my frown mattered at all (which it doesn't), I should not of course mean to frown on any of the musical promotion schemes that so much redound to our credit. They are good, but they are not good enough. I simply think we have carried to a criminal length our adoration of the individual performing genius and the expert performing organization—to say nothing at all of our quite undiscriminating mania for machine-music, whether in player-pianos, victrolas, radios or what-you-will. Music, as an experience, if it is worth while at all, demands that the experience be direct and to some extent creative and active; the experience by proxy is fine, but it is a lesser experience. What we need is not bigger and better concerts, by famouser and famouser artists, but a wider distribution of musical art in action. I mean, specifically, that for Daughter to play a Chopin Etude in the home, and for many Daughters in many homes to do so, is a healthier, fairer musical condition than for the same Daughter, totally ignorant of playing for herself, to "thrill" blindly and idly over Paderewski's performance of that Etude. I mean that congregational singing is essentially more musical—certainly more religious—than listening supinely to the all-too-ordinary and treacly solo by the paid star in the expensive choir. I mean to applaud and stand up for the group around the piano after supper; the informal orchestra assembled to "try out" some string quartettes; the college boys singing on the doorstep of the fraternity house (even jazz has this to its credit, that through its means men have taken up musical instruments); mountaineers with their ballads and guitars, Negroes singing at work, old-time fiddlers scraping in the backwoods; above all, too, children singing and playing, as a part of life's better pleasures, natural and accessible. By these participators of all sorts, in all extensions of skill and appreciation, let our progress in musical culture be measured.

Prose Style, *Blues* Magazine
Critic's Almanac
March 3, 1929

Good prose is being written in America, but it is not common. The main body of our prose has its tone and language from the magazines and newspapers. That is to say, it is journalistic prose, even when it is used by novelists like Sinclair Lewis and Theodore Dreiser. The eighteenth century would give enough examples to show that a journalistic prose does not need to be a bad prose. But in our day, journalistic prose has been damaged by two adverse influences, neither of which is bad in itself, but harmful in application. Science has filled the language with colorless terms that lose all the virtue of exactness as they pass into the general vocabulary of editors, preachers, novelists, biographers and other exhorters. I refer to words like "factor," "conscious," "complex," "element," "fundamental," "self-expression," "standardization," and all their tribe. The effect of such a vocabulary on all our most solemn and purposeful journalistic prose is to give it a pale veneer of Latinity and make it dull.

The contrary manner, which is of course rebellious and mocking, is best shown forth in Mr. Mencken's writings. He is a master of a style that is both explosive and vulgar; nor do I mean these terms as marks of blame. Mr. Mencken has given new life to the neglected Anglo-Saxon branch of the American language, bringing back into common use

the curt and husky vocabulary that pretentious journalism
steers politely clear of. The way he mixes in his Latinisms
is equally deft, for he makes them sound like parodies on
the grand style and smacks his lips gustatorily over "aber-
rant youth" and "salient anarchists" while he flings in hearty
vulgarisms to flavor the mass, inventing at the same time
his own pseudoscientific terms to give his sayings an air of
doctrine.

> Since the dawn of time, [Mr. Mencken says of the philosophers]
> they have been trying to get order and method into the thinking
> of "Homo sapiens"—and "Homo sapiens," when he thinks at all,
> is still a brother to the lowly ass (Equus africanus), even to the
> ears and the bray.

But Mr. Mencken stands quite alone in his field. Not to
say that he has not been imitated far and wide! But all the
imitations, all the near-Menckenese effusions written by the
poor fellows whose souls have been scarred by barbarous
America—these are for the most part sorry, cheap and vile
things, which borrow his tone but are without his force.
They are popguns to his cannon. One cannot believe that
Mr. Mencken has changed journalistic prose for the better.

Our literary prose is stiff and uneven, hardly ever sure of
itself. The elaborate prose of Elinor Wylie looks like fair
and shining stuff, but one sees quickly that it came from the
antique shop, where it underwent much patching and
polishing and brocading. Cabell comes nearer to writing an
easy prose, artistic without being obviously artful; yet he
can perform only by hypnotizing himself into a kind of
medieval twilight, whence the idiom of his prose flows
languidly forth. He, too, is an antique. Willa Cather's prose
is effortless and without affectation, as is Elizabeth
Roberts's, and it also has the virtue of striking a contemporary idiom. All of the writers of the Left Wing are
without exception musclebound. With great skill they copy
all the worst mannerisms of James Joyce. They are duller

and more dreadful than the Latinistical journalists who are eaten up by science, and they constitute, by and large, a graceless rabble. Mr. Ernest Hemingway, a little rebellious, gets out a prose that is all bones and guts.

My natural patriotism should make me hesitate to say this. Indeed I hate to admit that Americans are inferior. The bitter truth is, however, that I know of few Americans who could turn out such an effortless and altogether pleasing prose as Siegfried Sassoon does in his *Memoirs of a Fox-Hunting Man*. Lo and behold, too, it is Sassoon's first novel; and such a good writer as Louis Bromfield has not even in his fifth novel attained a prose as good as Sassoon's.

The state of Mississippi can now claim, or disclaim, a modern magazine. The first issue of *Blues, A Magazine of New Rhythms* has just come to me from Columbus, Miss., where it is edited by Charles Henri Ford and offered to the public at $3 a year. Its appearance in Mississippi is to me mysterious and odd. Of the eleven contributors, seven are recorded as living in New York City. One lives in New Hampshire, another in Arizona. Of the remaining two, one hails from New Orleans and the other, though born in New York City, has no residence recorded.

The contents of *Blues* remind one of the dullest and tritest parts of that sepulcher of modernisms, *The American Caravan*. The contributors to *Blues* repeat the vices and have none of the virtues of the forward and experimentalist cults that wax and sicken on the banks of the Seine or the Hudson. For example, the opening story, by Jacques Le Clercq, is imitation-Hemingway, touching wastrels, idiots, prostitutes, and cadavers. The poets glibly mention the unmentionable in imitation–*Dial–New Masses–Transition* verse. Their diction reeks pleasantly of underwear, nudes, blood, complexes, and E. E. Cummings's acrobatic punctuation. Joseph Vogel contributes a few vulgar Joycean interiors.

Vaguely but boldly, an editorial proclamation sets forth the magazine as the organ of certain persons "disgusted with literature as it is at present perpetrated in the United States." The plan of the editors is to "revitalize and introduce new rhythms in creative writing." They announce themselves as opposed with equal determination to the "sentimental" and the "forced, the far-fetched."

Being without information other than the magazine contains, I hesitate to offer an opinion as to whether *Blues* is a student prank; or the project of some exile from Greenwich Village, come down to winter in the South and to subject the Mississippians to his civilizing influence; or the effort of some native brother who has returned from a season among the enlightened spirits of the North and is now consenting to act as a sort of local Messiah of literature. It is too bad that the magazine itself betrays no evidence that anything very original is on foot. I have an unhappy feeling that neither Mississippi nor American literature can be saved from disaster by the publication of *Blues*. A quick and easy passing, with the least possible pain and inconvenience to the editors, is the best I could wish for the magazine.

Book-of-the-Month Club
Critic's Almanac
April 28, 1929

The Book-of-the-Month Club is being assaulted from various quarters. Mr. John Macrae, president of E. P. Dutton Company, quarreled vehemently with the club, the immediate occasion being the selection of *The Cradle of the Deep* rather than Henry Williamson's *The Pathway*, which was sponsored by Mr. Macrae's firm. But his attack went beyond the immediate occasion and delivered itself on general principles. Hardly was it well under way when some rude sailors piped up with the observation that Miss Joan Lowell's nautical terms, in *The Cradle of the Deep*, were landlubberish and wrong. Other old salts rushed to the rescue. But more serious was the charge that Joan Lowell fictionized her "autobiography" to the broad extent of wrecking the *Minnie A. Caine* and swimming to the beach, three miles distant, with kittens clinging to her bare skin—which things could not have occurred, as the *Minnie A. Caine*, far from being sunk, is now in a western harbor. And Joan has been forced to confess she was on it, not sixteen years but a year and a half.

In the meanwhile, Mr. Canby has been patiently explaining that this book club does not mean to pick out "the best" book of the month, but only "a best." In the latest *Saturday Review* an editorial discusses the need of recommending "best" and "good" books; and, perhaps as a concession to the hue-and-cry, the *Review* adds a new feature: a list of "recommended" books.

One hardly knows what to make of this furore. It is hard, however, not to take some pleasure in seeing the book clubs hounded a little. If they are really so altruistic as they claim to be, they ought to be able to stand some biting and chewing; if they are not—well!

Nobody ever charged, I suppose, that the book club did not offer "good" books. What one objected to was the swanky and authoritative air of their advertising and the siren persuasions by which thousands of American readers were lured into putting their book-buying power into the hands of a remote critical junto. It simply couldn't be called free trade.

There are other things that make one uneasy. The

suspicion of political jockeying will not down. Everybody who believes that all of the selecting committee of the Book-of-the-Month read fifty or sixty books a month, please (as we used to say in the country) give me a quarter. Think of lazy Kit Morley doing such day-labor for a book club; think of temperamental Heywood Broun doing it; think of busy William Allen White forsaking the *Emporia Gazette* to gallop through a half-hundred possible master-pieces, twelve times a year.

The 70 percent discount is a staggering revelation. It means that a publisher can sell a $2.50 book for 75 cents to the Book-of-the-Month Club and still make money. If that is possible, what a pyramiding of profits the regular retail price must mean! An ordinary book buyer and book reader stands aghast at such proceedings. But I suppose it all comes down to this: the Book-of-the-Month Club and its rivals are commercial, not artistic, organizations. If we can think of them as Big Business and take all their gorgeous palaver about culture as no more than the thrilling verbosity of a toothpaste advertisement, we shall have them down right.

Antiques, Handcraft
Critic's Almanac
May 18, 1930

Some people may think that the collecting of antiques is just another crazy American fad, sure to pass when buyers have had their fling. This is probably a shallow judgment that does little justice to the state of our society. The desire to collect antiques may proceed, and I suppose often does, from an honest dislike for factory-made articles and a preference for earlier pieces, the products of handcraft, as simply better in quality. Or it may take a speculative turn, and originate in a wish to make a "good investment." Or it may be merely fashionable. More likely, it represents a healthy nostalgia, a wish to connect oneself with a past more admirable than the standardized and blatant present, and as such it seems to be leading us to a sincere rediscovery and revival of the domestic arts, extending to other things than furniture.

The appearance of Henry Hammond Taylor's book, *Knowing, Collecting and Restoring Early American Furniture*, is a mark of the trend. This is no mere buyer's guide, but a series of explanations, made in the most winning manner, as to how the amateur, if sufficiently reverent and skillful, may "restore" his antiques, as well as, incidentally, know and collect them. It does not appeal to the power of money, but to the craft of hands. I know that no publisher would sponsor such a book if he were not convinced that it has an audience waiting. Its appearance signifies to me that there must be more people than we think in these United States who wish to work lovingly with old furniture and are not content merely with the collector's zeal.

To such people Mr. Taylor's book will be a Godsend. He proceeds on the assumption that many collectors want actually to live with and use their pieces. In that case, they are sure to find that their collections often need repairs— or rather "restorations"—and they may want to do the work themselves rather than resort to professionals. Mr. Taylor tells just how the job may be done; and, since he is himself a good amateur collector and restorationist and has dissected and put together again many an old piece, his advice comes with authority.

The "dissecting" is in itself of importance, he insists. It gives a firsthand knowledge of construction for which there is no substitute, and, furthermore, is a guide to genuine antiquity. And his philosophy of restoration is to save the smaller evidences of age and long usage—the old hand-wrought nails . . . burns, the marks of three-legged pots, old saw marks, crisscross knife marks, carved initials, and various and curious stains. All these things are history.

He is altogether against planing and scraping, which produce "skinned furniture"—a frightful tragedy. He insists, in his chapter on refinishing, that the outer surface of the wood must be saved. He tells what woods and what brass appurtenances will fittingly supply missing parts, and explains carefully what tools should be used, what methods of cabinet work, what materials in refinishing—all in the most explicit way. He concludes with a chapter on "Evidences of Age," which will be full of interest to all collectors, whether they "restore" their own furniture or not. The only possible reservation that might be made to his discussions is that he apparently is acquainted with New England antiques alone, for he does not once mention Southern pieces. The book is illustrated with photographs which exemplify his directions to great advantage.

As one inexpert in such matters—being a lover of old furniture but not a "collector" of it in any thoroughgoing sense—I am hardly fitted to discuss technical details. But the larger social meaning of books like this attract me very much—and they do have "larger social meanings" in a far more real sense than that of some pretenders to the phrase I could name.

We talk so much about "culture," as if it were altogether a matter of books and profound artistic tastes to be acquired by purchase or industrious application. But culture, as I think of it, affects our entire way of life in every detail and is not a robe we put on for special occasions. It can be and ought to be, a matter of pots and pans, of tables, chairs, and quilts, of cooking and sewing and carpentering, and numerous other things which our mechancial age tends to despise and cheapen for the promise of some "higher life" not yet visible on the horizon.

Before the industrial revolution set us all to spinning in our multitudinous narrow fields of specialty, the lives of Western nations had, comparatively speaking, a harmony of culture that extended from the lowest—if you will, the most vulgar—occupations to the highest. A patchwork quilt, a chair, a ballad, a sermon, a poem, an oration, a house, a portrait of one's grandfather—all partook of qualities closely akin. Art was not separated from life in the sense that it is today.

Then factory production, finally mass production in American style, intervened. And where is art today? It is in the art museum; it is not in the home. Where is the public taste? It is in the public purse.

Let us consult the oracle for further signs and omens. Wise and stupendous Henry Ford, God's gift to us Americans, what has he done in this emergency? It is a remarkable and pitiful thing to see. Henry Ford, who has pushed hard the processes of industrialization and standardization, has been seized with a fit of nostalgia. Frenzied with zeal for handcrafts, he collects old furniture, restores old inns, stands up for old-time fiddlers. Henry Ford does not know and never will know exactly what has happened to him. His rebellion is against himself. It is a rebellion going on, in one way or another, in many hearts. Let us be glad that Henry Ford is in this matter simple-minded and romantic. Perhaps his example will lead to something.

The market could certainly absorb, in my humble opinion, more books like Mr. Taylor's, for we are turning in his direction, pronouncedly if not yet *en masse*. There are other such books, for that matter—notably such a work as Ruth Finley's *Old Patchwork Quilts and the Women Who Made Them*, published last year, to say nothing of numerous books on antiques. Let them keep coming.

The Book Business

Critic's Almanac
August 3, 1930

One hardly expects to find the missionary complex in works of fact, but it is an indulgence that the most earnest researchers nowadays nearly always allow themselves. In *Books: Their Place in a Democracy*, Mr. R. L. Duffus sets out, originally under the auspices of the Carnegie Corporation, to study quite objectively the conditions of book reading, book selling, book publishing in the United States. He has accumulated and arranged—as clearly as the complicated subject would allow—a valuable and impressive mass of information. But he also has apparently worked under the pleasant illusion that, if Americans curiously refrain from buying and reading many books, many good books, and especially many new books, their condition is highly objectionable, and ought to be and can be remedied, by some kind of organized effort.

> I believe [he writes] that the failure of the democratic majority to accept intellectual and aesthetic ideals is due rather to a lack of will to do so rather than to a lack of ability. And I believe that the lack of will is due to false and imperfect systems of education and to other conditions in the environment which may be altered.

This is simply the common progressive notion of our day. We are to achieve civilization—a book-reading civilization—by determining to do so and heartily working according to a program. And always these advocates put the educational prescription at the top of the program. What ardent missionary souls they are! Little do they remember how missionaries of Christ, in the South Sea Islands, introduced measles and tuberculosis along with redemption, and often exterminated the natives they came to save.

It is a dubious thing to begin a study of the book situation in the States with high ideas about civilizing and saving.

184

It subtracts from the value of an otherwise sensible and good book, for again and again it is evident that Mr. Duffus will not be satisfied with our country until libraries and bookstores are as fully jammed as movie palaces.

Mr. Duffus, however, is quite another man when he once gets into facts and explanations and lays aside his complex. The tale he tells of course is of more interest to those engaged in the book trade, to authors, and possibly to educators, than to the public at large. But it has much general interest, too. The infinitely complicated factors that govern the system of publishing and distributing books; the use and function of libraries, as related to the book business; the part of book clubs—which Mr. Duffus rightly estimates as rather parasitical and unworthy; the hard condition of the bookseller; the "geography of reading"—these and allied topics are discussed in all their ramifications. This is all to the good.

Some of the information Mr. Duffus assembles may be a little surprising to the uninformed. For instance:

If an author works a year on a book and it sells 1,500 copies, his royalties will be about $325. If it sells 3,000, about $725; if 15,000 about $5,100. And out of thousands of titles published each year, not more than 175 on the average will sell 15,000 copies. In other words, an author may work a solid year and get no more than one of Ford's employees will earn in two months. The only profitable writing is magazine or textbook writing; in other fields, the author's rewards are decidedly insecure.

The publisher's margin of profit on a $2.50 book, with items of cost except general overhead deducted, can be figured at about 17 to 28½ cents and from this must still be deducted the book's share of general overhead and possible losses on other books.

The South, the Southwest, and large areas of the Middle West constitute the bad book market, comparatively speaking, and the East, with the Pacific Coast, the good market.

With the exception of the cultural island of the Pacific Coast, [says Mr. Duffus] the book market has lain to all intents and purposes within a territory bounded by a line drawn around Chicago, Cleveland, Washington, D. C., New York, Boston and Detroit. Though books have been distributed in fairly large numbers outside this enclosure, it was here that their fate has been determined and the fortunes of authors or publishers made or lost. Are these limitations inevitable?

(Mr. Duffus gives no figures on per capita consumption, or on the kinds of books bought.)

And then Mr. Duffus answers his own question by saying:

I cannot help thinking that the book trade has been suffering from a grave lack of imagination. If automobiles, collars, breakfast foods, toasted or untoasted brands of cigarettes, women's dresses, and a hundred other articles manufactured in a few important centers can be distributed throughout the country, so also can books.

With this view I heartily disagree, in the first place because it would be calamitous, if not insulting to the cause of literature in general, to have it "put over" by forced feeding and vulgar ballyhoo. It would tend to destroy whatever shreds of integrity literature still possesses. And in the second place, Mr. Duffus, who opines so glibly that mass education is the solution, along with mass propagandizing, overlooks completely the character of the social organization we have let ourselves in for. The reading of books (except as mere entertainment) demands a leisured tempo, a life economically secure and well integrated, if it is going to mean anything at all to serious individuals. We do not possess such a life, and the whole tendency of our time is against its cultivation.

The industrial regime demands specialists; and specialists must follow their specialty. They have no time and little inclination for the general interests represented in the more or less regular reading of good books—especially new books. Your doctor, your lawyer, your insurance solicitor, your luncheon club leader, your preacher, your representative in Congress and even the college professor—all must give feverish attention to the particular grind they are engaged in. They have to keep up with trade journals or scientific organs, and to follow a numerous round of engagements with people to whom the age of speed and mobility has made them agonizingly accessible.

They are always jostled, and their interests are continually being narrowed. If they wish to turn from their feverish business to seek relaxation, they do so without escaping from the fever, and they furiously launch into golf, bridge, wild parties, movies, motoring. They keep up with the times, a little feebly and nervously, by picking up a magazine or by reading a daily newspaper—and here, too, they are jostled, bumped, bewildered out of all possibilities of contemplation. They can be bookish people only by severe effort of the will—and who in these great days of modernity can enjoy the luxury of exercising much will power? Women, it is true, believe in culture almost as if it were a religion. They form, I should guess, the bulk of American readers. Certainly there seem to be two or three times as many women customers as men in bookstores that I know.

Only by a considerable reformation of our life, from the economic base up, can we begin to approach any of the ends that Mr. Duffus thinks are so desirable. But even the matter of what is desirable is a matter for discussion. I am not at all sure that we should be better off if ten million people should read Thornton Wilder where one million read him before. Nor do I see that anything is gained by urging people, in tones of concern, as if wheedling them into a duty they regard with suspicion, that they owe it to civilization to read more books, better books—especially new books. This may seem, in the editor of a book page, like rank heresy. But in an age of ballyhoo, I, for one, would prefer to see books exempt from noisy advocacy. And it might be better anyway, even in the sheer interest of widening the book market, to preach somewhat after this contrary fashion:

"My good friend, I should advise you, as a free American citizen, to have as little to do with books as the laws of compulsory education will allow. For books are dangerous. They will probably do you no good. They will disturb you and put ideas in your head, and they may corrupt your morals if you have any left to corrupt. Books are for idlers, and you are a busy man. Books are for poor people, who don't have the money to intoxicate themselves with bootleg liquor and must get drunk on words. Books are for the intellectually chosen—a class which you, as a democrat, despise. Let them alone."

Sassoon's War[*]

Critic's Almanac
October 12, 1930

Last week I wrote of Mr. Fredenburgh's *Soldiers March*, indicating in terms that I trust may be considered favorable, that I thought it an honest war book, observant and firm, not very "literary," and yet gaining, in comparison with many American books of the sort, in being quite without pose. We who read books like this as soon as they appear are always under some embarrassment. We read a book,

[*] This is one of many reviews of World War I books. Davidson read all of them and reviewed most of them himself, checking them carefully against his own experiences in France as a First Lieutenant, 324th Infantry, 81st Division.

and commend it. If the next week another book appears, on more or less the same subject, and is a better book than the first, we are commendatory again, but begin to wonder whether the public will get suspicious of our opinions if we say too much. That is my condition now. For here is Siegfried Sassoon's *Memoirs of an Infantry Officer*, as fine a war book as I have read; and having said so much already on the subject of war books, I ask myself whether I have anything left to say that will not be repetition. Well, it would be an injustice not to make a powerful effort.

But first, a little moralizing about war books! When war books give an honest and well-balanced report of the war, they are only too likely to be awkward in execution. Conversely, when they have a nice artistic finish they are often very far from being honest. For example, Mr. Fredenburgh's novel sees the war as a rough-and-tumble affair, a sort of school of hard knocks that matured young men much too rapidly for their own good but did not make whining, ungallant weaklings out of them, after all. This is an honest report on the war; but nobody can proclaim the novel a literary masterpiece. *All Quiet on the Western Front*, which is written with great skill, is to my mind a really dishonest report on the war. I offer this quite unpopular notion realizing that people will not believe me, for have they not seen *All Quiet* in the pictures? And how fetching, to see Frenchmen mowed down point-blank by machine gun fire, and to hear American youth dressed up in German helmets chattering noble sentiments. But *All Quiet* has always seemed to me a rather cloying piece of Teutonic sentimentality, turned a little upside down—I don't dislike it because it is German, either. Its beery blubbering simply puts my teeth on edge.

Mr. Sassoon does not blubber, and he does not have any special theory about the badness or goodness of war, though I daresay he has parted with more illusions and seen more dead men than Herr Erich Maria Remarque. Furthermore, he is an exceptionally fine writer. His style, thank heaven, does not get in the way of his honesty and his capacity for seeing and remembering all that we need to know about the war. People will think me an idiot, I suppose, for preferring Sassoon's *Memoirs of an Infantry Officer* to Herr Remarque's woeful story; but I do prefer it. And I also prefer it to Aldington's *Death of a Hero* or Hemingway's *A Farewell to Arms*, or even Robert Graves's *Goodbye to All That*, with which, for special reasons, it invites comparison, and almost any other war book you might mention with the possible exception of *The Case of Sergeant Grischa*.

These new *Memoirs* of course are really a continuation of Sassoon's previous book, *Memoirs of a Fox-Hunting Man*, which I trust all of us remember as one of the finest books of the past two years. Both Aldington and Graves used the first part of a single volume to give a prewar background to war experiences. Sassoon devoted the larger part of his *Memoirs of a Fox-Hunting Man* to the same purpose, and the idyllic mood of his fox-hunting days carried over into the war experience, which in the first book had no terribly repugnant features.

But the second group of *Memoirs* is all war. The idyllic mood is gone completely. Sassoon hardly ever thinks of fox-hunting days except as something incredibly far-off; and when he goes back to England at intervals, on leave or after being wounded, he has the experience of so many soldiers in finding the back-home atmosphere almost worse than the war itself.

At the outset of the book, he is attending an army school, somewhat in holiday spirit.

> I was like a boy going to early school, except that no bell was ringing and instead of Thucydides or Vergil, I carried a gun.

Amusingly, he records the "homicidal eloquence" of the

bayonet instructor, a Major who represented that man "had been created to jab the life out of Germans." But this is soon over. He returns to the front and is back among his old companions. From this time on, it is one engagement after another, for the Battle of the Somme is soon under way.

Sassoon's experiences were no different in fact from the usual run of trench duty, raid, attacks, and marches that fell to the lot of every infantryman. What distinguishes his account of all these things—which in so many British books are so dully related that one war book is just like another—is the exceptional clarity with which he sees everything and the perspective he gives it. And there is no querulousness. Although he finally rebelled against the war, as a war, or was persuaded to do so, Sassoon is never interested—as Graves nearly always is—in finding out and exposing the rotten side of war.

At one point he compares his own attitude toward the war (at the time) with Graves's attitude, for the two met on various occasions and swapped views. In Graves's book, the author speaks a little patronizingly of Sassoon's tendency, at this stage, to write somewhat heroical verses about the war. Sassoon now gives us his view of Graves, whom he calls David Cromlech:

> My attitude, (which had not always been easy to sustain) was that I wanted to have fine feelings about it (the war). I wanted the War to be an impressive experience—terrible, but not horrible enough to interfere with my heroic emotions. David, on the other hand, distrusted sublimation and seemed to want the War to be even uglier than it really was. His mind loathed and yet attached itself to rank smells and squalid details. Like his face (which had a twist to it, as though seen in a slightly distorting mirror) his mental war-pictures were a little uncouth and out of focus.

The difference is one of temperament, and Sassoon's superior balance—though he could be impulsive enough in action—keeps him from getting his own pictures "out of focus." I feel when I read Sassoon that I can trust him absolutely to set everything in a proper light, even his own personal feelings. His account of his own exploits, which he represents as originating partly in ignorant rashness, partly in blundering, and partly in just going ahead, may be taken as a typical piece of British modesty; but I think it is hardly mere modesty, though the modesty is there.

Sassoon accomplishes a really remarkable feat of objectivity. He examines himself as coolly and humorously as he examines his companions. When he rescues a wounded corporal, after an abortive trench raid, it is anxiety and solicitude that make him do it—a humane impulse, rather than bravado; but he tells the truth about the Military Cross that he got for his exploit. Frankly, he was not unhappy to get it—all the more because it helped him out of a tight place later on. Also, when he captures a section of trench single-handed and then sits down on the firestep, not knowing what to do next, or when, in the engagement near the Hindenburg tunnel, he rushes wildly about with his bombers and talks hysterically to everybody within reach after he is wounded, we can be sure that we are getting a true and honest account of the psychology of battle. This is the real thing—no eyewash, no pathos, no misplaced cynicism either.

Perhaps the most interesting part of the book, however, is his account of how, under the influence of the editor of the *Unconservative Weekly* and of Bertrand Russell (thinly camouflaged as Thornton Tyrrell), he decided to quit the war by openly publishing a written repudiation of it. I wish I could go into this episode fully. For those who can read between the lines, it is very instructive indeed. Without in any way impugning Russell's sincerity, Sassoon makes him appear a rather futile person who was able, a little too easily, to overawe and persuade an innocent officer of the line into a piece of useless heroics. It was Graves in the end—not Russell—who properly understood what was going on in Sassoon's mind, and Graves saved him, as we know, from a court-martial by deceiving officials into thinking that Sassoon was a little "touched" by war's terrors. It was a decent solution; and I urge all who think war is an evil, which must be met by pacifistic measures, to read carefully the closing parts of Sassoon's book—and, for comparison, Graves's as well.

It was a bad war, of course; but what made it extremely bad was the totally asinine way in which it was managed by most of the higher-ups concerned, on both sides. (See, in this connection, also Mr. William Seaver Woods's *Colossal Blunders of the World War*.) The soldiers of the line were splendid, always; it is their extraordinary fortitude and splendor of character that make the record of a book like Sassoon's something really glorious, if at the same time tragic. But the generalship was ineffably stupid; how can we ever explain such holocausts as the battle of the Somme or the German attack on Verdun, except as originating in the brains of military dotards. And here there is subject for a further discourse, which I must postpone until another day. The World War was the first war in history to be thoroughly mechanized, on a fully modern, presumably "efficient" basis. It was also the first war in all history to produce no great generals, no great leaders, and perhaps not a single piece of first-class strategy. In other words, the triumph of the machine!

Backgrounds of Agrarianism

Frank Lawrence Owsley

Extra Review
December 20, 1925

Like every other Southerner, I was brought up to believe in the gallantry and invincibility of the Confederate armies during the Civil War. The defeat of the Southern armies was to be attributed to the obscure manipulations of incomprehensible fate, or, at most, to pressure of numbers and resources. There was furthermore a picture in the mind of admirable and desperate loyalties; all the men and all the women of the South were beyond measure devoted to the Cause, and in the great drama of the Civil War the only villains were the Yankees.

After reading *State Rights in the Confederacy*, by Mr. Frank Owsley of Vanderbilt University, I still believe, just as much as ever, in the gallantry of the Southern armies and the greatness of military leaders like Lee, Jackson, and Forrest, but I am forced to revise considerably my notion of the elements which brought the Southern cause to defeat.

Mr. Owsley's thesis is that the Confederacy, which was founded on the principle of states' rights, died not only in behalf of, but because of, that principle, which in its particular application worked out most disastrously. In spite of all other circumstances, Mr. Owsley declares:

... if the political system of the South had not broken down under the weight of an impracticable doctrine put into practice in the midst of a revolution, the South might have established its independence. The Stephenses, Toombses, Browns and Vances could not wait till after the war to try out their theories and air their differences. Insisting upon the theoretical rights of their states, they sowed dissension among the people and destroyed all spirit of cooperation, finally, between the states and the Confederate government, and, at times, arrayed local against central government as if each had been an unfriendly foreign power.

197

Inexorably, methodically, and unemotionally, Mr. Owsley demonstrates this thesis. He writes as the calm historian who has examined all the evidence, and who seeks to reveal only the honest truth. He backs his assertions with a mass of data, letters, messages, state records of unquestionable authority. It is a brilliant study which to me (who do not claim to be an historical authority) is in the main quite convincing. And the story he tells, sad and sordid as it may be, must be accepted as a new contribution to the history of the Civil War. His claims may be too sweeping, and his emphasis may seem unfair to those who are accustomed to think of the Civil War as a record only of glory. But however much it may shock our sensibilities, surely we can afford to face historical truth.

How did the doctrine of states' rights work out within the Confederacy itself? Why, just as the principle of self-determination has worked since the World War! Flaunting the creed of states' rights in the very face of Jefferson Davis, the governors of various Southern states withheld arms, troops, supplies, ships, from the Confederate government. Instead of "pooling" their resources, the states, through their governors and legislatures of the states not only often refused to cooperate with the central government, but often actually worked at counterpurposes. They kept rifles for their own bodies of state troops instead of turning them into the Confederate arsenals. They enlisted great numbers of men in these state troops and kept them for supposed local defense against hypothetical invasions and thus rendered these bodies impotent for larger strategic purposes. They insisted on clumsy methods of supplying their own men that might be enlisted in the Confederate armies, and allowed the Confederate quartermaster service to remain impoverished.

They competed with the central government in blockade runners to carry much-needed supplies, and, through pressure in Congress, hampered and defeated the attempts of Davis and his cabinet to secure vessels for carrying goods. They resisted conscription in all sorts of ways, and devised means for getting around it. They hindered the application of martial law in war-threatened districts, fought the suspension of the writ of habeas corpus, and protected their own malingerers and deserters.

Governor Brown of Georgia was particularly notorious in using the cloak of states' rights to cover the most amazing anti-Confederate activities. The picture of him which comes out in Mr. Owsley's calm record is of a bigoted politician. Yapping "state rights" like an excitable fox terrier, he joyed in hindering Confederate operations at critical moments. For example, he sent Georgia troops home on a thirty-day furlough during one of the crucial periods of the fighting around Atlanta.

The Governor [writes Mr. Owsley] was taking care to mend his political fences even while Atlanta was falling into the hands of the enemy.

Governor Vance of North Carolina was another offender. While the Confederate armies in Virginia were ragged and ill-kempt, he was piling up stores for his "state troops."

At the time of the surrender, [writes the historian] Vance had, according to his own count, 92,000 uniforms, great stores of leather blankets, while Lee's troops were ragged and without blankets.

Other Confederate leaders suffer in like manner under Mr. Owsley's investigation. The political idols fall under his blades like weeds under the scythe, and like weeds fade and sicken. I have cited only one or two of the particular instances; in Mr. Owsley's book are literally hundreds, annotated, indexed and cross-referenced with the cold, clear logic of the scientific historian.

Of course the book is a study in shadows, not in brave colors. Like the physician, Mr. Owsley is concerned as to the causes of the death of the patient, and therefore gives his attention to dissection of bones and sinews, not to examining the character and virtues of the deceased. Therefore, the book is, from one point of view, depressing. But from another point of view, it is exhilarating. We need to be knocked flat on our faces, occasionally. I yield to nobody in my love of the South, and my loyalty to its best traditions. My blood-kin fought at Shiloh and Murfreesboro, and I claim a personal affinity with the soil of Middle Tennessee. But I believe I am aware that it is not well to keep on hugging a departed glory to your bosom and at the same time to overlook the frequently inglorious truth. Mr. Owsley has not discussed the valor of the Confederate armies, nor the loyalty of the thousands of Southerners who did devote soul and body to the cause. Neither has he impugned that valor and loyalty. He has shown us, rather, a fundamental consequence of a political theory which has figured importantly in the history of our country. And, more immediately, has shown us what a devilish handicap peanut politicians can be—peanut politicians such as exist in large numbers now, if I am not mistaken, within the bounds of every state in this buoyant new South. Let us hope the peanut politicians will not betray us again.

Stonewall Jackson's Way

Critic's Almanac
April 29, 1928

Turn your eyes into the immoderate past,
Find there the inscrutable infantry rising,
The demons out of the earth—they will not last.
Stonewall, Stonewall, and the sunken fields of hemp,
Shiloh, Antietam, Malvern Hill, Bull Run . . .

Thus wrote Allen Tate in a poem full of strange desperate questions, his "Ode to the Confederate Dead." I remembered those lines when I came to read his sturdy, biographical narrative, *Stonewall Jackson: The Good Soldier*, which is prose in form but really poetic in implication. I remembered, too, an admonition he once gave me. "Our past," he said, "is all but irrecoverable." But in *Stonewall Jackson* he has happily contradicted himself. This book is not troubled with desperate questions. It is a triumphant, unperplexed recapture of the heroic past as represented in a great, almost legendary figure.

But how is this? There is a certain surprise in this book. Nobody would have dreamed that Allen Tate's first volume would be a narrative about Stonewall Jackson. He was one of the leading spirits of the Fugitive group of Nashville poets, who at first could not be easily related to the older Southern tradition. In his own poetry he followed a difficult modern path. Later he went to New York and made his mark as one of the most brilliant critics there; in thoroughness and disinterestedness, in fact, he stands practically alone. One would think him more concerned about the French Symbolists, say, than the battle of Chancellorsville. Is he, then, playing a trick on us?

Not so! Somewhere he has found that the past is not only possible of recovery. It must be recovered, else we are lost

201

in a wilderness of a million barren novelties, the shouting, staring wilderness of bizarre frenzies and outlandish jollities, left without trace of footsteps backward or forward. The genius of place and the quiet guiding daemon of the artist will not be denied. With their help the past will be recovered. Look and see; it is recovered. Not whim, but inner necessity and conviction brought Allen Tate to Stonewall Jackson. The troubled modern turns with relief to a figure that wears no uncertainty of the heroic, and finds a cause to cleave to as well as true stuff for art. In this good sense Mr. Tate's *Stonewall Jackson* comes to us as a genuine book and is not, after all, so surprising. And we of the South all have Mr. Tate's problem: we must recover the past, or at least in some way realize it, in order that we may bring the most genuine and essential parts of our own tradition forward in contact with the inevitable new tradition now in process of formation. Only thus can we achieve vital continuity in the national life.

For this special reason, if for no other, Allen Tate's *Stonewall Jackson*, despite certain limitations, has more meaning and importance than most of the casual mass of biographies, now before the public, of Turk and Chinee, funman and president, wanton woman and evangelist. Many of these, like books of travel, are only mental ticklers and achieve no integration, are without social experience. But Mr. Tate aims at and, I believe, in large part accomplishes that integration.

He makes historical and biographical research serve this larger end, which of course is essentially artistic. He has grubbed through the documents and visited the battlefields, not with the purpose of turning up new facts but with the all-absorbing desire to throw the amazing story of Stonewall Jackson and his deeds compellingly forward into the clear strong light of narrative. In this respect he follows to some extent the method so highly developed by Maurois and others, but it should be remarked that he resists the temptation, much too common nowadays, to be ironically condescending, to chart complexes, to rattle skeletons in the closet; he does not even bother to dwell on old Jack's "obscure stomach complaint." The narrative is sharp, clean-cut, economical; at times, with its short, spare sentences, trimmed down to the very bone of simplicity, it has the brusqueness of the general himself. But it also has its moods of gentleness. Despite the terseness, almost saga-like in its omission of circumstantial details, the air of romance and heroic days filters in, a definite presence pervading the whole rather than any particular part. The lack of overtones is undoubtedly a defect. The background of the times might advantageously have been filled in more completely. But perhaps Mr. Tate wanted to let Stonewall do his own talking and did not care to be ingratiating. At least his method, though sometimes uncompromising and stiff, is preferable to the hints of jocosity in Gerald Johnson's recent book on Andrew Jackson.

Mr. Tate sets forth, but does not set out to "explain," the genius of Stonewall Jackson. Despite the psychologist, the secret of genius remains indecipherable. We can only examine the man with reference to particular events, such as wars and political movements, and let the personality remain, in its infinite values, mysterious; it is better so. Stonewall Jackson, as seen through Allen Tate's book, sprang from the semi-pioneer society of the Virginia Valley, where the Jacksons had been great people. The intense wish for distinction which marked his actions up to a certain point may have come partly from

the discrepancy between his inherited family pride and the poverty that had humbled his branch of the Jackson family. . . . Thomas Jackson's illusion made it out that his whole family had gone into a decline; it thus became his self-imposed duty to restore it.

But this was not egotism, any more than Jackson's religion

was, as some biographers have made it out, a sort of fanaticism. As a boy, Jackson had read both Parson Weems's *Life of Francis Marion* and the Bible. He had been eccentric in holding rigidly to a personal code of honor. "He did everything hard." He naturally wanted to live up to the Southern code of values, too, whereby a man's property, and not, as in New England, his "inner life," constituted character: since he had no property, he had to get education as a substitute, and thus was led to West Point eventually, and to the army. And thus in Mexico his only fear was "that I might not meet enough danger to make my conduct conspicuous."

But there were other peculiarities about Jackson besides the habit of intense concentration he had cultivated and the firm religious feeling which was a definite part of his nature.

It is the paradox of the great that the most ambitious are the most disinterested [writes Mr. Tate]. The exercise of character for its own sake becomes the unconscious aim of such men.

So with Stonewall. In politics as in religion he held good Virginia views; he believed in freeing the slaves, eventually; but he also believed in Virginia, and when the moment of conflict came, his genius, being in Mr. Tate's phrase "disinterested" and therefore undistracted by such petty ends as bothered Jefferson Davis and even J. E. Johnson, bent itself with burning, almost terrible intensity upon great ultimate ends. Nothing is more striking than the way in which Mr. Tate develops this point; at every crisis, in the tightest places, in what were apparently high moments of victory, even while lying wounded in the cannonswept thickets at Chancellorsville, Jackson kept his mind firmly on the larger ends. No wonder he seemed mysterious, even to his own troops. Men do not understand what vision means. But in the fierce satisfactions of conflict, Jackson's earlier wish for distinction had disappeared. Now he gave the credit to God. All that mattered was to defeat the enemy to the utmost.

I shall not attempt to summarize Mr. Tate's handling of the campaigns of Jackson. He is at his best, I think, in his narrative of First Bull Run and especially of Chancellorsville. His account of the valley campaigns seems oversimple; it does not satisfy me; but then it is difficult for a layman to visualize those very complicated movements, which require close map-work for understanding, and I have not found even the voluminous Col. Henderson fully satisfying. But in general Mr. Tate's account is shrewdly done; he is comprehensive, and he has a way of making scenes stand out in your mind's eye: the railroad cut at Second Bull Run, the Dunkard Church at Sharpsburg, the troops on the Valley roads. I do not find his explanation of Jackson's conduct in the Seven Days' fighting satisfying; but then, nobody's is; General Maurice's excuse of "poor staff work" is passable, but Jackson's delays are still unexplainable. Fate or the Hand of God held Jackson back, let us say. Mr. Tate does not say so explicitly, but I gather from this general tone of his treatment, and from significant details here and there that he may believe what others in their hearts know well, that but for the death of Jackson, the whole tale of the war would have been different.

And now I come to the most unconventional part of Mr. Tate's book. It is judicial, somewhat restrained, not narrowly partisan, but, so far as it steps aside from straight narrative to develop a point of view, that point of view is positively Southern. Mr. Tate is hard on Jefferson Davis, as on Lincoln, McClellan, Burnside, Hooker, and John Brown, distributing praise and blame where they duly fall. But in his philosophy of the situation he is Southern, and that is most unusual in these times. The South, he says, had the historical sense: the North, which believed in abstract right and was much too "privy of God," had no historical sense and "was trying to destroy the social and political structure of the United States by force of arms." Not the Southerners, but the Northerners were the "rebels," and Mr. Tate writes now and then of the "Northern rebels."

This is most astonishing. This is most daring. This is also most praiseworthy. Nobody wishes to reawaken the old sectional bitterness. Nobody wants to disturb the Union. Nobody proposes to unseat the monuments to Federal troops or desecrate the national cemeteries. But if the South's cause really was just, it is not being sentimental to say so. It is merely substituting a grand and honorable myth for a contrary and unnatural one. We shall not fight the Civil War over again; but there is no reason to believe that the North with its notions of upsetting the Constitution, was divinely appointed to preserve the destinies of the United States and that the South was the wrongheaded and unruly member to be suppressed. There is no reason to think that Lincoln and his aides had all the patriotism, and that Lee and Jackson had none. Mr. Tate in effect proposes to substitute the legend of the South for the legend of the North, building his mythology as it should be built around a grand historical figure. And all things considered, I rather welcome the change. The one is just as American as the other, and I must confess it suits the fiber of my native being better than the cold, intellectual stuff you find in history books. Then let us salute Allen Tate, the first Southern biographer of the younger generation who has had the courage to worship an old hero and to remember his fathers.

The Spotlight on the South

Critic's Almanac

June 2, 1929

In the past few years a change full of meaning has come over the great national magazines, like *Harper's*, *Scribner's*, and the *Atlantic*. They have almost entirely lost their earlier character as media for art. The best poets and the best novelists (unless lured to the *Cosmopolitan* by Mr. Hearst's dollars) simply wait for book publication as the only means of reaching an audience; or, if they are lucky enough to break into the magic circle, the poets may find a way into a liberal weekly, like the *New Republic;* or, if they are more experimental, they may try the more chilly and charmed circle of the *Dial*, or one of the fly-by-night magazines that sporadically appear and vanish.

But the loss of distinguished creative art to the sober ministers of our culture is made up for in a new direction. These tremendous monthlies, with their hundreds of thousands of devoted readers—the cream of American civilization, we have no doubt—have made themselves over into organs of opinion and controversy. Here, and not as of old, in the newspapers, do the burning questions of the day get their frankest and most thorough discussion. The giants of politics, science, business history, and even that but lately hushed and obscure sister, philosophy, stalk forth in full armor into the public arena and let fly their weapons. One fine and ambitious magazine, *The Forum*, makes a specialty of mortal combats, its successive issues being mainly a series of bloody duels between notables on every imaginable problem, from the religion of Al Smith to the structure of the atom. The artists, too, are in these pages, but, except in rare instances which one suspects are a sop to tradition, not in the role of artists. They, too, are ready with argument

207

and explanation, having often as much to do with politics as with literature. They have gone from art to articles.

Take, as a particularly exciting instance, the still unsolved problem of the relation of the Southern states to the rest of the Union—a problem that keeps bobbing up defiantly and that still survives the decision of arms which, it was once thought, settled things eternally. In "The Southern Legend" in the May *Scribner's*, Mr. Howard Mumford Jones, of the University of North Carolina, deals briefly but pertinently with the matter of sectionalism. Southern sectionalism lasts quite obstinately—and not altogether harmfully—he points out, for the plain reason that Northerners enforce it on the South by their persistent ignorance and misunderstanding. With delightful irony he pictures the items of Northern ignorance. On the unfavorable side, to Northern eyes the South is a "kind of immensely extended and rural Chicago"; it is the land of lynchings, Ku Klux Klan, night rider, mountain feud, voodoo murder, and fundamentalism. And strangely mixed with this dark picture is the curious romantic one, quite complimentary but equally overdrawn of

a land that is always afternoon, [where] platoons of perpetually grinning darkies line up in the cotton fields, prepared to burst out with "Swing Low, Sweet Chariot" the moment a white man appears; [or where] the simple Southern highlanders converse in sentences impartially compounded of "hit," "you-uns," and "tote," feeding their babies on moonshine licker and shooting at everything in sight with a rifle that saw service at King's Mountain.

The real South, which is neither so bad nor so picturesque, is left out of the picture. "Nobody knows what is going on in the cultural life of the South today," and "the most remarkable development in contemporary American civilization—this renaissance of the South" is by and large ignored. Then "Southern sectionalism is about the only defense which the progressive can turn to."

Mr. John Crowe Ransom, of Vanderbilt University, tackles the matter from a different angle, and his essay and Mr. Jones's admirably supplement each other. In "The South Defends Its Heritage," in the June *Harper's*, he offers what might be called a philosophy of Southern life, dealing with the whole question thoroughly and emphatically, and speaking his heresies against blind progress with such persuasive sincerity that he might be given as the finest available example of the deliberate sectionalism that Mr. Jones notes as necessary.

The South differs from the rest of the country, Mr. Ransom says, in that it has developed and maintained over a very long period "a seasoned provincial life" of its own, whereas the rest of the country has succumbed very rapidly to the influences of "our urbanized, antiprovincial, progressive and mobile American life that is in a condition of external flux." This typical Southern life is, according to his view, European in its quality, since its main feature is stability:

There are a good many faults to be found with the old South, but hardly the fault of being intemperately addicted to work and gross material prosperity. The Southerner never conceded that the whole duty of man was to increase material production, or that the index to the degree of his culture was the volume of his material production. His business seemed to be rather to envelop both his work and his play with a leisure that permitted the activity of intelligence.

But after having formed its own way of life—a way which despite disasters and deficiencies, offers a fair and continuable tradition, with much promise in it still—the South finds itself facing a new hazard, which Mr. Ransom does not hesitate to define. It is industrialism, which in its eternal flux represents a principle not native to this section. Granting that industrialism is inevitable, the question is

whether the South will permit herself to be so industrialized as to lose entirely her historic identity; or will accept industrialism, but with a very bad grace, and will manage to maintain a good deal of her traditional philosophy.

Mr. Ransom unequivocally favors making a fight for the latter alternative. He proposes two definite means of action. One would be "to arouse the sectional feeling of the South to its highest pitch of excitement in defense of all the old ways that are threatened," and to represent industrialism as "a foreign invasion of Southern soil, which is capable of much more devastation than was wrought when Sherman marched to the sea." But such a course is "hardly handsome enough for the best Southerners. Its methods are too easily abused." The other course, then, is for "the South to re-enter the political field with a determination and an address quite beyond anything she has exhibited during her half-hearted national life of the last half a century." And her political program, in consonance with her traditional stability, would be agrarian, joining hands with the agrarian forces of the West, and perhaps even reviving the Democratic party.

All I can do (in lack of space for discussion) is to urge the readers of this page to study Mr. Jones's and Mr. Ransom's articles in their entirety—the one for the satisfaction it will give their often sorely wounded spirits; the other for its wise analysis of the fundamentals of Southern life and its bold challenge to all of us not merely to think about our Southern life and our native traditions, as Stark Young not long ago urged us to do, but to act.

It is hard, after being quickened in ardor by two such essays, to drop to the flat level of reproach. Yet I cannot but reflect with some melancholy that there is no common medium of expression, reaching the general body of Southerners and drawing them together in the consideration of their peculiar sectional problems. Mr. Ransom and Mr. Jones had to go to New York to get their articles published, if they wished to reach any but a very small audience. And these same great magazines, which, correctly judging the national pulse to be throbbing at least momentarily with interest in things Southern, gave these two authors space, will on some tomorrow present, with admirable catholicity, the direct opposite of all that our two authors stand for. And the hundreds of thousands of readers, racing nervously from contemporary problem to contemporary problem—learning the mystery of glands, exploring the intricacies of Einstein, getting acquainted with Mussolini, delving into the sociology of crime, and occasionally slicing into a story by Hemingway or Callaghan as one tastes a pickle for its sour contrast—will simply continue to do that and nothing more. We thank our stars, of course, that the awe-inspiring monthlies are "public-minded," but we are scared to death of their terrific program of ideas, all the same. I wish profoundly (like a foolish sectional Southerner, devoted to the old home place) that there were something nearer home, if less efficient and famous—a general periodical with a definite policy, to give us some feeling of consistency and safety.*

* *The Southern Review*, edited by Charles W. Pipkin, Cleanth Brooks, and Robert Penn Warren, began publication in Baton Rouge in July 1935.

Phillips's *Life and Labor in the Old South*
Critic's Almanac
June 9, 1929

In the years from Appomattox to Al Smith the South has been visited with misfortunes that need no retelling here; and not the least of these, as John Crowe Ransom firmly points out in the current *Harper's,* has been the "toxic disturbance that attends industrial progress." Always the danger has been not only that the South should be exploited by unseemly hands, but that it should deny itself by losing its touch with the past.

Providence, cruel in some ways, has nevertheless allowed us the good fortune of having a record to appeal to. Often the appeal has been fumbling or shallow. It is one of the peculiar graces of the present that the appeal to the record has passed into the hands of a new generation of artists and historians against whom the old taunt of "Rebel" prejudice cannot be flung. Ulrich B. Phillips, a wise and skillful historian indeed, is of this new order. To the study of the record he brings a conscience that cannot be impugned, an even, gentle temper that makes his writing irresistible, and, with these, a historical technique of the first rank. His book, *Life and Labor in the Old South,* will at once take a high place among the important books of this generation that are giving the Southern tradition a contemporary meaning.

Speaking generally, I should say that *Life and Labor in the Old South* comes like a direct answer to a Southerner's prayer. Specifically, I might again refer to Mr. Stark Young's wish that the South should not take "boiler-plate thinking handed out all over the country" but "think on its own conception of what society is," and Mr. John Crowe Ransom's indication that the items of Southern tradition need to be studied in detail by historical and sociological experts. To the extreme partisan who may have overidealized Southern life, or to the jeering skeptic who argues—I have heard such—that the Old South was a mere pretense, Mr. Phillips's book offers the inescapable evidence of a record not colored toward either extreme. Naturally it is not a simple record.

Traditions are simple, conditions were complex, [he rightly says] and to get into the records is to get away from stereotypes.

The book deals not with wars and politics—the old pabulum of history. Its scope is geographical, economical, social. It is planned as the first volume of a group, the second of which "will trace the course of public policy to 1861." A third will consolidate social and political themes for the postwar period. In some chapters this book parallels Mr. Phillips's *American Negro Slavery*, published ten years ago, but, as he indicates, with new emphases and additions of material.

Mr. Phillips lays down no general thesis and comes to no sweeping conclusion. He seems to say, "Let whosoever will, declare the meaning; these are the facts." It is perhaps the defect of the book that few generalizations are attempted, but we are to suppose that this restraint comes not from timidity but from the modern historian's devotion to a scientific method, chary of speculations. Mr. Phillips's charming and never pedantic style does not wholly conceal the marks of that prosily efficient tool—the card index. His work, to describe it a little unjustly, is a casebook into which selected and typical items have been entered and arranged, under such headings as Climate, Soil, Staple Crops, Economic Origins and Growth, Conditions and Cost of Labor, Strains and Behavior of Population, and the like. Or, to use some of his own chapter titles: "The Land of Dixie" (with the emphasis on "Land"), "From the Backwoods to the Bluegrass," "Homesteads," "The Plain People," and "The Gentry."

As one not expert in history and economics, I may be considered rash to try to get a broad meaning from a miscellaneity of truths, where the reader is very often brightened by Mr. Phillips's conscientious zeal in noting the exceptional along with the regular. But if an historical work is to have any use beyond the "Believe It Or Not!" kind of excitement, somebody must generalize. For these precarious times, the meaning of Mr. Phillips's book seems to be as follows:

Ways of life in the Old South were no mere importations or engraftings. They grew naturally out of practice to meet local situations and were not devised according to some golden theory produced from a grand cabinet of philosophers. Let the emphasis be on growth, for the South took its time (in those days) about growing. Its peculiar institutions—among which was that especially peculiar institution, slavery—had their roots in economic necessity, some accident, and much plain sense. So far as the South was different from other parts of the country, it was different because it had to be.

The rest of the story is a lesson in the local differences that make a Southern tradition much more various than seventy-five years of history textbooks, produced mainly in non-Southern regions, have indicated. This sounds obvious, but it is the obvious that has most often been overlooked. For instance, the weather: Mr. Phillips's first sentence strikes me as very pertinent, with the temperature hovering around ninety degrees:

> Let us begin by discussing the weather, for that has been the chief agency in making the South distinctive. It fostered the cultivation of the staple crops, which promoted the plantation system, which brought the importation of negroes, which not only gave rise to chattel slavery but created a lasting race problem. These led to controversy and regional rivalry for power which produced apprehensive reactions and culminated in a stroke for independence. Thus we have the house that Jack built, otherwise known for some years as the Confederate States of America.

So Mr. Phillips considers the weather at length—and I could wish certain architectural theorists in our midst would do the same and would not put up buildings so uncomfortably out of harmony with this old Southern tradition. But I cannot begin to array the details with which our historian considers the weather, the soil, the crops, and everything else—the book is all detail anyway. Let me, rather, ask a few specimen questions and see how they would be answered from the evidence.

How are variations in the spread of the plantation system to be explained? Answer: by the crops, chiefly. Sugar cane could be grown profitably only on large plantations, because the manufacturing process was a part of production which the small farmer could not manage. Tobacco, on the other hand, required no machine process and could not be grown profitably in large quantities. A Virginian is quoted as saying: "A crop of tobacco that employs sixty hands always brings the farmer in debt." Wheat, which required less attention than any other of the staple crops, "promoted consolidation of units" in Virginia and North Carolina. Cotton "was adapted to cultivation on any scale great or small," so that "one-horse farmers and hundred-slave planters" competed on fairly even terms, acre for acre.

The result was that large plantations, with their accompaniment of economic problems, were the characteristic of what Hergesheimer calls the Deep South. Cotton was the most widely grown crop of all. And the farther north you went in the South, the smaller the plantations, which tended to become just farms.

Was life on the old plantation as gracious as it has been pictured? On the whole yes—especially for the Negroes. Though the plantation force was "a conscript army," the plantation was

also a homestead, isolated, permanent, and peopled by a social group with a common interest in achieving and maintaining social order.

It was a factory, a school, a parish, a pageant, a variety show, a matrimonial bureau, a nursery, a divorce court, a hierarchy—not without grievous episodes but surprisingly unsevere, as many travelers of a contrary bias were forced to admit.

The stringent laws governing slave life were by tacit consent not closely enforced: benignity was "somewhat a matter of course." As to what the masters did and how they managed their territories, Mr. Phillips has three excellent chapters on that subject, in which he lets the records do the talking—diaries, notes, letters, ledgers. Summing up, he says: "The slave regime was a curious blend of force and concession, of benevolence, of antipathy and affection." The overseers were another matter: "They were alike only in their weather-beaten complexions and their habituation to the control of negro slaves as a daily routine." James K. Polk, among others, did not find the management of his place, "Pleasant Grove," very satisfactory under the overseers system, and his series of difficulties is recorded as typical.

What about other strands of the population than the gentry and the slaves? Mr. Phillips estimates nearly six of the eight million whites as "out of proprietary touch with the four million slaves." His chapter on these "Plain People" is briefer than we should like, possibly because they did not, like the planters, leave good records. They are depicted mostly as strong substantial folks whether in the mountains or in the towns. I am especially grateful for Mr. Phillips's differentiation of the "po' white trash." He thinks that these

listless, uncouth, shambling refugees from the world of competition comprised only a small portion of the non-slaveholding population.

I should like to pass this sentiment along to Mr. Mencken, who imagines that the "poor whites" are today as numerous and powerful as Attila's hordes.

Question and answer might go in this fashion, with great satisfaction, except in certain matters. In this very distinguished book the only lack of proportion that I can find is that Mr. Phillips's conception of the Old South favors plantations and gentry too much and does not take into full enough consideration the strong Western character of the part of the South on our side of the Appalachians. Mr. Phillips passes by Kentucky, Mississippi and Tennessee rather lightly; he does not linger much in the regions we know best.

Bowers's *The Tragic Era*

Extra Review
September 15, 1929

In 1865 the South lost the war. During the next decade the South lost the peace. A third defeat endured longer. For sixty years and more, at the hands of New England historians, the South lost something imponderable and precious, whose absence from the minds of men made a nearly ineradicable gap between sections: the South suffered historical defeat. It saw monstrous legends persist, not to be refuted by Southern voices, for Southern voices were laughed down under the charge of sectionalism, sentimentalism, and the bloody shirt. It saw a powerful industrial civilization arise under the aegis of a political party whose principle was the dollar, and it knew that that civilization and that party were founded on the crime of Reconstruction. It saw the United States of America become the United States of the North and West, with the Solid South as a kind of embarrassing appendage to the "real" America, while children, even in many Southern schools, developed hazy notions that the center of gravity of American history, originally and mainly in New England, shifted a little west in 1865 and thenceforth reposed in the bosom of Lincoln.

One by one these defeats have been overbalanced by

victories. Even Appomattox has been resolved into something like a moral victory. The physical damage and some
of the political damage of the Reconstruction have been
repaired. Now the last defeat seems to have reached a turning point. The labor of Southern historians, which has had
more local and professional than general popular honor, is
reinforced by the work of historians, biographers and
journalists on whom the old suspicion of sectionalism cannot
be cast. Lloyd P. Stryker, a New Yorker, minced no words
in his vindication of Andrew Johnson, filling out his portrait
against a background of Reconstruction times as handily
as a Southerner could wish; and lo! his book was well
received. Now Claude Bowers, the distinguished editor of
the *New York World*, follows his studies of Jefferson and
Hamilton and of Jackson's political battles with a powerful
book that covers the same period as Stryker's and that
also expresses with relentless clarity and overwhelming
array of facts the malignancy of the crime committed
against the South and the nation in the years after 1865.

   Mr. Bowers's title, *The Tragic Era, the Revolution After
Lincoln*, gives in brief his intent. History books, especially
history textbooks, have given the vague impression that the
Reconstruction policy forced upon the South, against
Johnson's will and with Grant's full connivance, was unwise
and unfortunate, and there they leave the subject, with a
few mild deprecations, as something hardly worth discussion in later high-minded days. Mr. Bowers shows the
episode for what it was: a conspiracy of mad partisans
willing to go any length for power, a complete subversion
of American institutions, a crime to which the slightest
gilding of mistaken idealism cannot possibly be applied.
The action of the Radicals, under Thad Stevens and
Sumner, backed by Beast Butler, treacherous Stanton, dis-
reputable Ashley, grotesque Ben Wade, was revolution,
deliberately conceived.

Within eight hours of Lincoln's death a caucus of Radicals was framing plans "to rid the Government of the Lincoln influence," as too conciliatory toward the South. Their popular cry was "punishment for the rebels." Their program, which had secret ends, included measures partly idealistic in appearance, like Negro suffrage; others vengeful and stringent, like confiscation of Southern property, subjection of the states under military rule, which military rule in turn was naturally to be controlled by Radical party leaders. If Andrew Johnson got in the way, as he of course did, his head must fall under trumped-up articles of impeachment. If the Constitution hindered, it was "a league with death and a covenant with hell," and it would be abrogated, suspended, or—as a more technical and decent concession—amended. Even the Supreme Court was not to be inviolate, and the principle of preserving the Union, for which the war had presumably been fought, was to be contradicted and pitched overboard whenever the political game so required.

I shall not here recapitulate the steps by which Thad Stevens and his fellow-conspirators gained their ends, or draw the picture of the results that followed. Mr. Bowers gives these in great detail, stopping now and then to draw a portrait, either of a conspirator or of a courageous figure who fought back, or to paint the social background of Washington in Johnson's and Grant's administrations or to trace the turbulent and foul conditions under which the Reconstruction scheme operated in the Southern states, or the firm, skillful, and intrepid measures by which the carpetbaggers and scalawags were finally routed. Mr. Bowers's method is simply to weave together the numerous strands of fact, without heat and practically without comment. His book, indeed, is almost overloaded with facts, carefully pegged down and annotated. I, for one, should have liked more expansiveness, which would have made the work longer but would have allowed for the interpretative comment that I conceive it to be the function of the historian, as an expert in full possession of the facts, to give.* But I do not blame Mr. Bowers for being perfectly objective. The facts themselves are tragic and damnable enough in many a case—and in other cases, heroic. They are the safest instrument for presenting the unvarnished truth that, as the author says, "makes so many statues in public squares and parks seem a bit grotesque."

The distinction of Mr. Bowers's book, as I see it, is three-fold. First of all I put the firmness and courage with which he has assaulted the citadels of the smug and complacent and brought into the light a subject too often discreetly hushed up. Mr. Bowers puts that subject unequivocally before us, and makes it possible—yes, makes it of high public importance—to reconsider its painful and terrible incidents, as well as its strange underlying motives, in relation to issues now before us.

Second, the fullness and the concentrated vigor with which he presents men and motives, as well as accumulated incidents, bring this "tragic era" before us on a national scale and enable us to study Reconstruction in its bearing on the entire national life of the period. Such a brief study as Dr. Walter L. Fleming's *The Sequel of Appomattox*, published some years ago, leaves nothing to be desired so far as all the major facts are concerned. Mr. Bowers's study does not surpass Dr. Fleming's in historical quality or in penetration of the issues, but its array of facts is bulkier and its pictorial background more extensive. Mr. Bowers's thousands of ordered facts, gathered from unpublished

* Bowers explained his attitude as follows in a letter of September 15, 1929, to Davidson: "I note what you say about absence of editorializing. . . . Being well known as a Democrat I would be open to debate—on opinions. But by giving the story, raw and ugly, they must quarrel with the facts of the record and not with the opinions of a benighted Democrat."

sources such as the Julian diary as well as all the usual documentary sources, suggest the many thousands more from which he made selection. On page after page one feels the impact of the unsaid. He has furthermore emphasized the deeds of many men often neglected, Southern and Northern alike. The central figures do not have the stage to themselves.

Third—and here I return to the major theme—Mr. Bowers makes plain beyond question the meaning of the entire Radical scheme which eventuated in the attack on Andrew Johnson and the nearly successful destruction of Southern society.

How did the Radicals, under the malign leadership of Stevens, manage to get support in Congress for a program that was obviously unconstitutional and even more obviously evil and inhumane? How did they manage to deceive many good and otherwise decent-minded Northern citizens into giving aid and applause—the rather stuffy James Russell Lowell, for instance? The answer is easy, though it seems incredible.

These wolves in sheep's clothing were able, first of all, to capitalize the hysteria that followed the assassination of Lincoln, in whose death they actually rejoiced because it served their purpose. In this and in the so-called "outrage" that later occurred in the South when black soldiers and white police (as at Memphis) or black freedmen and white Klansmen (as nearly anywhere) clashed, or in all the induced or natural disorders that either existed or were fabricated for their ends, they found provender to feed the already inflamed imagination of the public. Their oppressive program was thus actually strengthened, for a long while, by its very oppressiveness, and we may contemplate the spectacle of an American people, in apparent possession of their senses, condoning and even applauding the subjection of eleven states, inhabited by their brother Americans, to the rule of their late slaves, egged on and instructed by venal white invaders who were often worse than the blacks themselves.

Thad Stevens and his crew had a stronger weapon still— the lure of power!

We may ask, did they actually believe in the principle of Negro suffrage for which they clamored? Possibly Stevens did, though I doubt it somewhat. Mr. Bowers claims Stevens was sincere, and though in general scoring him heavily, also touches him lightly, as he touches Sumner, with the whitewash brush. If Stevens was sincere, his sincerity was a monstrous thing that worked cunningly and brought profitable results. Negro suffrage and the slogan of black heels on white necks were the *sine qua non* of the Radical plan, because only through Negro suffrage and corresponding disenfranchisement of the Southern whites could the political security of the Radicals be established. Here is the clue, openly admitted by Thad Stevens himself. He wished to view the Southern states as "conquered provinces" (convenient trick!) and to institute Negro suffrage in order "to secure perpetual ascendancy to the party of the Union."

Here was the bait—the appeal to the loaves and fishes, the spoils counter, the job market. By this means were recalcitrant party men whipped into line, even for so miserable a device as the impeachment proceedings and the various force bills. The appeal to power, especially when it is camouflaged with a show of humanitarianism, is always attractive, and among politicians it always wins over principle. The profligacy of Grant's administration, the general mismanagement in the initiation of the Negro into his new rights, the depletion and the humiliation of the South under carpetbag governments backed by Federal bayonets, the virtual prostitution of Congress and its subsequent decay in statesmanship (even to this day), the increasing trend toward overcentralization of government, and social and political evils too many to enumerate—all may be traced, I feel after reading this book, in large degree to the vindictive ambition and evil genius of Thad Stevens and his gang. No American, I feel sure, whether of North or South, can read the record and think on its results without a deep sense of shame and revolt.

Nor can we, with Mr. Bowers's book in hand, regard our present enlightened stage of progress with much more comfort. The Reconstruction tragedy was ended by the determination of Southerners who by actual show of arms, backed at last by the awakened sympathy and disgust of more thinking Northerners, put the rascals out. Yet the results stayed on. Let me quote from Mr. Bowers:

> Power had passed, during the revolution, from the agriculturist to the industrialist and the financier, and these, more powerful than the politicians, had become the party's allies. A degree of centralization not dreamed of in other days had been realized. State rights were to be denounced for forty years as the equivalent of treason. A new order had been established, built upon the ruins of the old. The Jeffersonian Republic that came in with the revolution of 1800 gave way to the Hamiltonian Republic brought in by the counter-revolution of 1865-76. The tables had been turned. The age-old fight would continue, the spirits of Jefferson and Hamilton leading as before, but the advantage, under the new order, had passed to the latter.

So at last here we stand, with the shades of Jefferson and Hamilton beside us, the one surely thoughtful and melancholy, the other smiling a little too triumphantly. This able book, that brings the issues of the past so graphically before us, by strongest implication bids us to regard the issues of the present. Whither shall we turn now? And what will the future historian write of our choice in an era which likewise has its tragedies of greed and malignancy, its foul triumphs of expediency over principle, while the cloak of idealism, ornamented with misappropriated words like

"service," "prosperity," and "progress," often hides a low
purpose and a selfish creed?

The South, at least, in the day when history is doing
belated justice, might well revive, especially in its younger
generation, the historical consciousness that has always been
part of its peculiar genius. Thinking on its past, always
inevitably involved with its present, is the South not likely
to find, while it views its old foe of the North with friend-
ship and generosity, the Southern shade of Jefferson a more
comforting one for the future than the other shade which
with all its material grandeur is, as of yore, a little too much
kin to the powers of darkness?

What Does History Mean?

Critic's Almanac
October 20, 1929

Much has been said on this page recently about Southern
authors and Southern books. To impatient readers who
may want a discussion of such contemporary writers as
Ernest Hemingway and Al Smith, I can only say that the
end is not yet. Their time will come, but for the moment
Southern issues are red hot. Hard blows are being struck,
and it is no time for folding of the hands in pure aesthetic
contemplation. Passing over the obvious dominance of the
South in the field of the novel (see Stark Young, Ellen
Glasgow, and others), I call attention to the no less remarkable swing to the field of Southern history and social
problems.

Powerful books have tumbled upon us in rapid succession, from the hands of Winston, Stryker, Bowers and

others—and now again from Allen Tate, whose *Jefferson Davis* goes far beyond his *Stonewall Jackson* in penetration of historical issues and in force of presentation. The very favorable reception of these books throughout the country is in itself an exciting phenomenon. It means, one supposes, that they are being read by the thousands of copies and, one hopes, duly absorbed and understood.

But are they being understood? If the public read but as the reviewers read, something is being missed. The reviews of Mr. Bowers's *The Tragic Era*, for example, are almost unanimous in outspoken praise, but with equal unanimity they fail to comment on the contemporary meaning of his book. The Reconstruction is discussed like some remote horror in China, the "revolution after Lincoln," to these critics, concerns our present affairs as little as a revolution in the architecture of igloos.

This restraint has a diffidence in it with which I can sympathize. After all, the chorus of Northern praise represents a generous open-mindedness that Southerners should appreciate and often might emulate, and it is too much to ask, at the same time, for interpretations that might be locally embarrassing to the interpreters.

Nevertheless, if the works of Winston, Stryker, Bowers, Tate do not mean something in our society here and now, they have no meaning and are only so many adventure stories. If history so near to us as this, is dead history, then no history is alive, and we had as well depend altogether on the comic strips for our social philosophy. Maybe I have a wrong answer to propose to the question of meaning, but such as it is, it shall be rendered—first, in a roundabout way.

One authority, at least, has said in effect that Mr. Bowers's book has no present meaning whatever—that it is, in fact, totally irrelevant.

In the October tenth issue of the *New Republic*, Pro-

fessor Arthur M. Schlesinger * of Harvard offers a review
of *The Tragic Era* that is gently caustic and wholly unfavorable. He hands Mr. Bowers left-handed compliments.
Mr. Bowers is "the greatest living practitioner of personal
history," a genus which by direct inference is not to be
taken seriously. His conception of his task "clearly sets
him apart from the professional historian and clearly accounts for his wide public backing," (i.e., Mr. Bowers's sin
is being unprofessional and popular). Bowers's method is
all wrong, for

while it lends itself to vivid and dramatic recital . . . it becomes
almost necessarily episodic, the great impersonal tides in human
affairs are neglected, and the wholesome averages of life . . . receive
no attention.

Furthermore, Bowers says nothing new. Other historians
(presumably quite professional) have made known the
secret this good while.

And now comes an extraordinary passage. Professor
Schlesinger says:

The reader would never realize that the process of reconstruction
was, as a matter of fact, exceptionally mild as such things go in
history. The Radicals stopped short of the crowning blunders; they
confiscated practically no enemy land and put no one to death for
a political offense. Furthermore, as Allen Nevins pointed out . . .
the progress of the South did not halt, for "a great part of the
producing areas had been little affected." . . . Even the much
execrated black-and-tan state constitutions had the useful result
of requiring the establishment of public school systems in the
Southern states. When has the signal failure of so great a rebellion
been attended by such light penalties for the conquered? It was
the unexampled forbearance, indeed, which made possible the
spiritual reconciliation of South and North within the lifetime of
the generation which had waged the war—one of the miracles of
history.

Could any "amateur" historian, one asks, make worse
blunders than this eminent professional one? If Reconstruc-

* Arthur M. Schlesinger, Senior.

tion was mild, Nero was a Christian gentleman. In what previous civil war were the conquered parties placed under the rule of their own black slaves, newly freed? It is news indeed that progress did not halt. As for the carpetbag school systems, what nonsense! In his *Sequel of Appomattox*, Dr. Walter L. Fleming wrote:

> Free schools failed in reconstruction because of the dishonesty or incompetence of the authorities and because of the unsettled race question. It was not until the turn of the century that the white schools were again as good as they had been before 1861. After the reconstruction native whites as teachers of negro schools were impossible in most places. The hostile feelings of the whites resulted and still result in a limitation of negro schools.

And as to Professor Schlesinger's "miracle" of reconciliation, one awesomely wonders whether he, naively, as Mr. Mencken, attributes the Solid South to the influence of Fundamentalism!

These errors refute themselves by their own absurdity. But they are, I should like to point out, perfectly consistent with the theory of history that Professor Schlesinger holds in common with many progressive historians of the Beard school. In his own book, *New Viewpoints in American History*, he writes:

> The full force of these new energies (economic) was not immediately apparent because the attention of the public, after the emotional experience of the Civil War, was for the time being riveted upon certain perplexing questions. But with the truer perspective made possible by the passage of the years the historians are beginning to give less attention to Southern reconstruction and more to Northern reconstruction, since the financial and industrial reorganization of the North has proved to be of greater enduring importance.

This means that Professor Schlesinger's interests are economic and, in the curiously vague contemporary sense, social. For him the course of history is determined not by "personalities" and politics, leaders and battles, but by vast impersonal movements tagged with names that flavor of science, "forces," "energies" and the like. History becomes the bloodless study of population pressures, food surpluses and scarcities. Everything reduces finally to food, shelter, sex. Every great figure, every great invention, every theory of government arrives only as a kind of automatic product of overwhelming circumstance—almost like a chemical precipitate.

Obviously, such a historian, busy with drawing economic graphs, would shelve Mr. Bowers's book as irrelevant and would be irritated with it as totally ignoring the beauty of his own doctrine. He would disdain the irregularities of those who make concrete Man rather than abstract Cause their study. And like the medical experimenter who views with calm the unhappiness of an inoculated dog, he would look unmoved on war and civil oppression, saying, "Just what one would expect . . . really, not so bad, eh!"

Without denying the value of economic interpretations of history, I should humbly make the claim that Professor Schlesinger's methods reduce history to a thing of no practical importance. If there is no human control of society, if everything depends on vast economic forces that automatically and anonymously make everything happen, it is useless to go to history for lessons as to conduct. For the "forces" act, whether we will or no, and we had just as well save our strength and sit around and wait for the forces to do their stuff.

Significantly, Professor Schlesinger comes originally from the Middle West, which is unconscious of any historical past, and which, with the industrialized East, has committed America to the worship of certain abstractions: notably money and success.

Professor Schlesinger believes that these "personal" historical studies have no meaning. To me—and I believe to anyone brought up in the South—they are full of meaning for the specific thing that Professor Schlesinger so dislikes. They brush aside abstract forces, and center our attention on human beings of our own near past who, for good or ill, foolishly or wisely, took responsibility into their hands and by their personal, particular force determined the scheme under which we live today. And if they did thus, have we not an equal liberty of procedure which ought to be wiser by the benefit of their bad or good example? No one can read Mr. Tate's book or Mr. Bowers's without the profound conviction that history would have been otherwise if men had acted otherwise. These works surely restore to us the feeling of responsibility that science and historians of the scientific school seem to want to take away. We should be ashamed before God and man not to take such books to heart.

James Truslow Adams's *Our Business Civilization*
Ralph Borsodi's *This Ugly Civilization*
Critic's Almanac
December 1, 1929

Mr. H. L. Mencken's criticisms of American life have never lacked point. They have been always pungent, nearly always irritating, often amusing, sometimes nasty. Perhaps they have never been really effective, even when directed at obvious evils, because one was never sure of any grave central wisdom or genuine enthusiasm behind them. They have been criticisms of manners, verbal bombs hurled at particular objects of Mr. Mencken's aversions; they never have gotten down to fundamentals, and nobody has the slightest idea what kind of Utopia Mr. Mencken would build, if he could build one. Mr. James Truslow Adams and

Mr. Ralph Borsodi have, I daresay, fully as much wrath as
Mr. Mencken ever had. But their criticism of American life
is healthier than his, and in the long run is bound to be more
effective, because they do get down to fundamentals. Their
reasonableness, their wise analysis of conditions, their positive views put their volumes in the class of necessary books.
We should read them as Mr. Mencken recommended that
we read *The Tragic Era*—"on our knees."

Of the two, James Truslow Adams is likely to be the
more widely read, and he is far the better writer. He is also
less quixotic in his notions and less "Utopian"—if the charge
of Utopianism may be brought against Mr. Borsodi's rather
practical vision of things. Both of the writers have already
attracted great attention and aroused much controversy
through publication in magazines—Mr. Borsodi in the
New Republic, Mr. Adams in numerous places.

Our Business Civilization, though it contains essays on
divergent topics like "The Mucker Pose" and "Is America
Young?" is really an examination of class rule in America
and its social results. The ruling class is of course the businessmen; the social results, even to the most cheerful apostle
of service, must seem excruciating and messy.

Our civilization, says Mr. Adams, is remarkable for "its
extreme structural simplicity." It is governed for and by the
businessmen, and businessmen, by capturing the strong-
holds of social activity one after another—school, college,
church, professions like medicine and law—now set the tone
of our society from top to bottom. In this latter point we
differ from other modern industrial communities; in England, for example, the prestige of business is by no means
complete, and it does not dominate the tone of English
society. But with us, for the first time in history business
rules all with utter frankness and self-satisfaction.

Well, then why not—especially if business rules benevo-
lently? Doesn't it create wealth, dispense jobs, endow uni-

versities and hospitals, elect nice presidents like Mr. Hoover? Doesn't it shower us with service, prosperity, and progress, and make us all happy little robots?

Oh, yes, nobody can deny such obvious virtues, says Mr. Adams, and he makes no quarrel with pleasant by-products of business. The criticism is directed against the rulership of business, not against business in itself, as a "purveyor." For the rulership of business never can be an enlightened one, because business exists only by Profit. Whatever charities or high-minded promotions business may indulge in, its final concern must be with Profit. Therefore, its entire view of government, art, religion, education, whatever-you-please, is bound to be colored by a basically selfish philosophy.

What are some of the results? The leisure essential to a humane civilization is confused with idleness and is depreciated or filled with material things, the sale of which "helps business." The professions lose dignity and give up social responsibility for the ideal of wealth. The arts are commercialized or atrophied. The older generation, busy with money-getting, lets ethics dissolve and then tries to make a foot-free "younger generation" the scapegoat for its own sins. Education becomes a muddle of mob snobbery—

exactly the same mental attitude that makes the laboring class talk of "colored wash-ladies" and "garbage gentlemen," that makes them want to be dubbed Bachelors of Arts after studying business English and typewriting.

Politics lets go of all principle, becomes hypocritical, practices time-serving. Even prosperity itself is a doubtful gift, when it leaves an immense gulf between the Mellon family with its annual income of $300,000,000 and the family of the college professor with (possibly) a bare $3,000 and when that prosperity rests on the dubious basis of "making people want more, and work more, all the time."

Worse than all, perhaps, is the vulgarization of society represented in "The Mucker Pose"—which affects newspapers, manners, conversation, and nearly everything else mentionable.

Mr. Borsodi, I am sure, would agree with Mr. Adams in all essentials, but his line of attack is quite different. He is an economist and statistician. His carefully organized indictment of our "ugly civilization" is directed at the focal point of modern industrial society—the Factory, with its technique of mass production, piece work, sales stimulation. He is not against the machine, and he does not condemn business; rather he criticizes, in a lengthy series of analyses well bolstered by statistics and examples, our infatuated devotion to the factory as the mainspring of industrialism.

His discussion of the evils that come from overfactorization is not exactly new. Mr. Adams says much the same thing in this chapter on "The Cost of Prosperity"; Ruskin and Carlyle talked along the same line many years ago. But he is more specific in his charges, and his criticism is the more telling because he points out in great detail the monstrous difficulties which the factory system brings upon itself.

The logical end of the now popular doctrine of ever-increasing consumption is, he points out, eventually a one-day week, a regime under which a faithful citizen will work one day only and spend his other six days in a patriotic effort to consume (first buying, of course) the numerous products that simply must find a market.

But it is Mr. Borsodi's counterproposition that is most exciting. It just happened, he says, that in the nineteenth century man's great servant, the Machine, got turned into the Factory and was there pretty well confined, with the final result that the servant became master. No need for this to have happened, says Mr. Borsodi. Machines have always existed, but before the days of industrialism they were domesticated, like the spinning wheel, to home use, and they promoted and did not destroy the happiness and well-being of human society.

To regain our lost happiness we have only to begin ardently to domesticate the machine, which now can be more easily adapted to home use than ever before, and which is bound to be available in increasing efficiency and variety—washing machines and electric irons being only minor examples of an already apparent drift towards domestication. Mr. Borsodi proposes, therefore, to agitate for a consumer's revolt, a return to the home as the production unit of the major essentials of a decent living, and, based on this, a veritable Jeffersonian economy (in modern terms) which would finally eliminate all but the "essential" factories and free us from the tyranny of having always to buy—buy—buy, besides doing away with congested cities, stock market crises, wild sprees of inflation, and all such evils. And he shows just how you may carry out the experiment yourself, and backs his discussion with a philosophical plea for a "quality-minded" instead of a "quantity-minded" civilization.

There is little doubt that each of these books has flaws in its argument. The Defenders of the Faith will be quick enough to point them out, for the Defenders of the Faith can always prove the Prophets wrong. I myself would certainly admit some suspicion of Mr. Borsodi's evangelistic enthusiasm, and Mr. Adams looks a little too fondly to England for his comparisons. But I have little doubt that these two men, with such other well-balanced critics as Stuart Chase, are in a real sense Prophets. It is too much to hope that the impact of their ideas will be immediately felt, but gradually it will be, for they put into our hands the goodly weapons that our better natures will want to use in the ever-continuing and now ever more supremely necessary war against our worse.

The World as Ford Factory

Critic's Almanac
November 9, 1930

There is magnificence in this new book of Henry Ford's
—this book of the splendid title, *Moving Forward*, which
comes to us with the additional signature of Samuel Crow-
ther as a kind of shrewd Boswellian collaborator. The title
itself is a magnificent rebuke to Mr. Ford's fellow-indus-
trialists, now wallowing sadly in the trough of business
depression. And with what magnificent gall does Mr. Ford
advise us, at this time of all times, that "the day when we
can actually have overproduction is far distant"; that the
five-day week and the eight-hour day must be still further
curtailed; and that the familiar Ford doctrine of raising
wages and lowering prices must go on indefinitely. Whether
these pronouncements are wise or foolhardy, I am not
enough of an economist to say. I can well imagine that they
may seem almost wicked to some merchants and manufacturers. I am more concerned with the theories of industry and of human life that lie back of the Ford-ideas, and
that perhaps have never before been so persuasively stated
as in this book.

Yet since Mr. Ford's book is not all doctrine, let me first
pay tribute to the part which is not. The middle chapters
of the book, such as "Changing Over an Industry," "Flexible Mass Production," "A Millionth of an Inch," give us
rather full glimpses into the workings of the Ford plants.
Here Mr. Ford appears as the honest mechanic—or factory
manager—who has an all-consuming zeal for his work.
Herein, who will say that Ford is not a genius—a genius
who scraps overnight "the largest automobile plant in the
world," in order to replace Model T with Model A; who
founds rubber plantations in Brazil, against an evil day;
who commands the services of the admirable Johansson,

measurer of measurers, in order to gauge to the millionth of an inch the delicate operations upon which the quantity production of Ford cars must finally depend? One cannot but admire the gusto and the not immodest pride of this Henry Ford. Yes, even though one is obliged to reflect that the fruit of these stupendous operations is nothing more magnificent than a Ford car, buzzing along the highways and no doubt transporting quite as many fools as wise men. It is comforting, too, to have Mr. Ford's insistence that it is the excellence of the product which should come first in the manufacturer's mind—and not the disposal thereof, or the profit, which will result necessarily. Let us give Mr. Ford all the credit we can in the fields where he may speak with some authority. It is only as Mr. Ford may be taken as an oracle on other matters that he is dangerous—in fact, very dangerous indeed, and subversive of the better part of life as I conceive it.

In the first place, Mr. Ford sees the world as a gigantic Ford factory, or as some kind of factory, in which people manufacture Ford cars, or other articles, for the sole reason of getting the money to buy the articles that they manufacture. This is a very pinched and narrow view of life to begin with. It leaves out the vastly interesting departments of human life that can hardly ever be expected to submit themselves to a factory regime. Of that life and of professional life, of politics and government, of housekeeping, lovemaking, motherhood, fatherhood, literature, history (to say nothing of philosophy and religion and such pleasant trivialities as conversation and good digestion), Henry Ford takes no account. And we may presume, from his childish comments on Prohibition and his naive views of leisure, that he has no thoughts on these various subjects and no valid information about them.

If Mr. Ford's book were merely a book on economics or on methods of manufacture, I would not raise this point at all. But his theories of manufacture are all tied up with his views of life, which have the simplicity of fanaticism. Furthermore, Mr. Ford has the impertinence to suggest, at least implicitly, that we had better give up our shabby ideas of life and adopt his glittering ones; and he ludicrously puts himself forward as a missionary to Europe, who is now prepared to confer on little agricultural Denmark and disturbed England and stable France the questionable benefits of a Ford regime.

Let me now examine rather hastily some of the principal Ford-ideas.

Of the greatest importance, perhaps, is his distinction between "labor-saving and labor-serving" as applied to machines. Mr. Ford thinks that we are nowhere near the end of our ingenuity in devising machines that will substitute machine work for human work. There will be more and more machines, always more efficient ones, which will be manned by skilled technicians and made by even more skilled technicians, so that unskilled labor will eventually be quite unwanted. That this development of machines will therefore displace workers even Mr. Ford is obliged to concede; but he holds that the displaced workers (now known as the "technologically unemployed") will be taken care of by the new industries that must continuously arise, to meet the eternal new demands for new products.

Meanwhile, the skilled laborers who are retained in the factory have their tasks made physically easier; that is the meaning of "labor-serving." Their hours are short, and their pay is high—in 20 years it may reach $27 a day. They are given more leisure, which they are supposed to use in consuming the surplus products ingeniously devised for them; and for this purpose, too, they are paid high wages. And all of this must go on forever, more and more, with no limit at all in sight.

Now this is all very clever, and one cannot deny that, to

some extent, the scheme has worked for Henry Ford, who has profited not only by his own genius but by the circumstances of a war-fattened, expansive period distinctly favorable to his independent experiments.

But there are serious implications behind these ideas.

What is the result for the laborer? The "labor-serving" idea is a mere quibble. Actually, Henry Ford's machines are labor-saving. This means that they are operated under the theory that labor is bad and men ought to do as little of it as possible. It implies that enjoyment is not connected with labor but must be pursued apart from it. One can only conclude that the introduction of more and more labor-saving machines signifies that labor will be held in more and more contempt. Or, still worse, that our lives are to be severely split between work and play, when as a matter of fact the two ought not to be put into opposition. In the ideal life work and play are not at odds, but harmoniously blend and interchange. God save us from the day when we may become convinced that work is an evil.

What is the result for the laborer who is thrown out of a job by the newly created machine? Mr. Ford passes lightly over this feature, in the face of a "technological unemployment" that is now giving thoughtful persons the gravest concern. Presumably, the laborer may get into some other industry, also newly created. Again, he may not. The prospect is one of fairly continuous unemployment, of both skilled and unskilled hordes milling painfully around our industrial centers. That this is already the case we know very well. And such a sharp and distressing study of unemployment as Clinch Calkins's *Some Folks Won't Work* is in severe contradiction to Mr. Ford's glib assurance.

What is the effect on industry itself? It is one of continual disadjustment and change. The manufacturer must always be scrapping his old plant and building a new one. He must put away his old machines and install better ones.

This, says Mr. Ford, must be the normal procedure. There must be eternal experiment, eternal change. And what does this mean but a condition of furious uncertainty and instability, with the industrial structure always in a rickety and perilous shape?

And what, above all, is the effect on the consumers—the largest class of all, including not only laborers and capitalists, but all the immense public not engaged in factory production?

Under the Ford economy, it will be their duty to be even more thriftless than they are at present. They must spend and spend unceasingly, in order to consume the never-ending stream of new products that industry hurls upon them. They will be encouraged to make a necessity of every luxury that the clever industrialists may devise. For industry of the Ford type has no regard for actual and fundamental needs! It seeks to create two or even twenty demands where none at all existed before.

The result of all this, almost inevitably, will not only be a terrifying expansion of the abstract money economy, now already puzzling in its weird ramifications. It will be to corrupt the public life, throughout its entire body, by persuading people to believe that life is made up of material satisfactions only, and that there are no satisfactions that cannot be purchased. On the one hand, we shall have financial chaos; on the other, a degraded citizenry, who have been taught under the inhumane principles of Fordism always to spend more than they have, and to want more than they get.

Mr. Ford means well, of course. So did old John Brown of Ossawottamie, when he proposed to arm the Negro slaves with pikes and guns. But Mr. Ford (who has exactly the John Brown type of mind, applied to mechanics and money) is more dangerous than John Brown, for he proposes to disrupt a whole nation by offering to its citizens precisely the same temptation that Satan offered Christ.

The book page June 17, 1928, after syndication.

Criticism Outside New York

The provincial literary editor turns out his page a week under handicaps that would throw a Humanist critic into a fit of chills and fever. Whatever the final product, his actual working methods are a perfect example of motion perpetually lost and of decorum eternally foundered in petty exasperations. Nine times out of ten, his book page editing is a part-time job, for no managing editor in his senses would think of giving a book editor an equal status with a sports editor or a society editor. So he is generally an editorial writer, or a Sunday editor, or sometimes merely a copyreader or a reporter, who does the book page on the side; or, as is more and more getting to be the case, he is a college professor who is called in to furnish a little genteel window dressing for the comic strips and the murder stories. Probably he has no clerical help, except what he can beg or pay for out of his own pocket. He must write his own letters, which will be numerous if he really keeps up with the new books and his reviewers; and more than likely, if he mails out review copies to selected critics instead of casually handing them out to staff members and friends, he will have to do the wrapping and posting himself. Merely the physical handling of the books is a trial to the flesh, for at the height of the spring and fall seasons they come in by the cartload and must be put in decent order. They must above all be put in a safe place, away from the casual thievery of the staff, who will think nothing of walking off with anything from a Zane Grey novel to Colonel House's memoirs.

But such minor afflictions are nothing in comparison with

Davidson wrote this article, originally called "Provincial Book Reviewing," for *Bookman*, May 1931. The editor asked him to use this less controversial title. Several paragraphs at the beginning are omitted.

239

the major ones, quite out of the class of inconveniences. These all come from the fact that books are published mainly in New York, which is located in a sort of No Man's Land claimed by the United States but belonging only technically within their jurisdiction.

The provincial literary editor is a thousand or two miles away from this crankily located "center." Advance copies of important books reach him belatedly, or not at all. He cannot be as prompt in his reviewing as the New York literary sheets, because he does not have their space and their facilities. From the flood of books that reach him, accompanied by bales of chatty "publicity notes" and all imaginable promotional devices, he is made aware that the publishing world of New York is not geared to his tempo. Apparently it is geared to suit the pace of a monstrous book-consuming machine that ravenously demands a fresh banquet of best-sellers every day in the week. The impression he gets is that people in the metropolitan areas spend the greater part of their waking hours in reading books. With a public so voracious, it is no wonder that New York reviewing is reduced to the desperate formula of recommending books as fast as the books appear. Reviewers become professional shopping guides, because they must.

In the South, the public is not so eager. At times the editor may wonder whether it has any appetite at all. When it perks up and shows an interest in its victuals, the editor knows that the victuals have been sealed and recommended in New York. When this book becomes a best-seller and that book a worst-seller, he can discover little evidence as to whether his own opinions have mattered. He guesses that publishers do not base their estimates on any approval he may give, and that booksellers do not wait upon his remarks to do their buying.

Then why should he exist at all? Can he be anything but a humble satellite of New York, repeating meekly, in his own distant orbit, the equinoctial procession of its blazing fashions?

To such questions my general answer would be a defense of provincialism. Without underestimating the power of New York and without denying that its influence is often beneficent, I should still hold that it is a perversion of function for the provincial editor to consider his book page simply an irrigating ditch, wholly obedient and conductive, through which the arts and learning of the metropolis gurgle into the sterile hinterland. Circumstances compel him to be an outsider, and he might as well never pretend to be anything else. Let him be an outsider, with all the force and discretion he can muster. Let him be a Westerner or a Southerner, frankly but not overbearingly. He need not rage against the sins of Babylon in order to cherish the integrity of his own Jerusalem, but he does need to keep his self-respect in the only way possible to honest men. The vague quality called "point of view"—reputed to be so prized of critics—will then be his without seeking, as much a native part of him as the accent and features he got from his own father, from his own land and people.

Of such provincial independence, however, one will naturally demand that it be effective. This is a hard demand to make, because effectiveness can never be proved by statistics. Yet I have grounds for believing that the provincial editor can be effective—and often is—if he will be quite patient, quite content to see the years go by without any display of quick and tangible results.

Certain limits must be granted. Publishers' lists are made up in New York and in Europe. They are bound to reflect the New York estimate of what the public wants and what it ought to want. That this is often a narrow estimate, even when it is most shrewd, the provincial editor knows all too well. It is self-evident that New York sells its wares to the provinces without being very well acquainted with the

various kinds of people that live, die, and occasionally read
books in the vast region that lies outside of a circle described with a hundred mile radius from New York. But
if he is defending his right to provincialism, he cannot very
well deny New York's right to its own provincialism, which
is simply a coat of another color. He cannot change New
York.

This apparent impotence will not matter very much if he
reflects that his duty as a critic—and as an editor—leads in
exactly the direction toward which his natural self-respect
has already inclined him. The critic must have an open
mind—that is true. But independence is as needful as
catholicity. If one can judge from the evidence, critical
independence may be harder to win and harder to keep in
New York than in the provinces, where the critic is exposed to few temptations, hidden or open. To be independent and to be provincial, in this sense, are the same thing.
Remoteness becomes, after all, a kind of good fortune, if
he knows how to use it well.

He cannot be prompt to the minute in reviewing books.
Very well, then, let him practice deliberation, within rea-
sonable limits. Does he know few of the modern authors
at sight? All the better reason for having little personal
bias for or against them. He has no fear of disfavor from
the great and the powerful, and is not much annoyed with
the importunities of the little. If he doesn't like Mr. So-
and-So's novel, he can say so without fear of political consequences. There is equally little reason for him to ignore
merit because it happens to be unfashionable or unpro-
moted. He cannot be seduced, even unconsciously, by publishers' advertising, because publishers do not advertise in
his page.

If these things are not true of every provincial literary
editor, they ought to be. I believe they are oftener true than
not, and so far as they are true they point toward an in-

dependence which in time may have a healthy effect. I do not look for any open schism, which will vent itself in a series of violent secessionist movements, assembled around the banners of provincial literary editors engaging in a species of guerrilla warfare against New York. But imagine fifty provincial literary editors, in as many cities, devoting themselves independently, with a corps of independent-minded reviewers, to the most obvious task of a book page, which is to criticize books and care nothing at all whether the books sell or whether the opinions are quoted. Imagine such a condition—and guess what a checking, balancing effect it would have upon publishing and criticism in New York, which nowadays simply attempts to sell the provinces what the New York reviewers and publishers happen to like. In that direction—a winding road, very long and quiet —lies the legitimate way of the provincial literary editor. It is a way of being "effective." It is his only reason for existing.

From a newspaper standpoint, one of the tests of the popularity of a feature is the quantity of letters from readers who volunteer abuse or applause—it does not greatly matter which, so long as they write in. A "colyumist" of my acquaintance gets such letters literally by the barrel; he keeps several barrels in his cellar to put them in. A literary editor enjoys no such profusion of correspondence. His efforts, no matter how earnest or blasphemous, are generally received in utter silence. He is left to carry on in a kind of negative bliss, presuming that silence indicates no disapproval and that, as long as there is no outcry for his ejection, he must be behaving himself acceptably.

Yet he has a fair notion about the people who compose his audience, since he mingles with them a good deal and can guess what their attitudes are. He can divide them, in his mind, into three groups.

First, there are the strictly fashionable crowd, who read

the new books simply to keep up, without caring much whether the books are good or bad. All they want is to have the new books on the table, or to patter brightly about them in the monthly "discussion group." For these folks, the local book page is a supererogation. They read the New York reviews and accept what is said. Or they subscribe to a book club and take what is sent. Probably they feel a little superior, on the whole, toward the local book page. They like to feel metropolitan, or they think quite seriously that New York knows what is fitting and proper for "cultured" circles.

At the opposite extreme are honest provincials who read only the local book page if they read any. By and large, these are of the order of a Mississippi gentleman who wrote me with disarming frankness: "I always peruse your page with interest, but I seldom read books any more. I read the page more to learn the trend of opinion than to select reading matter." These people make up a very large group, from whom the provincial literary editor may hope to make a few dubious converts. But the support they give is a little too casual to be satisfying.

For the purpose of establishing an informed and independent provincial opinion, a third group is the most important. These are persons of education and sensibility who "keep up," like the clubwomen and the best-seller infatuates, but with reserve and deliberation. They are slow to buy books. They do not join book clubs. They do not make a fuss over fashions, and are not rushed off their feet very easily. Secretly or openly, they are a little dissatisfied with New York opinion, detecting in it, perhaps, a certain amount of hollowness and chitter-chatter. Without defining their attitudes very precisely, they are really ripe for rebellion and need little encouragement to make themselves felt.

These are the people for whom a provincial book page

can really mean something. They offer a nucleus, if only a nucleus as yet, for building up an expressive and sympathetic body of readers who in turn will influence other readers and form at last a bloc of literary Jeffersonians ready to conspire against the complacent literary Hamiltonianisms of our day.

The problem of the provincial literary editor is to diminish the size of the first group by jarring its complacence, and to increase the size of the third group by additions from the first and second.

But no perfunctory handling of books will avail to achieve this end. Nor will any solo editorial performance, however brilliant and passionate, be enough in itself. The provincial book page must be as good in quality as the New York reviewing sheets; if possible, it must be better. The provincial editor must be a real editor. He must attract the services of able reviewers who will have public respect and who will give his page, week in and week out, a consistent excellence. If he is able to enlist such people, he will be doing something more than acquainting an invisible public with the new books. He will be affording provincial criticism an outlet. He will provide a forum of literary opinion where unprofessional critics may try out their ideas in print. Gradually, with many haltings and backslidings, his reviewers and he may shape provincial opinion until it is not only in touch with modern literature but expressive of itself.

Provincial reviewers are not so glib or knowing as the happiness boys and girls who discover new masterpieces every week in the columns of New York periodicals; but they are also less bored, less opinionated, possibly more painstaking. They review books for what the books are worth, because it never occurs to them to do anything else. They are undistracted, they have leisure and freedom, they have no ax to grind.

That is, when they can be discovered and put to work, their best work is of this order. Even their bad work is likely to be honest work. The great vice of provincial reviewing, of course, is its perfunctoriness and shallowness. I know that a great deal of this kind of reviewing exists, but I am not talking about blurb-copying female sentimentalizing, all the petty practices that are an affliction to the authors, the public, and the publishers.

I do not say it with any particular pride; it was always obvious enough that a diligent book page editor need not condone such practices. It was always easy, in fact surprisingly easy, to secure a good review for a worthy book. During my seven years of up-and-down, I suppose there were as many as three or four hundred individuals on my list of reviewers. The marvel was that these people, many of them busy persons, were apparently ready enough, upon my simple request, to drop their work and write a book review—for which, after the inconsiderate fashion of provincial newspapers, they got no pay except the possession of the book. In my editorial solicitations I tried to keep this in mind. If the reviewers were to have only the books, then they ought to have the books they wanted, and I catered to their private tastes, so that for this man I helped build up a library of travel books, for that one religion, for another one Proust, and so on.

Of course some of the reviewers were writers who from time to time contributed to national periodicals. The first number of the page ever issued contained reviews by Allen Tate and John Crowe Ransom. Other authors who reviewed occasionally or frequently were Edwin Mims, William S. Knickerbocker, Newbell Niles Puckett, Kate Trimble Sharber, Grant C. Knight, Nicholas Van der Pyl, William E. Barton, Roy L. Garis, Robert Penn Warren, G. B. Winton, John D. Wade—poets, biographers, novelists, academicians, if not professional critics. But there were many other quite unprofessional persons whose work was

equally good and just as faithful, people for the most part
unknown outside their own locale. I recall no better estimates of Cabell, anywhere, than those written by Jesse
Wills for my page. I doubt whether Mr. Canby or Mrs.
Van Doren get many reviews of better quality than those
that were done for me by Elizabeth Wheatley, Lacy Lock-
ert, Ruth F. Moore, Ellene Ransom, Richard S. West, Sue
White, Henry B. Kline, Dorothy Yarnell, Abbott Martin.

On the whole I am inclined to think that the amateur
reviewers, when they have the knack, are preferable to professional ones, because they are more impressed with the
obligation of doing a good review (not necessarily a favorable one) and have not yet learned the sad lesson that
criticism is one of the most impermanent and least respected
forms of writing. This is particularly true of the young
people in the first flush of literary enthusiasm, who have
just discovered that they can write and are foolish enough
to think book reviewing a good beginning. To these I gave
all possible encouragement. They were often a mainstay
when the graybeards failed me, and their reviewing often
put the graybeards to shame. Perhaps one of the best by-
products of the page was the opportunity it afforded these
young people to quicken their literary interest and try out,
for what it was worth, the kind of writing that a book page
permits.

But their importunities were sometimes embarrassing.
Sometimes there were college students who could do better
writing than the very professors under whom they were
supposed to be studying. I published reviews—good ones—
from a sophomore at the University of Tennessee long before I discovered her immature station in life. Finally I
had to make a rule that I would assign no books to undergraduates. It would not do to have reverend age and
ebullient youth joggling each other too intimately on a
book page.

There was never any lack of reviewers, excellent re-

viewers, willing and eager to write for no pay, ready to
thank me humbly for the "privilege" of doing reviews, or
glad to write out of a sense of public duty. They were
people of all sorts and stations: college presidents, editors,
lawyers, judges, insurance and bond salesmen, authors, clubwomen, housewives, clergymen, gentlemen farmers, army
officers, teachers, politicians, and of course college professors. The reviewers were distributed in all parts of the
South, with a sprinkling from the East and Middle West,
but most of them, of course, represented the western South
and might be taken as a cross-section of it. Through them
it was possible to make the book page, over a course of
years, an expression of intelligent Southern opinion in regard to books—and perhaps in regard to the questions, social, political, religious, that the books of these turbulent
years raised.

In the earlier days of the page, when review copies came
but sparsely in response to my fitful pleadings, it was easy
for me to review all the books that came in. I had too fine
a conscience then. It seemed to me that whatever somebody
had gone to the enormous trouble in writing and printing
ought to have a notice, even though a disapproving one.
Inevitably, fine conscience was blunted and replaced by
something that may have been either wisdom, cynicism, or
practicality. In the last four or five of my seven years, books
came in ever-increasing numbers. It was impossible to review all the half-worthy or the nearly good books. It was
hard enough, it was almost impossible to get around even
to the apparently deserving ones within a decent period.
Before the fall books could be assigned and reviewed, they
were obscured by a tide of spring books in full spate. In
November the ardent publishers hurl masterpiece after masterpiece at the book editor, and dutifully he crams his
copy-folder with reviews that will take him three months
or more to finish printing. But in January the publishers

are already assuring him that the books of the fall are faded and gone.

The literary editor's task is not lightened at all by the system, or rather the lack of system, which a great many publishers use in sending out review copies. During the latter years of my experience I tried to solve the problem in part by furnishing each important publisher with a list of titles, chosen from catalogues. With about half the publishers this arrangement worked rather well on the whole. To the other half, the preference of the local editor meant nothing, and books arrived for review, or did not arrive, in a perfectly insane fashion. Some of the publishers—especially the older, more conservative houses—studied rather carefully the peculiarities of the local page; but these were few enough. We always had a plethora of books that were not worth reviewing or that we were not interested in reviewing—a book of Yiddish hymnology, or a history of Gloucester, Massachusetts, or the speech defects of school children in a Brooklyn high school, or German diction in singing. And we were always missing important books, frequently books of local interest, for no intelligible cause, and being greeted, upon complaint, with a formula—"Our supply of review copies is exhausted," or a quarrelsome "Our records show that this book was sent you . . ."

Publishers should know their own business, and, having enjoyed many courtesies at their hands, I feel sufficiently respectful toward them. I know how complicated and elusive their business is, and I understand how they must study sales sheets. But I shall never be able to comprehend an economy that will permit one publisher to send for review the two hefty volumes of James's *Charles W. Eliot* and will forbid another to furnish *The Adams Family*. I can recall getting numerous review copies of obscure Scandinavian or Polish novels from a certain publisher and missing entirely a novel by a Tennessean, published by the same firm. I remember being refused a review copy of the diary of President Polk, whose tomb is a few steps away from the newspaper I worked for; but I was always getting diaries or biographies of other worthies in whom I could take no possible interest.

Occasional quarrels and disappointments over review copies are minor irritations. But the provincial editor's general experience makes him inevitably aware of some weaknesses in the publishing system. Book publishers go blithely about their seasonal enthusiasms like so many manufacturers of automobiles and millinery, chirping continually about new models in biography, fiction, and pseudo sciences; but they seem to know the manufacturing end only. They know little about the book-consumers—who they are, or where they are, or what they are like. When the market fails to absorb a publisher's wares, he seems to think something very mysterious is in the wind. It is a "bad market" for books, and that is all he can say.

The provincial editor is not concerned with sales, which are somebody else's business entirely. But he can see some of the troubles. Strangely enough, many reasonably well-educated people, after reading a book review, have no idea as to how to go about buying the book in question. They have forgotten that books are sold in bookstores, or do not know where the bookstores are. To make matters worse, a vast number of potential book-buyers have been educated to think of only two varieties of books: school books and library books. The free school system may have taught them to respect books, but it has not taught them to want to own books. They have been subtly led to believe, instead, that the Declaration of Independence and the Constitution imply that books are to be furnished, like roads and farm relief, as a sort of communal right. They are encouraged in this belief by modern architects, who do not include private libraries among the appurtenances of the average American home.

Furthermore, in the South at least, the population is still mainly agricultural. It includes many Negroes, and many persons both white and black who do well to read a news-paper. This population, being agricultural, lacks spending money, and if it had the money, it would have no inclina-tion to invest it in books. Yet when all these classes of nonreaders and book-borrowers are subtracted, there remain enough people to make a good-sized body of book-consumers. Still the publishers complain. Figures prove, they say, that the South buys only 5½ percent to 7½ per-cent of the books issued from New York—a bad showing in comparison with other sections.

I do not trust these figures implicitly. They do not include the purchases that many Southerners make by mail directly from Brentano's and other metropolitan stores. They do not include, I imagine, the orders that Southern booksellers place directly with book-jobbers like Baker and Taylor. And they are calculations for *new* books only, and therefore are not a complete commentary on reading habits. Besides, they take only quantity into account, and are no measure of quality. For publishers assume, with pardonable vanity perhaps, that all their wares are of uniform excel-lence. If the South does not buy their books profusely, then the fault must be the South's and nothing could possibly be wrong with the books offered for sale! I should like to think that the South's taste is the main ruling factor here; I am afraid it is not, but it would certainly be proper to argue that the reading public of the South is not so easily "panicked" as the more congested centers of population. Its tendencies are conservative. It is slow to take up the more violent modernities.

But when the South makes up its mind to buy, it will keep on buying indefinitely. If Aunt Emma once decides that Sinclair Lewis is all right, she will get every Sinclair Lewis novel that comes out; and she will see that Cousin Sue and Uncle George get copies at Christmastime and on birthdays. It is the quick turnover, the dizzy shifting from fad to fad between seasons, that finds the South most unresponsive. I am unable to shed many tears over this reluctance to be stampeded. I shudder at the thought of book publishers "developing" the Southern market in the fashion apparently contemplated by Mr. Melrich V. Rosenberg in a recent article in the *Publishers' Weekly*. "The trade in the South," he says, "has yet to concern itself seriously with the aggressive merchandising of books." And I hope it never will, if "aggressive merchandising" means a lot of noise and hurrah about one's duty to civilization and one's obligation to buy Skeezick's new series, "Novels in the Nude," as highly recommended by the usual group of sponsors.

The truth is, I have found myself in tight corners at times, when called on to suggest current books for the reading of gentle ladies, brought up with Victorian decorum, or good country gentlemen like the farmer I used to know, who made it a rule to reread *A Tale of Two Cities* every autumn when he fired his tobacco and had to stay up all night. When the lady from upstairs used to call on me and ask for something to read of a winter evening, it was embarrassing to discover that practically every novel on my shelves was an improper book. When I went a hundred miles into the country to visit my father, what could I possibly take him, in the way of current reading, that would compete with the Shakespeare, the Plutarch, the Thackeray, that he knew so well? For the lady upstairs I might occasionally manage a Booth Tarkington or a Galsworthy. For my father there was nearly always some biography and history of more or less merit; but I shrank from offering him *The World of William Clissold* or *My Life* or *Marriage and Morals*. It may have been my own innate conservatism that restrained me; it may have been an unconscious admission that Wells was after all no adequate substitute for Thackeray, and that Isadora Duncan and Bertrand Russell were featherweights in comparison with Plutarch and Shakespeare. Coming right down to it, I was inclined to be a little ashamed of some branches of modern literature before my own people, no matter how boldly I championed it in print. And for all I know there may be some fundamental division of taste between the literary East and the provincial South, not particularly to the discredit of either section, but a profound division nevertheless, a chasm not to be easily bridged by venders of books who believe fanatically in "salesmanship" simply because salesmanship works in the metropolitan areas.

Even so, grant that the situation is as bad as can be from the publisher's standpoint; I fancy they will never improve it much by their present procedure. Their one hope is in the bookstores, whose scanty numbers they are doing much to diminish and nothing to increase. Your Southern reader, I think, is not yet ready (if he ever will be) to respond buoyantly to mass sales schemes. He wants to know his bookseller, and he wants his bookseller to know him (or her). When he comes into the store, he wants to be called by his right name. He wants to gossip, to consult and be consulted. The bookseller's success rests largely on building up a clientele of persons whose family histories, professions, tastes he knows as well as he knows his stock.

Against this inclination, which means a small and dispersed but a very steady trade, the publishing system unfortunately throws its whole weight. The extraordinary policy of pushing nothing but "new" books, as if books were as perishable as chewing-gum and automobiles, is discouraging to the bookseller, who cannot possibly carry every item in stock. The remote high-and-mightiness of some publishers; their repeated errors in handling orders and shipments; the compartmentalizing of their business—which means, often, the handling of correspondence by subordinates who know neither the geography of the United States nor the contents of the books they are publishing; their deadly opportunism in permitting the rise of book clubs that cut heavily into booksellers' trade; their eagerness to rush books into cheap reprints while expensive editions are still on bookstore shelves; their general unacquaintance with the South, or with any part of the United States outside New York— all this hurts the booksellers just as it frets and hampers the book-editor.

Two or three times a year—sometimes less often—the publisher's field agents make the rounds of bookstores (at least of those that still have good credit) and struggle against conditions as best they may. These are generally sensible and gallant souls, with a passion often for good literature. They lug huge suitcases around in tropical weather and cover, in gigantic leaps, a territory half as big as Europe. They are well liked, and they are well received; but they touch only a few cities, and hastily at the best. Their salesmanship is not much helped by the fact that they frequently are obliged to solicit orders for books they have never read—probably because the manuscript has not been received at the publisher's office, and the book exists only as a dummy.

It is a strange, almost a messy business. I have no solution for it. But one recommendation might be made. If the heads of the publishing houses would occasionally omit one of several annual jaunts to Europe, and journey through the highways and byways of their own country instead, they might profit a good deal. They would at least learn the map of the United States.

In so mixed-up a situation, the book page is an unknown quantity, no matter how good its intentions. Sometimes I have been driven to think of it as a survival only—a last gesture of decency that the modern newspaper is ready to make before it becomes all promotion, all advertising, all sensational entertainment. "Dramatic criticism" has about passed away in provincial newspapers. Instead there is a "movie page" consisting of blurbs written by Hollywood pimps—perhaps with the addition of a syndicated column or so. It is promotion merely. The advertisers—that is, the movie theaters—would allow nothing else. Perhaps book pages are destined to undergo the same transformation. After all, a newspaper publisher may argue, books are now a commercial product. Why should they be discussed any more critically than other commercial products: furniture, patent medicine, stocks and bonds, radio programs—all of which are advertised and promoted but never reviewed? A great many large newspapers have already taken exactly this view—see, for example, the "book pages" of certain dailies in Cleveland, Atlanta, Cincinnati, Louisville.

But perhaps the book page may survive long enough to catch the turn of the tide in another direction, when the country is at last surfeited with advertising and newspapers have to change their present policy.

As long as it does survive, it is one very important place where a last stand may be made against vulgarity and crass standardization. It may not serve to "sell" this or that book by a specific review. But it will encourage decent people to think that decency remains somewhere and can lift up its head, even in the columns of a Sunday newspaper. It should give such people a confidence in themselves and help them to be critical in a time when the main tendency is to conform to the shallow mores of big business. It may not reform taste by driving people dictatorially, but it may help taste to form itself.

In our time, however, when there is so much more emphasis on ideas than on art, and when art itself has a pronounced social bias and propagandist turn, the book page—especially the provincial book page—has a chance to assume to some degree the function that the editorial page has about dropped. Presumably the literary editor and his staff are reviewing books; but the books they review are so full of ideas that the reviewers often become editorialists in practice. More than likely, the newspaper owner will be quite indulgent toward such social philosophizing on the book page, which he does not take very seriously. During my seven years I recall only one instance in which a review was suppressed by the owner. That was a review of Stuart Chase's *Your Money's Worth*, which was cut out because it "might offend the national advertisers." I remember no instance in which I was scolded after the appearance of a review. But I published many a review that might have called for a scolding, if the owner had not been either too careless, or too indulgent, or too high-minded to notice—I do not know which!

Now that this particular book page is wiped out, one casualty among many casualties of the Great Depression, I could not argue with perfect and ultimate certainty that all the things I have speculated about are true. I can only say that they seem to be true, or might have been true, or certainly may still be true for any book page founded and administered by persons who are willing to take pains. Clearly, there are such persons, in the South and elsewhere, and I like to think that they may prevail. But as I look at their pages and see little invasions of crossword puzzles and underwear advertisements among the book reviews, I begin to wonder whether their days, too, are numbered.

APPENDIX

The following list of contributors to the book page is incomplete. A great many of the shorter reviews were either unsigned or marked with initials which are no longer recognizable. Numbers after each name cover all identifiable reviews.
V Member of Vanderbilt faculty or staff during book page years.
S Vanderbilt student during book page years. (Only two or three undergraduates contributed before graduation.)
F Vanderbilt student prior to book page years. (Most, but not all, so designated were associated with the Fugitive group.)
T Member of the *Tennessean* staff.

Jane Allen	5	Ashton Chapman	21
John Paul Abbott (S)	8	P. L. Cobb	1
Walter P. Armstrong	16	W. C. Cobb (S)	6
George Bally (V)	1	Hazel Cole	2
William T. Bandy (S)	6	Douglas H. Corley (V)	6
William F. Barton	1	Walter F. Coxe	4
Denver Ewing Baughan (S)	8	Compton Crook	2
Maxwell Benson (S)	6	Walter Clyde Curry (V)	11
Dorothy Bethurum (F)	1	Sidney Dalton	2
Lucius J. Bircher (V)	2	Malcolm Dana (V)	1
Carlos Bissell (T)	2	John Daniel (V)	1
Lawrence Blair (F, V)	1	Thomas H. Davidson	11
A. G. Bowen	1	William Davidson (S)	1
Mildred Brantley (S)	4	Ethel M. Davis	2
Pollye Braswell	4	Lillian Perrine Davis	5
William R. Breyer	13	Olivia Dorman	1
Cleanth Brooks (S)	1	Herbert Drennon (S)	7
Byron C. Browder	1	Ernest J. Eberling (V)	2
O. E. Brown (V)	1	John Tyree Fain (S)	3
Helen Buquo	3	Nell Fain (S)	14
Charles Bell Burke	2	James I. Finney (T)	31
Irene Malone Cain	8	D. F. Fleming (V)	2
D. C. Cabeen (V)	6	Walter L. Fleming (V)	1
Thelma Campbell	8	John Fletcher (V)	7
Sam Carson (T)	1	Charles E. Forbes (T)	5
Thomas Carter (V)	3	William Frierson (F)	25

James Street Fulton (S)	2	John M. McBride	1
R. J. Gale	5	J. C. R. McCall, Jr. (S, T)	2
Roy Garis (V)	10	Walter McClelland	2
P. W. Gaunt (S)	2	Paul T. Manchester (V)	1
F. M. Green (V)	1	J. W. Manning (V)	3
R. A. Haden	3	Abbott C. Martin	13
Katherine Hall (S, T)	32	H. F. Martin	3
T. Graham Hall	1	George R. Mayfield (V)	6
Philip Hamer	2	Susanna Miller	3
Albert Mason Harris (V)	74	Edwin Mims (V)	13
Coleman A. Harwell (T)	9	Puryear Mims (S)	5
Lucile Heath	1	Samuel H. Monk	1
George S. Heller (V)	8	Ruth F. Moore	3
Robert S. Henry (F)	16	Marshall Morgan (F)	11
John L. Hill	6	Barr Moses (T)	66
Sherlock Hope	1	Charles Moss (S)	2
Stanley Horn	5	G. O. Mudge	1
Mason Houghland	2	H. C. Nixon (V)	24
William S. Howland (T)	3	Emily Olmstead	1
Arthur Palmer Hudson	2	D. M. Owens	1
Robert Hunt (S, T)	4	Frank Lawrence Owsley (V)	10
Alice James	4	L. G. Painter	1
A. Theodore Johnson	10	Edd Winfield Parks (S, T)	64
Stanley Johnson (F, V)	24	James R. Peery	5
Willoughby Johnson (S)	6	Charles W. Pipkin	1
Eugene Kayden	6	Newbell Niles Puckett	12
Lewis H. Keller	2	Paul Radin	1
J. L. Kesler (V)	1	Anne Rankin (T)	19
Warren Kingsbury	1	Ellene Ransom (F)	14
William W. Kingsbury (T)	50	John Crowe Ransom (F, V)	64
Winifred Kirkland	2	Walter Cade Reckless (V)	1
Henry B. Kline (S)	14	Willis Lee Reeves	1
William S. Knickerbocker	4	E. E. Reinke (V)	2
Grant C. Knight	9	T. L. Rettger	10
Charles E. Krutch	2	Linda Rhea	22
Lyle H. Lanier (F, V)	8	Paul Ritter	1
Elizabeth Margaret Latch	1	William J. Robertson	2
Tom Little (T)	4	Charles A. Rochedieu (V)	1
Lacy Lockert	7	Bert Roller	6
Roberta Dillon Lyne	1	Robert Rowlett (T)	9
Andrew Nelson Lytle (S)	12	W. T. St. Clair	11

Appendix   259

Herbert Sanborn (V)	1	Florence Tyler (F)	1
Hugh W. Sanford	1	Nicholas Van der Pyl	14
H. B. Schermerhorn (V)	6	Charles Wade (V)	1
Theodora Scruggs (S)	14	John Donald Wade (V)	1
L. B. Shackleford	2	Frank Waldrop (T)	14
Kate Trimble Sharber	22	Harold R. Walley	1
A. M. Shaw	3	Leone Warren	3
George Simmons (S, T)	6	Robert Penn Warren (S)	6
Mrs. George Simmons	9	Samuel Weingarten (S)	2
L. B. Smelser (V)	1	Richard S. West (S)	35
R. S. Smith	9	Elizabeth D. Wheatley	29
Alfred Starr (F)	24	A. P. Whitaker (V)	10
R. B. Steele (V)	2	Margaret C. White (F)	1
Richard M. Stern	2	Sue S. White	13
Alec B. Stevenson (F)	7	Albert Williams (F)	6
Alice E. Stockell	10	O. E. Williamson	1
Kate W. Stone	7	Jesse Wills (F)	34
J. W. Stovall	9	Virginia Winkleman	3
Thomas W. Talley	1	G. B. Winton (V)	11
Allen Tate (F)	27	G. P. Winton	7
Eric Tatum	1	Katherine Witherspoon (S)	1
Warren Taylor (S)	50	M. T. Workman	1
Pauline Townsend	1	Arthur M. Wright (V)	2
Charles Turck (V)	5	Dorothy Atwood Yarnell	17

INDEX

261

COLOPHON

THE TYPE FACES *used in this book belong to the group known generally as Old Style, though neither is truly a reproduction of the designs of the two type designers whose names they bear. The text is set in eleven-point Janson, two points leaded. This face, which dates from about 1690, was originally thought to have been cut by Anton Janson, a Dutch printer who worked at Leipzig. It was actually designed by Nicholas Kis, a seventeenth-century Hungarian typefounder working in Amsterdam. It is a good example of the sturdy Dutch faces that prevailed in England until the designs of William Caslon became popular. The title page and display matter are set in several sizes of Garamond Bold, a face not actually based on the designs of the sixteenth-century Parisian designer, Claude Garamond, but having much of the quality of the French typography of that period.*

The trademark was designed for Vanderbilt University Press by Theresa Sherrer Davidson, the wife of Donald Davidson. It is a form of the triskelion encircled by the traditional laurel wreath. Besides appearing in the arms of both Sicily and the Isle of Man, the triskelion has been employed in many cultures, and a form of it was used by the Indians of Tennessee. The Fugitives, the group of writers who flourished at Vanderbilt in the early 1920s, adopted it informally as their emblem. The symbol was originally three legs joined together, and to the Fugitives it was evidently seen as three legs running. It also bears a relation to certain sun symbols and may have signified the light which the Fugitives were seeking, for they saw themselves as fleeing towards as well as away from something. In some representations, the triskelion is seen as three V's joined together, making it especially appropriate for use by Vanderbilt.